HTML & XHTML

DeMYSTiFieD®

About the Author

Lee Cottrell started programming in 1982. Since this time, he has worked in many different programming languages. Lee has a Master of Science degree in information science from the University of Pittsburgh. Currently, Lee is the Program Manager for Computer Programming and Computer Networking programs at Bradford School in Pittsburgh. His teaching duties include networking, hardware, programming, database design, and web development. Lee also develops and writes curriculum for Bradford Schools nationwide. During his free time, Lee coaches baseball, softball, and soccer for his community athletic organization.

About the Technical Editor

Les Graves has been a technology instructor at a variety of schools for 10 years teaching programming, including HTML, and networking. He also has 17 years of corporate business and programming experience. He received his Bachelors of Science in Computer Science from the University of Pittsburgh and his Masters in Information Systems from the University of Phoenix. He resides in Pittsburgh, PA.

Les has had the privilege of working side by side as a technology instructor at Bradford School with the author, Lee Cottrell, and can attest to what an awesome instructor Lee is with great depth of experience and passion for his students' success.

HTML & XHTML
DeMYSTiFieD®

Lee M. Cottrell

New York   Chicago   San Francisco   Lisbon   London   Madrid   Mexico City
Milan   New Delhi   San Juan   Seoul   Singapore   Sydney   Toronto

Cataloging-in-Publication Data is on file with the Library of Congress

McGraw-Hill books are available at special quantity discounts to use as premiums and sales promotions, or for use in corporate training programs. To contact a representative, please e-mail us at bulksales@mcgraw-hill.com.

HTML & XHTML DeMYSTiFieD®

1 2 3 4 5 6 7 8 9 0   DOC DOC   1 0 9 8 7 6 5 4 3 2 1 0

ISBN 978-0-07-174804-9
MHID   0-07-174804-0

Sponsoring Editor
Roger Stewart

Editorial Supervisor
Janet Walden

Project Manager
Vipra Fauzdar, Glyph
International

Acquisitions Coordinator
Joya Anthony

Technical Editor
Les Graves

Copy Editor
Bob Campbell

Proofreader
Madhu Prasher

Indexer
Claire Splan

Production Supervisor
James Kussow

Composition
Glyph International

Illustration
Glyph International

Art Director, Cover
Jeff Weeks

Cover Illustration
Lance Lekander

DeMYSTiFieD® Series

Advanced Statistics Demystified
Algebra Demystified, 2e
Alternative Energy Demystified
ASP.NET 2.0 Demystified
Astronomy Demystified
Biology Demystified
Biophysics Demystified
Biotechnology Demystified
Business Calculus Demystified
Business Math Demystified
Business Statistics Demystified
Calculus Demystified, 2e
Chemistry Demystified
College Algebra Demystified
Data Structures Demystified
Databases Demystified, 2e
Differential Equations Demystified
Digital Electronics Demystified
Earth Science Demystified
Electricity Demystified
Electronics Demystified
Environmental Science Demystified
Everyday Math Demystified
Forensics Demystified
Genetics Demystified
Geometry Demystified
HTML & XHTML Demystified
Java Demystified
JavaScript Demystified
Lean Six Sigma Demystified
Linear Algebra Demystified
Logic Demystified
Macroeconomics Demystified

Math Proofs Demystified
Math Word Problems Demystified
Mathematica Demystified
Matlab Demystified
Microbiology Demystified
Microeconomics Demystified
Nanotechnology Demystified
OOP Demystified
Operating Systems Demystified
Organic Chemistry Demystified
Pharmacology Demystified
Physics Demystified, 2e
Physiology Demystified
Pre-Algebra Demystified, 2e
Precalculus Demystified
Probability Demystified
Project Management Demystified
Quality Management Demystified
Quantum Mechanics Demystified
Relativity Demystified
Robotics Demystified
Signals and Systems Demystified
SQL Demystified
Statistical Process Control Demystified
Statistics Demystified
Technical Analysis Demystified
Technical Math Demystified
Trigonometry Demystified
UML Demystified
Visual Basic 2005 Demystified
Visual C# 2005 Demystified
Web Design Demystified
XML Demystified

The Demystified Series publishes more than 125 titles in all areas of academic study. For a complete list of titles, please visit www.mhprofessional.com.

I would like to dedicate this book to my family. Larry, my father, pushed me to ensure I succeeded. My wife, Laurie, has always supported me through good times and bad. Finally, my children Lizzie and Chris provide me the inspiration to continue to excel.

Contents

Acknowledgments

Countless people contributed to the success of this book. It seems impossible to thank everyone. If I missed someone, I apologize.

First, I need to thank Kerri Moriarty. Kerri encouraged my love of writing and continued selling the idea of me writing another book to our book representatives. Kerri introduced me to Nancy Marr, a representative of McGraw-Hill.

Nancy talked with me at length about books I wanted to write. She provided the format for a book proposal and provided the e-mail address of acquisitions editor Roger Stewart. Roger talked with me at length about the DeMYSTiFieD® series. Shortly thereafter, I wrote a proposal for this book.

Sponsoring editor Roger Stewart and acquisitions coordinator Joya Anthony at McGraw-Hill walked me through the successful completion of the book. They provided templates, insight, and good advice on how to complete the book. Joya and Roger kept me on task throughout the completion of the book.

My friend Les Graves handled the technical editing of the book. Les found all of the little mistakes I made in my code. He simplified several of my examples and suggested several items that dramatically improved the book.

Kara Kleid, a former colleague at Bradford School and a phenomenal artist, introduced me to JQuery. Without JQuery, the JavaScript portion of this book would be much more complex.

My grammatical editor, Bob Campbell, converted my sloppy Pittsburgese into good, readable English. He took awkward sentences and turned them into graceful statements.

Finally, I need to thank Vince Graziano and Linda DeFalle. These two have pushed me and made me into a much better employee and geek.

Introduction

Congratulations! Your purchase of this book shows that you are a highly motivated student. You want as much out of your HTML class as possible. This book will help you to become the best HTML developer possible.

Who Should Read This Book

Everyone should read this book, of course! My kid needs braces! Seriously, though, HTML is the primary communication medium of our time. Nearly everything you do—be it study, play, or work—has an online component. Understanding how these online components work is crucial.

This book is not just about HTML; it actually covers three languages very well. This book covers HTML, its cousin XHTML, and the web formatting language CSS. You cannot learn HTML without encountering CSS. The book seamlessly integrates the three technologies. By the time you finish the book, you will be very proficient in all three languages.

How to Use This Book

I remember taking a programming course in college from a very bad professor. When I approached him for help, he said to "read the book." Great, thanks for the help. Well, I did read the book. I found out that there is a proper way to read a programming book.

The proper way to read a programming book is to skim over the text. Get the gist of what the technology can do. Then you need to type the code presented by the author. Do not go on until the code works. The code is the most important part of a programming book; everything else simply supports the code. In a nutshell: if you understand the code, then you can understand the language.

Knowing this, I molded each chapter around code. Each chapter has three main components. First, the chapters start with an overview of the topic, and if possible, a real-world analogy. From there, the basics of the topic are presented, along with working code. After the basics are presented, you will encounter the first of several practice exercises. These exercises guide you through creating a web site. After the basics are covered, the technical level increases slightly. After at least two practices with the topic, you are introduced to how to format using CSS. The last component of the chapter is the quiz. A ten-question multiple-choice quiz ends each chapter. Test yourself. If you do well, go on. Otherwise, revisit the topics you missed.

So while reading my book, skim over the prose. I won't mind; I would do the same for your book. Then type the code in your favorite text editor and test it out. Compare your browser screen to mine. If they match or are very close, then you did the code right. If you find yourself with code that simply will not work, you can download all of the code from www.mhprofessional.com/computingdownload.

Once you get my code to work, start making little changes and see what happens. This tinkering will teach you more than any other method.

In addition to the code, each chapter has several practice sections. The practice is a guided exercise in creating a web page. Each step has a description of what you are doing, why you are doing it, and how to do it. I provide the exact code I wrote. If you get confused, the end of each practice has a code block showing the finished product.

Chapter Synopsis

There is no set order to the book. Once you complete Chapter 3, tackle the chapters in any order you need. I organized the book based on how I teach HTML to my students. I paid very close attention to avoiding using topics from a previous chapter in a later chapter. Each chapter ends with a discussion on formatting using CSS.

Chapter 1 teaches the history of the Internet. It emphasizes the main technologies that created and still sustain the Internet today. It is very important to understand where our technology has come from. In addition to a history lesson, Chapter 1 introduces the tools of the trade and most of the languages on the Internet.

In Chapter 2 you will create your first web page. From this page, you build a template usable in the remaining chapters. You encounter tags and other HTML elements for the first time. HTML attributes for tags are defined. Finally, you find an overview of CSS.

Chapter 3 introduces color and graphics. You learn how to define any color you desire. The chapter presents best practices for graphics and color. Legal methods for acquiring images finish the chapter.

Chapter 4 introduces hyperlinks. You learn how to build links to external web sites. Links to pages on your own site are covered. Formatting the links with CSS ends the chapter.

Chapter 5 shows how to create lists. The three current list types, ordered, unordered, and definition lists, are covered. Chapter 5 also introduces nesting lists. Formatting lists through CSS ends the chapter.

Chapter 6 brings tables to a web page. Tables allow the presentation of columned data. Chapter 6 shows the tags for rows, columns, and captions. Included is merging multiple cells into one cell.

Gathering data with forms is the focus of Chapter 7. You will learn how to create text fields, radio buttons, and other form objects. Controlling where and how to send data is a major point. Not covered is the scripting language that receives the data.

Chapter 8 uses CSS to lay out your web page. The box model aligns objects on the screen. Your page is broken into pieces through div and span tags. Combining the div tags with the box model, you will develop three different page layouts.

Chapter 9 introduces JavaScript. JavaScript has many uses. Complete coverage of JavaScript is beyond the scope of this book. Instead, the use of preexisting scripts is emphasized.

Chapter 10 is one of the few chapters in the text that requires completion of earlier chapters. You must complete Chapters 8 and 9 before attempting DHTML. DHTML merges scripting and page layout to achieve very cool visual effects.

Chapter 11 introduces how to include multimedia elements to a web page. Since this is an easily abused technology, you learn the best practices for each multimedia object. You will learn to use sounds and movies on your page.

Chapter 12 covers frames. Frames are a technology that allows simple page layout and functionality. Frames are not as popular as they once were. Creating and controlling frames are covered in the chapter.

Chapter 13 ends your exploration of web pages by teaching you how to acquire and populate a web domain. You contrast Go Daddy's and 1&1's domain registration and hosting services.

How to Contact Me

The best way to contact me is through e-mail. My primary e-mail address is lee@leecottrell.com. Feel free to send criticism, praise, comments, errors, or questions. I will do my best to respond in a timely manner.

chapter 1

HTML and the Web

This chapter defines the origins of the Internet. Additionally, common tools and languages used in building web pages are introduced.

CHAPTER OBJECTIVES

In this chapter, you will

- Read a brief history of the Internet
- Define HTML
- Contrast versions of HTML
- List web development languages and tools

The Internet and the World Wide Web are an ever-present factor in our lives. We learn, work, and play using the Web. Through services like Facebook and YouTube, we interact with our peers in ways never imagined by our parents. Many people believe that their lives would be incomplete without access to the Internet.

A professor of mine in college stated that to understand where a person or thing is, one needs to understand where it came from. Understanding why the Internet works the way it does today requires a little understanding of where it came from.

The beginnings of the Internet lie in the Cold War. The United States Department of Defense (DOD) wanted a way to communicate with its bases in the event of a nuclear war or natural disaster. In 1957, the DOD formed the Advanced Research Projects Agency (ARPA) to solve this problem.

A Brief History of the Internet

It took 12 years until ARPANET, the first viable solution to the DOD's problem, was developed. In 1969, four universities connected to each other over ARPANET at a whopping 50 Kbps. The University of California at Santa Barbara and Los Angeles, Stanford, and the University of Utah were the first "netizens." By 1973, ARPANET boasted 23 hosts. In 1974, Vint Cerf and Bob Kahn jointly coined the term Internet.

Still Struggling

TCP/IP addresses contain four sets of digits called *octets*. The IP address for a very popular social networking site is 69.63.189.16. This is very difficult to remember. DNS allows an easier name for the site, www.facebook.com.

When you type in a web address, your computer will ask a DNS server to convert it to TCP/IP. From there, your computer will then use the converted address to request the web documents.

To see this in action open up a web browser. Enter in the address www .facebook.com. Now open another browser window or tab and type in the IP address 69.63.189.16. Both addresses will take you to Facebook.

It is not imperative that a web designer understands how DNS works. You do need to understand that it is part of how the Web works.

Between 1974 and 1990, a large number of technical developments improved the Internet. More and more hosts joined the network. Higher-speed networks handled bigger messages and more users. 1983 saw the implementation of TCP/IP and DNS. TCP/IP assigned numerical addresses to Internet computers. TCP/IP ensured that each site had a unique name, while DNS allowed humans to more easily remember those addresses. Internet traffic was noncommercial at this time.

In 1990, Tim Berners-Lee, a researcher at CERN in Geneva, implemented a version of hypertext that worked over the Internet. The goal of this project was to allow easier access to research papers. In 1992, CERN renamed Berners-Lee's creation the World Wide Web and released it to the world. In the next year, Marc Andreessen and the NCSA released the first graphical browser, Mosaic. This browser is the grandparent of all modern browsers.

By 1994, commercial sites began appearing on the Web. With the combination of an easy-to-use Internet and powerful yet inexpensive home computers, the Web began to move into the average person's home. By 1995, there were over six million Internet hosts, offering a vast array of services.

The mid to early 1990s were the dot com era. In this time, thousands of commercial entities started with a .com idea. The extension .com signifies a for-profit business. Prior to the Web, most new businesses had a physical presence. Web businesses often attempted to lure customers without a physical presence. Many of these companies died without making any money. Some, like yahoo.com and amazon.com, succeeded beyond anyone's wildest dreams.

TIP *It is interesting to see how bad web developers were at designing web pages in the 1990s. Start by visiting www.yahoo.com and seeing its current look. Then visit the Wayback Machine at www.archive.org to see how Yahoo's first page looked.*

The Internet and the World Wide Web are firmly entrenched in our lives. Every day, thousands of new sites are developed. Users find new ways to use the Web that its implementers did not imagine. With the material contained in this text, you will learn the basic language common to all web sites. Perhaps, you will take this material and develop the next big web site.

TIP *For a more detailed look at the history of the Internet, visit Hobbe's Internet Timeline at www.zakon.org/robert/internet/timeline/.*

What Is HTML?

HTML stands for Hypertext Markup Language. *Hypertext* is the technology that allows for links on the Web. On every web page visit, there is likely a link to another resource. These links contain a Uniform Resource Locator (URL) to another document. The URL is simply the web site name and the page. An example URL is www.google.com.

The second half of HTML is *Markup Language*. Markup languages provide format and structure to a document. In HTML, a series of tags controls the markup. Each tag has a meaning. The browser will read the tag and render the page appropriately. Tags are groupings of letters or numbers surrounded by angle braces. An example tag is the heading 1 tag, <h1>. Consider Code Block 1-1. There are three distinct tags, the H1 tag, the ordered list (OL), and the list item (LI). Figure 1-1 shows the output of this code rendered in Internet Explorer 8.

CODE BLOCK 1-1

```
<h1>Reasons to learn HTML</h1>
<ol>
<li>It is fun</li>
<li>It can lead to a great career</li>
</ol>
```

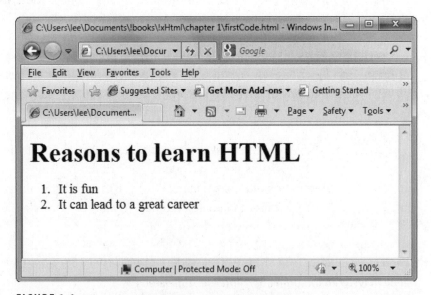

FIGURE 1-1 · The output of Code Block 1-1 in Internet Explorer 8

HTML's component parts completely define its nature. It provides formatting and structure to web pages. Hyperlinks access other elements. As long as the developer provides a correct address to a web resource, HTML will retrieve it. Provided the HTML is correct, a browser will render it.

Versions of HTML

Communications among humans are constantly changing. Styles of writing change and new words develop. When we stop using a word, we drop it from our lexicon. The same is true of HTML. New tags are developed and obsolete ones removed with each revision of the language.

The World Wide Web Consortium, better known as W3C, maintains most web languages. W3C publishes recommendations that define how the language should work. It is up to the individual browsers to implement the recommendations. The recommendation is not a rule, the community is free to interpret and implement the recommendation as they see fit.

When the W3C wishes to remove an element from the language, they deprecate the element. Deprecation means the element will not be supported in future versions of the language. Most textbooks and all web sites will clearly identify deprecated elements. Web page developers should never use deprecated elements on a web site.

The current version of HTML is 4.01, as of this writing. W3C formally recommended version 4.01 on December 24, 1999. It added several elements, corrected some mistakes from version 3, and deprecated several elements.

Extensible HTML (XHTML)

HTML is an extraordinary language. However, it has some flaws. The flaws allow developers to use bad syntax, and not follow the HTML rules. HTML coded in this fashion may render incorrectly in different browsers and computers. XHTML solves this problem.

XHTML is nearly identical to HTML but requires developers to write all pages with proper syntax. The syntax for XHTML is much stricter than for HTML. When a web designer uses XHTML properly, that will result in a page that is well-formed.

NOTE   *"Well-formed" means several things: All tags must be closed; tags contained within another tag must be nested properly; all tags are in lowercase; all documents have one <html> tag called the* root *element; and attributes must be set to a value, held inside of quotation marks.*

Code Block 1-2 contains a complete XHTML document. It contains one root element, the <html> tag. All other tags are nested within this tag. To understand nesting, think of the toy dolls that fit inside of each other. Opening the largest doll reveals a slightly smaller doll. These dolls are nested. The last <p> tag has a <b> tag properly nested within it. The first two <p> tags are not closed. Browsers will likely render this correctly, but it is not correct. The second set of <p> tags are correctly closed.

CODE BLOCK 1-2

```
<html>
<!--There is one html tag.
Everything is contained inside of this tag-->
<head>
<title>xHMTL examples</title>
</head>

<body>
<!--an improperly closed tag -->
<p>This is a paragraph.
<p>This is a second paragraph.

<!--the same code properly closed -->
<p>This is a paragraph.</p>
<p>This is a second paragraph.</p>

<p id="para5">This paragraph uses an attribute.</p>
<!--Improper nesting-->
<p><b>The b tag should be closed before the p.</p></b>

<!--proper nesting-->
<p><b>The b tag is closed before the p tag.</b></p>
</body>
</html>
```

XHTML is the language taught in this book. If you are new to web development, it is in your best interest to start with XHTML. Experienced developers are strongly encouraged to switch to XHTML. If you use XHTML for all of your development projects, your site will run well on all browsers on every computer.

TIP   *The XHTML rules seem harsh. They are easy to implement. All of the tools used by modern web developers will develop well-formed documents. You will have to go out of your way to write bad XHTML.*

HTML 5

HTML 5 is the upcoming replacement for HTML 4.01. It merges HTML and XHTML features. The new standard has deprecated several tags and introduced several new tags and design elements.

W3C has not recommended HTML 5. It is still changing. Several commercial sites, including www.youtube.com, have switched their code to HTML 5. Throughout this book, you will find tips discussing the likely changes from XHTML syntax in HTML 5.

Other Web Languages

HTML is the premier language on the Internet. However, it is far from the only language. Several other languages exist. Some are helper languages, while others allow developers to create dynamic web pages. Most of these languages are beyond the scope of this book. However, it is important as a web designer to know what these languages do.

Cascading Style Sheets (CSS)

The most important helper language for HTML is CSS. CSS makes web pages look nice. Ideally, HTML will hold the data for a web page while CSS will describe how the document looks. Usually whenever W3C deprecates a tag, a CSS element replaces it. I will use CSS in this book to format the web pages.

TIP   *CSS is best experienced. Visit www.csszengarden.com for a tour of what CSS can do for the web designer. This site contains a short essay regarding CSS. Do not read the essay. Instead, try the different designs to see the power of CSS.*

JavaScript

JavaScript is a programming language. Web developers use JavaScript to create small programs that run within a web page. Quite often, JavaScript is a client-side scripting language. This means these small programs run on the computer viewing the page. Chapters 9 and 10 will introduce how to use JavaScript in your pages.

Active Server Pages (ASP)

ASP is a programming language that builds dynamic web pages. ASP is a Microsoft product that runs on Microsoft operating systems. ASP runs on a server and creates an HTML page based on the user's requests. ASP runs online stores. Since the code runs on a server, ASP is a server-side scripting language.

PHP: Hypertext Preprocessor

PHP is another server-side language. It handles all of the same tasks as ASP. One big difference is the systems that can run PHP. PHP can run on any server, not just Microsoft.

NOTE   *PHP is both a hobbyist language and a serious development language. PHP powers both online gaming guilds and web stores.*

Web Editing Tools

When HTML was new, the only tool a developer could use was a text editor like Notepad or vi. Today, you have many choices with HTML editing tools. They generally can be broken into two categories. The first category is code editors. Code editors require you to type the HTML. The second category is WYSIWYG editors. These tools visually build the page, without your writing the code.

Neither category is perfect. Code editors require you to know the code and the proper syntax but allow you complete control over your design. WYSIWYG editors, while easy to use, can offer less flexibility than an editor offers and often write bad HTML. In this book, we will concentrate on code editors. Writing HTML using a code editor will allow you to learn HTML, which is why you purchased the book in the first place.

Code Editors

Code editors allow you to type the code for your HTML page. Most modern code editors offer syntax highlighting and code hints. Syntax highlighting will color your code as you write it. This makes it easier to read your code. Syntax errors are identified as you type. Code hints appear as you type. Usually all you need to do is type the first few letters of a tag or attribute and the editor will fill in the rest for you.

Notepad/Simpletext

Notepad, shown in Figure 1-2, is included with all versions of Microsoft Windows. Simpletext is included in Mac OS X. Both will allow you to type a web page. However, neither offers code highlighting or code syntax. Only use these products if you are desperate!

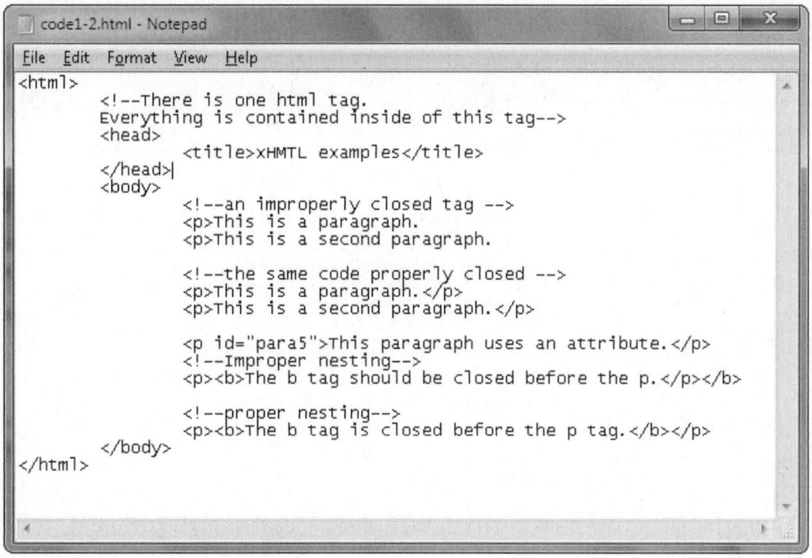

```
code1-2.html - Notepad                                    _  □  X
File  Edit  Format  View  Help
<html>
        <!--There is one html tag.
        Everything is contained inside of this tag-->
        <head>
                <title>xHMTL examples</title>
        </head>|
        <body>
                <!--an improperly closed tag -->
                <p>This is a paragraph.
                <p>This is a second paragraph.

                <!--the same code properly closed -->
                <p>This is a paragraph.</p>
                <p>This is a second paragraph.</p>

                <p id="para5">This paragraph uses an attribute.</p>
                <!--Improper nesting-->
                <p><b>The b tag should be closed before the p.</p></b>

                <!--proper nesting-->
                <p><b>The b tag is closed before the p tag.</b></p>
        </body>
</html>
```

FIGURE 1-2 • Microsoft Notepad in Windows 7

Gedit

Gedit is included with most modern distributions of Linux. It offers code highlighting but not code hints. Gedit is appropriate for web development.

Programmer's Notepad

Programmer's Notepad is a free program available from www.pnotepad.org. It offers code highlighting in color for nearly every programming language, and some code hints. Additionally, it offers a tab system to allow you to work on several documents at the same time. I have been using Programmer's Notepad for my classes for several years. My students love using it. The newest version automatically closes your tags for you. A screenshot of Programmer's Notepad 2.10.1010 is shown in Figure 1-3.

Taco HTML

Despite its odd name, Taco HTML is a fully featured editor for the MAC OS X. It offers code completion, syntax highlighting, and multiple tabs. Unfortunately, it is not free, and costs $25 for a license. Visit www.tacosw.com to download the 30-day trial.

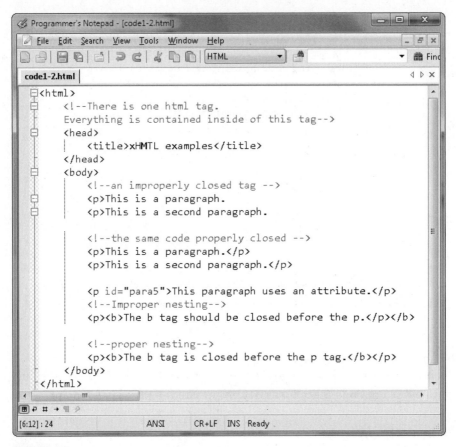

FIGURE 1-3 • Programmer's Notepad 2.10.1010

WYSIWYG Editors

WYSIWYG editors are very popular with web designers. They allow fast development of web pages. However, they tend to hide the HTML behind a series of dialog boxes. I recommend avoiding these editors until you are very comfortable with HTML.

Adobe Dreamweaver

Dreamweaver, shown in Figure 1-4, is probably the most used WYSIWYG editor in the world. It is very fast, produces beautiful pages, and manages most web site creation. Versions exist for both Windows and Mac OS X. Purchase a copy from www.adobe.com/products/dreamweaver/. At press time, the package cost $399.00. Student pricing might be available from your school. See your instructor for details.

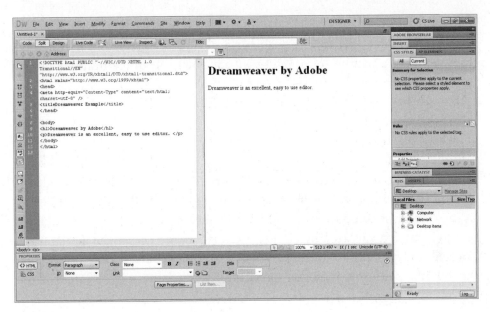

FIGURE 1-4 • Dreamweaver

Microsoft Expression Web

Expression Web is a relatively new tool from Microsoft. While slightly less powerful than Dreamweaver, it handles all of your web page creation needs. Additionally, it is much less expensive than Dreamweaver. At press time, the software was available from www.microsoftstore.com for $79.00. If your school belongs to the Microsoft Academic Alliance, you might be able to get a free copy of this program. See your instructor for details.

Web Browsers

The last items you need to build web pages are web browsers. All operating systems come preloaded with at least one browser. As a web designer, you should have all of the modern browsers installed on your system. The three most popular browsers are Internet Explorer, Mozilla Firefox, and Safari. For all practical purposes, all do the task of surfing the web admirably.

Remember that HTML is a recommendation. Web browser manufacturers are free to render tags as they see fit. Thus, a web page that looks fine in Internet Explorer may look terrible in Firefox. Coding a page for a particular browser is not a smart move. Some users are devoted to their browser. A page that only renders in Internet Explorer will chase away Firefox users. If your site is selling a product, you have chased away at least 40 percent of your potential customers.

Microsoft Internet Explorer

Internet Explorer (IE) is only available on Windows platforms. It is a good browser, with a number of usability enhancements. It offers multiple tabs, a private browsing mode, and several security enhancements. IE gets a lot of bad press as being insecure. While it is true that IE is hacked more often, it is overall a good browser.

Mozilla Firefox

Firefox is typically the browser of choice among computer professionals. It is a fast browser, with many security enhancements. What makes Firefox different is its support of add-ons. An add-on will change how Firefox works. Add-ons are free programs written by Firefox users. Figure 1-5 shows the add-on page located at https://addons.mozilla.org/en-US/firefox. Firefox comes installed on most Linux platforms. For other operating systems, get a copy of Firefox from www.mozilla.org.

FIGURE 1-5 · The add-ons page in Firefox

Safari

Safari is the browser loaded onto OS X computers. It is a good basic browser. One of its main features is its ability to track your favorite sites. Upon opening Safari, you see a preview of your favorite sites. It is reasonably secure with good features. A Windows version is available. Safari on Linux is possible, but requires the installation of a helper program titled Wine.

CAUTION   *IE and Firefox are the two most popular browsers in use worldwide. It is difficult to determine which is more popular. Several sites track which browsers visit them. Visit www.w3schools.com/browsers/browsers_stats.asp and www .thecounter.com/stats/ for some insight into browser usage.*

Summary

This chapter briefly described the history and origins of the Internet. It defined HTML, its developer, and its purpose. It discussed several different versions of HTML and identified the preferred version. Finally, you grew acquainted with a list of development tools and web languages.

QUIZ

1. _____ is a client-side scripting language.
   A. CSS
   B. PHP
   C. JavaScript
   D. ASP

2. This organization controls the development of web languages.
   A. W3C
   B. CERN
   C. DOD
   D. ARPA

3. The address for a web page is more correctly known as a _____.
   A. link
   B. hypertext
   C. URL
   D. nest

4. _____ developed the fundamental principles of the World Wide Web.
   A. Vint Cerf
   B. Tim Berners-Lee
   C. The United States Department of Defense
   D. Bob Kahn

5. Which of the following lines of XHTML code is correctly nested and closed?
   A. \<p\>\<b\>First line\</p\>\</b\>
   B. \<b\>\<p\>Second line\</p\>
   C. \<p\>\<b\>Third Line\</b\>\</p\>
   D. \<b\>Fourth line\</p\>

6. This helper language formats web pages.
   A. CSS
   B. JavaScript
   C. PHP
   D. Dreamweaver

7. The Internet first became functional in _____.
   A. 1960
   B. 1969
   C. 1973
   D. 1993

8. **This is the version of HTML I recommend using.**
   A. HTML 5
   B. HTML 4.01
   C. XHTML
   D. HTML 1

9. **Which of the following is not part of the definition of well formed?**
   A. All tags must be closed.
   B. Tags must be properly nested.
   C. Attributes may be null.
   D. Tags are in lowercase.

10. **"Not to be supported in future releases" is the definition of _____ .**
   A. obsolete
   B. deprecated
   C. extensible
   D. nested

chapter *2*

Your First Web Pages

This chapter will create your first HTML pages. You will use the standard HTML tags. Finally, you will create a template for use throughout the rest of the book.

CHAPTER OBJECTIVES

In this chapter, you will

- List the components of a web page
- Build an HTML template
- Create your first web site
- List and use common HTML tags
- Format using CSS
- Perform validation

17

The journey of 1000 miles begins with a single step. For web development, the first web page is that first step. You must learn the component parts of a web page before you can begin writing web pages.

In this chapter, you will explore the basic components of a web page. Additionally, you will build a template to simplify future development. You will encounter tags and formatting rules. At the end of this chapter, you will have a nicely formatted page with which you can amaze your friends and family.

Components of a Web Page

All web documents are composed of at least the same two elements. All web documents have a head and a body. The *head* describes the content type of the document, while the *body* holds the actual content. Your documents will have a head and a body. This rule holds regardless of the type of web document. Images, streamed songs, and standard web pages have headers and footers.

Doctype

Web pages have a third component. All web pages should have a line that indicates the version of XHTML used by the page. This line is the *doctype*. Using a doctype is mandatory for all XHTML pages.

The doctype is probably the most confusing line of code in your web documents. The doctype indicates the URL to the document type declaration (DTD) used by the document. DTDs are the rules this XHTML document follows. Good analogies to DTDs are the ground rules in a particular softball field. Each field has different rules regarding dead balls, book rule doubles, and home runs.

There are several different DTDs usable in your documents. The most current is the XHTML 1.1 document DTD. This doctype, originally called the strict doctype, rigorously applies all of the rules for XHTML. This DTD, while harder to work with, results in the most correct XHTML. Pages using this DTD cannot use any deprecated elements or framesets. I recommend using the strict DTD for all of your documents. Code Block 2-1 shows the correct doctype for the strict XHTML DTD.

CODE BLOCK 2-1

```
<!DOCTYPE html PUBLIC "-//W3C//DTD XHTML 1.1//EN"
"http://www.w3.org/TR/xhtml11/DTD/xhtml11.dtd">
```

The transitional DTD helped web developers migrate from older versions of HTML to XHTML. Deprecated tags and elements will work with this DTD. While this DTD is easy to work with, your pages may not work in newer browsers. Unless you have a very specific need, avoid the transitional DTD.

The frameset DTD works like the transitional DTD but adds frame support. Frames are a method in XHTML that allows multiple windows in the web browser. This technique of dividing the page lost favor in the early 2000s. As with the transitional DTD, you should avoid it unless you need to use frames.

Still Struggling

The doctype lines are hard to remember. Whenever I need to type a doctype, I copy one from the Web. The doctype page at www.w3schools.com/tags/tag_DOCTYPE.asp is a good choice.

Head

Creating the head for your web pages is rather easy. Headers are fairly consistent from page to page. The head contains one required element and several optional elements.

The head for your XHTML page follows immediately after the doctype, inside of the head tags. Code Block 2-2 contains the minimum head for an XHTML document. Notice that the html tag is opened but not yet closed. It will be closed after the body tag in Code Block 2-3.

CODE BLOCK 2-2

```
<html>
<head>
    <title>This is your title</title>

</head>
```

Code Block 2-2 will work if you are coding a web page in English and it will be viewed on a computer listing English as its primary language. The page will render poorly if you are writing in Cyrillic. To compensate for regional differences, the html tag uses attributes to describe the language of the page.

An *attribute* is a part of an HTML tag that further describes the tag. A simple analogy is with your clothes. It is likely that you saw several people wearing shirts today. The shirt is comparable to the HTML tag. Now, each shirt has a color. This is the attribute of the shirt.

Attributes are written inside of the <> for the tag. It is a place in your HTML documents that I call the attribute space. Proper XHTML etiquette requires that all attributes have a value. Code Block 2-3 shows a correct <html> and <head> section. The <html> tag uses two attributes. First the XML *name space* is set. This, along with the doctype, completely defines the rules used by the document. Second, the English language is specified with the xml:lang attribute. For a complete list of language codes, visit www.w3schools.com/tags/ref_language_codes.asp.

CAUTION *Not listing the lang tags within the html tag will result in your page defaulting to the English language.*

CODE BLOCK 2-3

```
<html xmlns="http://www.w3.org/1999/xhtml" xml:lang="en">
<head>
        <title>This is your title</title>

</head>
```

Title

The head may contain several elements. Only the title is required. The contents of the title element will appear in the very top of your browser window. Figure 2-1 illustrates where the title will appear in Internet Explorer 8. Notice

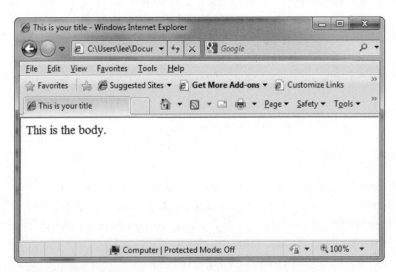

FIGURE 2-1 · The title element displayed in Internet Explorer 8

that the title appears in the title bar for Explorer and in the tab for the page. Additionally, the title may appear in your taskbar if you minimize the page.

TIP   *There are two ways to open a page from your computer in a browser. The first is to drag the page into the browser. The second is to File | Open the page. For Internet Explorer 8 users, the File menu is visible if you turn it on. Turn the menu on under the Tools drop-down, and then select the Toolbars option. Select the menu bar option.*

Meta

The meta tag is used to hold information about the web page. Information contained within the meta tag will not be displayed on the screen. Instead, computer programs can read the meta tags. The meta tag requires a content attribute and should have a name attribute. While the meta tag is completely optional, I recommend using the meta tag to describe the author of the page. Code Block 2-4 shows common usages of the meta tag.

CODE BLOCK 2-4

```
<meta name="description" content="Brief description of the page"/>
<meta name="author" content="Lee M. Cottrell" />
```

Optional Head Elements

Table 2-1 lists the remaining optional elements for the head section of your web page. Many of these elements are used later in the text.

Body

The header section of a page describes the document. The body section contains the actual content of the page. This is the section of your HTML document to focus upon. You will spend nearly all of your web development time working on the body.

TABLE 2-1 Optional Head Elements

Element	Description
style	Holds formatting information for the current page.
link	Holds the URL for an external style sheet document.
base	Used for scripting languages to set the home page for the script.

An HTML Template

Creating a new web page is rather daunting. You have to enter the correct doc-type, add head elements, and create a body. Since all web pages have the same elements, it can simplify your life to create a template. Code Block 2-3 lists a standard XHTML template. It includes the correct doctype, a title, language choice, and meta tags holding your name and a description of the page.

You should create this document. Start by creating a folder on your computer called HTML. Fire up your web editor of choice and enter the code in Code Block 2-5. To simplify finding this document later, name it **!template.html** and save it into your HTML folder.

TIP   *The ! at the beginning of the filename will ensure that it is always at the top of the File Open dialog box. This is a handy trick for documents or folders of current projects.*

CODE BLOCK 2-5

```
<!DOCTYPE html PUBLIC "-//W3C//DTD XHTML 1.1//EN"
"http://www.w3.org/TR/xhtml11/DTD/xhtml11.dtd">
<html xmlns="http://www.w3.org/1999/xhtml" xml:lang="en">
     <head>
          <title>This is your title</title>
          <meta name="description" content="Page description"/>
          <meta name="author" content="Lee M. Cottrell" />
     </head>
     <body>
          <p>This is the body.</p>
     </body>
</html>
```

TIP   *Several web sites provide proper XHTML templates. One of the better sites is www.webstandards.org/learn/reference/templates/xhtml11/.*

This template will create a basic black-on-white web page, shown in Figure 2-2. The title tag appears at the top of the page, and the contents of the body are visible. The meta tags are not visible.

Using the Template

Now that you have the template, creating web pages will be a little easier. You will have to worry less about the tedium of web pages, and be able to concentrate

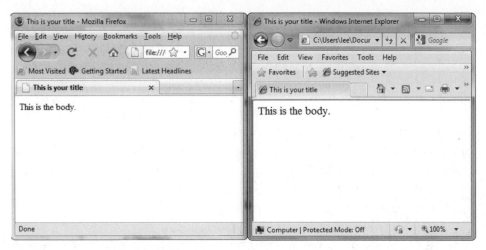

FIGURE 2-2 · The template as viewed in Firefox and Internet Explorer

on the fun part—designing the page! However, as with all good tools, you need to learn how to use the template.

Start using the template by opening the !template.html file in your web editor. Then select File | Save As. Name the document whatever you wish, but end with the extension .html. Change the title text and the description. Delete the contents of the body tag. Save the document again and you are ready to begin.

CAUTION   *One of the hardest things about web development is file management. For your own sanity, save all of your filenames with lowercase letters and do not include spaces.*

Creating Your First Web Site

Now we can get to the fun stuff. We can build web pages and web sites. In teaching HTML, I have found that students have a very hard time getting started. I have countered that by creating a simple checklist to follow every time you create a site. By following the checklist, you will create a properly organized web site that has room to grow and is easy to manage.

Web sites typically have dozens of files. Without a folder structure, you are likely to get confused. Create a folder for every project you work on. Name this folder after your project. This habit will help you keep project files separate.

TIP *Creating a folder per project is useful in all aspects of your life, not just HTML!*

The first file loaded on every web site is index.html. Regardless of the name of your project, name your first file index.html. This habit will allow you to build links later and will allow your page to work if you purchase web space.

Name additional files whatever you desire. However, you should stick with short, easy names that describe the page contents. Use lowercase letters, and avoid using spaces. Like the index page, they will end with the extension .html. For example, if you are creating a page about your friend Dave, you should name the page dave.html or friend.html.

TIP *While browsing the web, you may see sites that use extensions other than .html. Most of these extensions refer to the scripting language that generates the HTML for the site.*

Practice Creating a Web Site

In the following steps, we will create a multipage web site about my family's pets. Currently we have one cat, one dog, and a varying number of fish. The web site will have four pages. There will be the index page, a page each for the cat and dog, and one for all of the fish. There will be no content as of yet.

1. Open up your web editor.
2. Select File | Open. Browse to the folder containing !template.html. Open it into the editor.
3. In the next steps, you are going to rename the template file and build the folder structure for the web page. Start by using your editor's menu to Select File | Save As.

   a. Browse to your HTML folder.

If you are using Windows, create a folder by right-clicking inside of the white area listing the files. Select New Folder. The following illustration shows the creation of the folder in Windows 7:

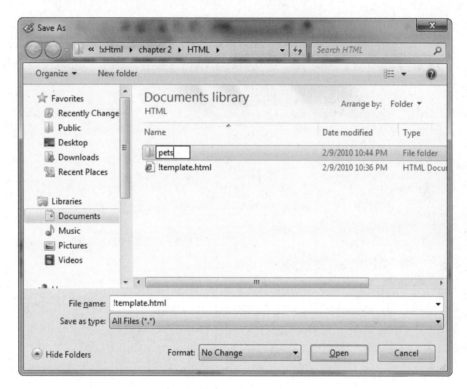

If you are using OS X, click Action and select New Folder. In either case, name the folder **pets**.

TIP *You can create folders in any way you are comfortable with.*

b. Open the pets folder.

c. Save the file in the pets folder as **index.html**.

4. Change the title tag to read **Cottrell's Pets**, as shown next.

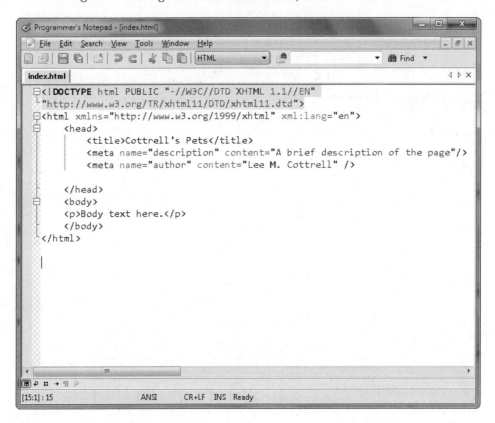

5. Change the meta description to read **"A site dedicated to Lee Cottrell's pets"**.

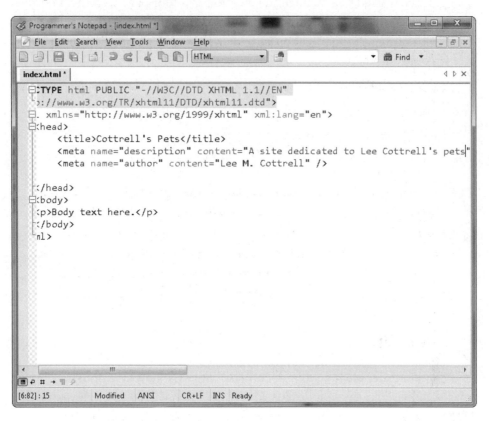

6. Delete the text "Body text here." from the body tag.

7. Save the file again.

8. Reopen the !template.html file. Save it as **cat.html** in the pets folder.

9. Change the title of the document to **Shadow Kitty**. Change the meta description to read **"A page about Shadow Kitty"**.

10. Save the document again.

11. Repeat Steps 8 to 10 to create dog.html and fish.html. Use **Alex the dog** for the title of the dog.html file. Use **School of Fish** for the title of the dog.html file. Create an appropriate meta description.

Web Site Creation Checklist

The practice walked you through the creation of a four-page web site. In order to create this site, you followed a short series of steps. These steps, when followed will ensure proper creation of your web site. With practice, these steps will become automatic.

1. Create a folder for the project.
2. Open the !template.html file. Save it in the folder as index.html.
3. Modify the title, description, and body content.
4. Repeat Steps 2 and 3 for every page in the web site.

TIP   *The best way to learn something is to practice on something you understand. One of my most successful students was a devoted fan of anime. Every time he learned a new technology, he applied it to a different anime cartoon. He was successful because he took the technology and learned it on his terms, in his world. By doing so, he gained a complete understanding of the technology. Emulate this student. Find something you care about and build a web site about it.*

Common HTML Tags

Tags contain the content of your document. Tags exist for paragraphs, headings, images, links, and many other categories. This section will focus on the common HTML tags. After this chapter, you will be able to build a basic web page for any topic!

Recall from Chapter 1 that Tim Berners-Lee developed HTML as a method to share research papers. Most of the core HTML tags make publishing a research paper on the web easier. The most used tags will focus on text handling.

Proper Use of Tags

A tag in HTML is typically composed of three elements. Figure 2-3 describes the components of a typical tag. The opening tag comes first. Any attributes needed by the tag are in the opening. Attributes always have a value, contained within double quotes. In the

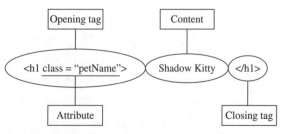

FIGURE 2-3 · Component parts of an HTML tag

illustration, the value is petName. Following the opening is the content. Content will differ based on the tag. Paragraph tags will hold text, while table tags will hold additional tags. Finally, the tag is closed. To close a tag, place the forward slash in front of the tag name. Note how, for instance, </h1> in Figure 2-3 closes the <h1> tag.

Notice that the tags in Figure 2-3 are in lowercase. This is very important. Proper XHTML requires the use of lowercase for all tag and attribute names. If you use uppercase, the HTML will probably work, but your page will not pass validation. Validation is discussed later in the chapter.

Some tags are a little different. They have no content. These tags are called empty tags. An empty tag will self-close. The three empty tags are <br />, <hr />, and <img />. Notice that the closing / is placed after the tag name.

CAUTION *Not closing tags can lead to unpredictable results on your web site.*

<p>

The <p> tag holds paragraphs for your web site. Each paragraph will be contained within the open and close tags. HTML will render the paragraph as one complete unit, followed by a blank line. If your site needs five paragraphs, then your HTML code will have five <p> and </p> tags. Code Block 2-6 shows two paragraphs about my cat Shadow. Figure 2-4 shows the output of the paragraph tags in Internet Explorer.

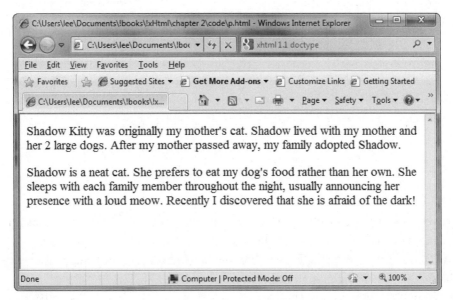

FIGURE 2-4 • Output of two paragraph tags

CODE BLOCK 2-6

```
<p>Shadow Kitty was originally my mother's cat. Shadow lived with
my mother and her 2 large dogs. After my mother passed away, my
family adopted Shadow.</p>
<p>Shadow is a neat cat. She prefers to eat my dog's food rather
than her own. She sleeps with each family member throughout the
night, usually announcing her presence with a loud meow. Recently
I discovered that she is afraid of the dark!</p>
```

There are two important things to notice in Figure 2-4. First, notice the blank line following the paragraphs. All browsers will add two line breaks after the end of the </p>. Second, notice how Internet Explorer created its own line breaks. All browsers will decide where the line should break based on screen size. In a larger window, the line would break in a different place. At this point in your web development career, you have very little control over how browsers render your text.

In addition to controlling new lines, browsers will ignore most of the white space in your code. White space includes tabs, newlines, and multiple spaces. Pressing ENTER, TAB, or SPACEBAR multiple times will have no effect on the output in your browser. Consider Code Block 2-7. It is the same as Code Block 2-6, but I added a number of newlines and tabs within the <p> tags. Despite these changes, the output in Internet Explorer is identical to Figure 2-4.

CODE BLOCK 2-7

```
<p>          Shadow Kitty was originally my mother's cat.
Shadow lived with my mother and her
2 large dogs.

After
 my
 mother passed away, my family adopted Shadow.</p>
<p>Shadow is a neat cat. She prefers to eat my dog's food rather
than her own. She sleeps with each family member throughout the
night, usually announcing her presence with a loud meow. Recently
I discovered that she is afraid of the dark!</p>
```


Sometimes you need to force a new line in your document. The <br />, or line break, tag provides a new line wherever you place it. The <br /> tag is one of XHTML's empty tags. It has no content and it self-closes. Code Block 2-8 shows the <br /> tag in action. The output is shown in Figure 2-5.

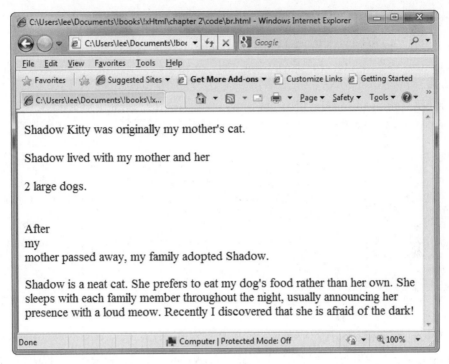

FIGURE 2-5 · Example of the <br /> tag

CODE BLOCK 2-8

```
<p>Shadow Kitty was originally my mother's cat. <br />
<br />
Shadow lived with my mother and her
<br />
<br />
2 large dogs.
<br />
<br />
<br />
After<br />
 my<br />
 mother passed away, my family adopted Shadow.</p>
  <p>Shadow is a neat cat. She prefers to eat my dog's food rather
than her own. She sleeps with each family member throughout the
night, usually announcing her presence with a loud meow. Recently
I discovered that she is afraid of the dark!</p>
```

<hr />

The <hr />, horizontal rule, tag produces a rule (line) across the screen. Like the <br /> tag, the <hr /> tag first produces a newline wherever it is placed. The rule is then drawn across the screen below the <hr />. Last, another newline follows the rule. In Code Block 2-9, the <hr /> tag is placed between the two </p> tags. Figure 2-6 shows the output.

CODE BLOCK 2-9

```
<p>Shadow Kitty was originally my mother's cat. Shadow lived with my
mother and her 2 large dogs. After my mother passed away, my family
adopted Shadow.</p>
<hr />
<p>Shadow is a neat cat. She prefers to eat my dog's food rather than her
own. She sleeps with each family member throughout the night, usually
announcing her presence with a loud meow. Recently I discovered that she
is afraid of the dark!</p>
<hr />
```

<h1>, <h2>, <h3>, <h4>, <h5>, <h6>

Paragraphs are important elements on a web page. However, a web page with too many paragraphs is very difficult to read. Headers, created by the <h#> tags, provide a way to break up the text and alert the reader to the information that follows. There are six levels of headers. As the heading number increases, the

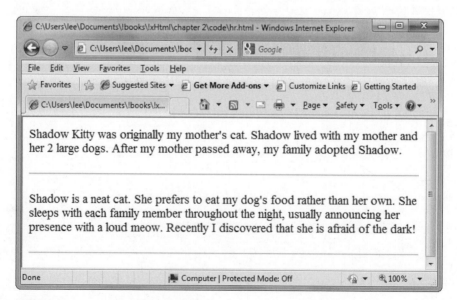

FIGURE 2-6 · Example of the <hr /> tag

size of the header font decreases. Figure 2-7 shows the relative sizes of headers in both Explorer and Firefox.

In both Firefox and Explorer, header sizes decrease down the page. However, notice that Firefox's font is a little smaller than Explorer. This is your first real experience with the differences in how browsers render HTML. This difference will become a problem, as we get deeper into HTML.

CAUTION *If you forget to close your header tags, all of your page will be rendered as a header.*

Having six levels of headers gives you a great deal of flexibility. Technically, you can use the headers any way you see fit. Traditionally, each has a particular role. See Code Block 2-10 for an illustration of these roles. In general, <h1> tags display the title of an entire page; <h2> tags are subheaders under the title; <h3> tags are sub-subheaders under the <h2> tag; and so on. Finally, <h6> tags contain footer text or legal disclaimers.

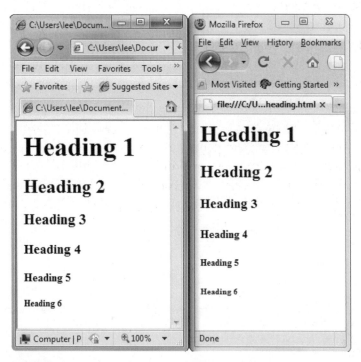

FIGURE 2-7 • Headers in Explorer and Firefox

CODE BLOCK 2-10

```
<h1>Chapter 1</h1>
     <p>Brief description about chapter 1</p>
     <h2>Section 1</h2>
          <p>Paragraph about section 1</p>
          <h3>Subsection 1</h3>
               <p>Paragraph about subsection 1</p>
          <h3>Subsection 2</h3>
               <p>Paragraph about subsection 2</p>

     <h2>Section 2</h2>
          <p>Paragraph about section 1</p>
          <h3>Subsection 1</h3>
               <p>Paragraph about subsection 1</p>

     <h2>Summary</h2>
          <p>Summary Paragraph</p>
<h6>Copyright 2010 Lee Cottrell</h6>
```

Headers should never directly follow each other. Place a paragraph or image between the headers. If this proves to be impossible, merge the headers together. The paragraph between the <h1> and the <h2> in Code Block 2-10 shows the correct usage of headers. The indentions in the example are for clarity only. Recall that HTML will simply ignore them.

<!-- -->

The comment tag is confusing to beginning developers. Browsers will ignore your comments, having no effect on your output. Given this, you may wonder why you should use them. The comment describes portions of your code, provides notes to future developers, or simply identifies the source of content on the page. Professional developers use comments to describe what they did and, more important, why they did what they did. Code Block 2-11 shows two comments.

CODE BLOCK 2-11

```
<!-- Information found on w3.org, written by Eric Johnson.-->
<p>Big paragraph here.</p>
<!--This multiline comment hides paragraphs that are not working.
<p>Not complete paragraph</p>
<p>Another not complete paragraph</p>
-->
```

In addition to describing your code, comments can help you fix your code. Imagine that you are working on a large web page for your boss, and the fourth and fifth paragraphs are not finished. Your boss calls and "requests" that you show her what you have done. Requests are simply nicely worded commands, so you get ready for her visit. Rather than show her partially completed paragraphs, use the comment tag to hide them from her. The second set of comments in Code Block 2-11 demonstrates this trick.

TIP *Comments are typically green text in your editor.*

Attributes of Tags

Attributes, as defined previously, are codes that modify the current tag. You first encountered them earlier in this chapter inside of the meta tag. The name and content are attributes of the meta tag. You will use them in several ways throughout your exploration of HTML. Table 2-2 lists the attributes common to all tags.

Refer back to Figure 2-3. The h1 tag used the class attribute. The attribute is within the angle brackets of the tag in the area I call the attribute space. The correct usage of all attributes, as shown in Code Block 2-12, is to use the name of the attribute, followed by an equal sign (=), and then the value of the attribute in double quotes (").

Figure 2-8 shows the effect of the style and title attributes. Notice that the h1 tag is italicized. The style attribute changed the text-style to italic. The lang

TABLE 2-2 Attributes Common to All HTML Elements

Attribute	Description
class	This attribute applies formatting to the element Class and sets a group of formatting rules to the element.
dir	When used with the lang attribute, this indicates whether the text reads from Right to Left or Left to Right. Its values are either ltr or rtl.
id	The Id attribute names the object within the HTML document. Id can also apply formatting rules.
lang	This attribute identifies the language of the object. It is very important when the language of the object is different from the rest of the page.
style	This attribute applies formatting to the element. Use style when you have a small number of formatting rules.
title	This attribute specifies a title for the tag. It will render as a tooltip in most browsers.

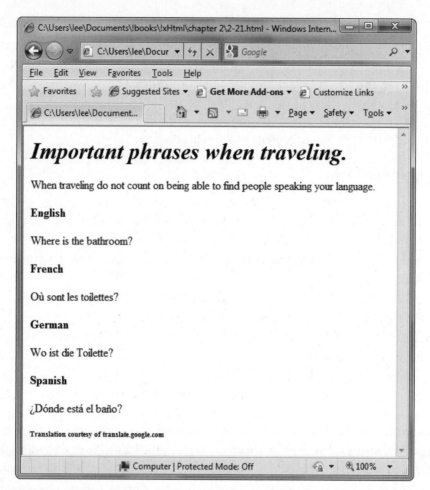

FIGURE 2-8 • Important phrases displayed in Internet Explorer

attributes have no visible effect, but the browser recognized the lang and displayed the text properly. Finally, the title attribute is visible as the tooltip at the bottom of the screen. The tip appeared when I hovered over the h6.

CODE BLOCK 2-12

```
<h1 style="font-style:italic;">Important phrases when
traveling.</h1>
<p>When traveling do not count on being able to find people
speaking your language.</p>
<h4>English</h4>
<p lang="en">Where is the bathroom?</p>
<h4>French</h4>
<p lang="fr">Où sont les toilettes?</p>
<h4>German</h4>
```

```
<p lang="de" >Wo ist die Toilette?</p>
<h4>Spanish</h4>
<p lang="es">¿Dónde está el baño?</p>
<h6 title="Legal Disclaimer">Translation courtesy of translate.
google.com</h6>
```

In general, you should not use attributes that modify the appearance or layout of the element. Most of these attributes were deprecated, in favor of using CSS. If you need to set color, or align an element, use the CSS in the style or class attributes. The next section introduces CSS.

CSS Formatting

Cascading Style Sheets (CSS) represents the correct way to format your web documents. CSS applies a series of rules to your web documents. These rules, defined by you, will change how browsers render your code. You are able to change where your elements appear on the page, their color, font, and many other elements.

CSS Properties and Values

CSS rules are set by using properties and values. A property is a predefined CSS element. This element will change how a tag renders. The value represents what you want the property to do. To use the property, you will need to type the property name, followed by a colon (:), and then the value. The rule ends with a semicolon (;). Refer back to Code Block 2-12. The h1 is styled to use italic font. The code font-style:italic; tells the browser to display this h1 in italics.

Learning how to use CSS initially means learning the properties and their associated values. Most properties accept a limited number of values, while some accept any user input. CSS, while challenging at first, will become your trusted ally in web development.

TIP   *Visit devguru.com at http://devguru.com/technologies/css2/index.asp for a complete list of usable CSS properties.*

CSS Font Families

Fonts, describe how the letters look. A modern computer has hundreds of different fonts. Unfortunately, the fonts on your computer may not be on another person's computer. As such, you need to choose web-safe fonts. Figure 2-9 shows fonts common to all computers. If the font you want is not listed, there might be an equivalent.

FIGURE 2-9 · Fonts common to all computers

Fonts belong to families. The three families most useful on the web are the serif, sans-serif, and monospaced. *Serif* fonts have small lines at edges of the top and bottom to finish them. Look at the Georgia font in Figure 2-9. Look at the first word, The. The *T* in "The" has serifs at the ends of the top line, and as feet. The *h* also has feet. These are serif. The serifs make it easier to read when printed on paper.

TIP *Visit ampsoft.net at www.ampsoft.net/webdesign-l/WindowsMacFonts.html for a good description of web-safe fonts and equivalents.*

The Courier New font in Figure 2-9 is a monospaced font. *Monospaced* fonts use the same amount of space for each letter. Unless you need to display programming code or wish your page to look like a typewriter, avoid monospaced fonts.

The most common font families used on the web are *sans-serif* fonts. Sans is a French word meaning "without." Thus, a sans-serif font does not have the little lines at the edges of the characters. Sans-serif fonts are easier to read on a computer screen. Look at Figure 2-9 again. The Verdana and Arial fonts are very clean. No serifs are present.

TIP *A common use for fonts on the Web is to use a serif font for headings and sans-serif fonts for everything else. This makes the headings stand out, while keeping the paragraphs on the site easier to read.*

The CSS font properties control how your text renders. Eight properties directly deal with fonts. I will list the four common properties in Table 2-3.

TABLE 2-3 Common Font Properties

Property	Description	Allowed Values	Example
font-family	This property sets the desired font for the element. You may list several fonts and a default font. Using multiple fonts is recommended to ensure your page looks as you want it.	You may use any font on a computer. However, you should limit your choices to web-safe fonts. The last entry is the font family.	font-family: "Times New Roman", Times, serif;
font-size	The font-size property changes the size of the text.	Several different sizes are possible. For simplicity, use a number followed by a pt. Larger points are bigger. Point values between 10 and 12 are optimal for reading.	font-size: 18pt;
font-style	This property allows you to make the font normal or italicized.	Italic, normal, oblique. Use oblique if italic fails.	font-style: italic;
font-weight	Font-weight describes the thickness of the letters.	Bold, bolder, lighter, normal, 100,200,300, 400,500,600,700, 800,900. The numbers represent the relative boldness of the letters. 400 is normal.	font-weight: bold;

How to Use CSS on a Web Page

There are three methods to apply CSS. The first method is to use the <style> tag in the <head> section. This method, called embedded styles, allows you to set rules for the tags on the entire page. For single-page web sites, this is the best method.

Second, you may use the style attribute and apply rules directly to an element. Use this method when you have an element with a unique style need. This method is far too tedious to apply to an entire page. Rules applied in this manner will override those set in the style tag.

For web sites with multiple pages, embedding the style on each page is tedious. The correct implementation here is to create a style document. To access the rules, you place a <link> tag in the <head> section. Style documents are covered in Chapter 4.

Use Embedded Styles

To embed a style section into your HTML document, you need to add a new element to the <head> section. The new element is the <style> tag. Enclosed within this tag are the rules and tags associated with the rules.

Embedded style elements provide a very efficient way to format your web page. You will set rules in the CSS for each HTML tag you wish to format. Once set, every matching tag in your HTML document will use the same rules.

Consider Code Block 2-13. I provided a rule for the <p> and <h1> tags. Be sure to notice the syntax. The p tag is present, *without* the angle braces. The CSS properties and values are set within a set of curly braces ({}). Every property set inside of these braces will apply to every <p> tag in the document.

CODE BLOCK 2-13

```
<style>
     p
     {
             font-family:Verdana, sans-serif;
             font-size:12pt;
     }
     h1
     {
             font-family:Georgia, serif;
             font-variant:small-caps;
             text-align:center;
     }
</style>
```

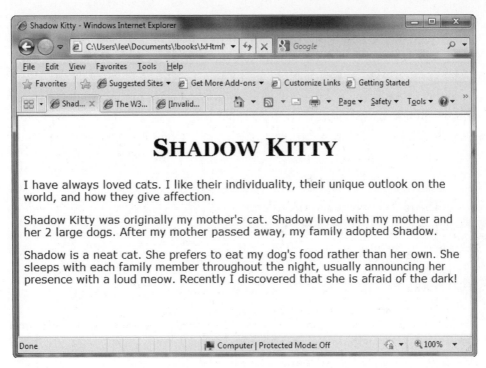

FIGURE 2-10 · The style tag in action

Figure 2-10 displays the results of this style applied to an HTML document. Notice that the header uses capital letters for all letters, but larger capital letters for the beginning of Shadow's name. This is the small-caps value being set. Refer back to Figure 2-9. The Shadow Kitty is indeed in Georgia, and the paragraphs are Verdana. Shadow Kitty is centered across the page, as text-align indicates.

TIP   *Neither text-align nor font-variant have been introduced in the text. There are more CSS properties than I can cover in the text. My recommendation is to find a web site or CSS reference book that lists the properties. From this starting point, start experimenting with the properties.*

Use the Style Attribute

The style attribute will allow you to set individual rules to tags. The attribute rules will either merge or override the embedded rules. This combination defines the term *cascading*, the C in CSS.

A good way to understand cascading is to consider the plight of a toddler. Imagine that a toddler asks Daddy for a cookie. Daddy says, "Yes" and sends him to the kitchen to get one. Mommy is in the kitchen and tells the toddler no. Since Mommy was the last rule applied, the toddler does not get a cookie. However, if Mommy says yes and allows the toddler a glass of milk, then both rules apply and the toddler is both eating and drinking.

In HTML, like the toddler, the last rule applied wins. In our <style> tag, the font-family is set to Verdana. If we wished to change our first paragraph, we could add a style attribute to the first <p> tag. Code Block 2-14 sets a style attribute to a paragraph. Figure 2-11 shows the resulting CSS rules for the first paragraph:

- The font-family remains Verdana.
- The font-size increases to 14pt.
- The background-color is light gray.

CODE BLOCK 2-14

```
<p style="font-size:14pt;background-color:lightGrey;">I have always
loved cats. I like their individuality, their unique outlook on the
world, and how they give affection.</p>
```

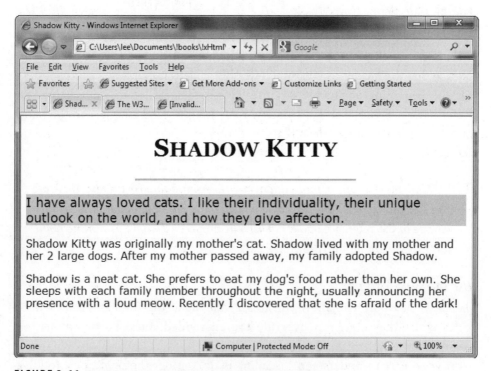

FIGURE 2-11 · The first paragraph changed using the style attribute

CSS and HTML Tags

Nearly all HTML tags have CSS properties devoted to them. As mentioned earlier in the text, CSS handles any attempts to format or change the layout of a tag. Code Block 2-15 shows how to format the <hr /> tag to be 50% of the page, 2 pixels high, and solid black. Figure 2-11 illustrates the code.

CODE BLOCK 2-15

```
hr
{
      width:50%;
      height:2px;
color:lightGrey;
      background-color:lightGrey;
}
```

Throughout the rest of this book, tags and CSS properties are introduced together. However, do not wait for me to introduce CSS. Visit devguru.com or another online reference page to learn CSS tags.

Bringing It All Together

This chapter developed several tags. We learned about creating an HTML document. The <p>, <h1>–<h6>, <br />, and <hr> tags were presented in isolation. CSS was introduced as a set of rules applied to an HTML document. Code Block 2-16 presents the complete cat.html document. I recommend completing cat.html on your own.

CODE BLOCK 2-16

```
<!DOCTYPE html PUBLIC "-//W3C//DTD XHTML 1.1//EN"
"http://www.w3.org/TR/xhtml11/DTD/xhtml11.dtd">
<html xmlns="http://www.w3.org/1999/xhtml" xml:lang="en">
      <head>
            <title>Shadow Kitty</title>
            <meta name="description" content="A page about my cat"/>
            <meta name="author" content="Lee M. Cottrell" />
            <style type="text/css">
                  p
                  {
                        font-family:Verdana, sans-serif;
                        font-size:12pt;
                  }
```

```
                       h1
                       {
                              font-family:Georgia, serif;
                              font-variant:small-caps;
                              text-align:center;
                       }
                       hr
                       {

                              width:50%;
                              height:2px;
                              color:lightGrey;
                              background-color:lightGrey;
                       }
                   </style>
             </head>
             <body>
                   <h1>Shadow Kitty</h1>
                   <hr />

<p style="font-size:14pt;background-color:lightGrey;">I have always
loved cats. I like their individuality, their unique outlook on the
world, and how they give affection.</p>

<p>Shadow Kitty was originally my mother's cat. Shadow lived with my
mother and her 2 large dogs. After my mother passed away, my family
adopted Shadow.</p>

<p>Shadow is a neat cat. She prefers to eat my dog's food rather than
her own. She sleeps with each family member throughout the night,
usually announcing her presence with a loud meow. Recently I discovered
that she is afraid of the dark!</p>

             </body>
       </html>
```

Validation

Writing HTML text is time consuming and error prone. To make your life more
difficult, different browsers will render your code differently. To help remedy
this problem, you need to write perfect HTML code.

Perfect, or valid, HTML code is the ideal of web development. To achieve
this, you need to avoid using any deprecated tags. Additionally, all tags and
attributes you use must be correctly typed. Finally, use the correct doctype. All
of the complete code blocks presented in this book will pass validation.

To ensure that your code passes validation, the W3 offers a free validation
service at validator.w3.org. This site allows you to check your HTML or XHTML.

Errors in your code are presented, along with a solution. Figure 2-12 shows the output of an HTML document that failed to place text inside of a <p> tag.

To validate your code, you need to visit validator.w3.org. From there, click the tab that applies to your situation. I usually use the "validate by direct input." Using this tag, I need to copy and paste my code into the box. Once the code is on their site, hit Check. Read and fix the errors, one at a time.

TIP *Just because your code works, it does not mean it is valid. Check all code before describing it as done!*

This process can take a long time. Many beginning students do not feel that it is necessary. They are quite incorrect. First, validated pages will work in all browsers on all operating systems. Valid code will have the fewest inconsistencies

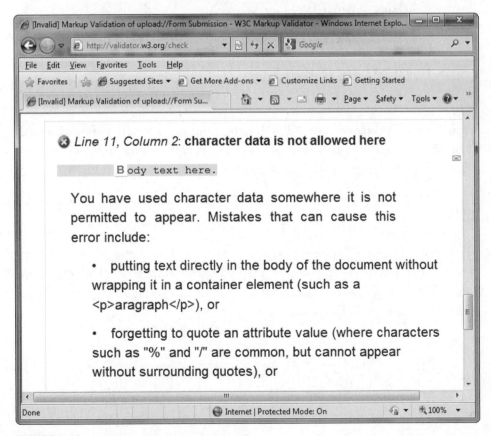

FIGURE 2-12 · Error output from validator.w3.org

Document type	"Gold"	Blue
HTML 2.0	W3C HTML 2.0 ✔	W3C HTML 2.0 ✔
HTML 3.2	W3C HTML 3.2 ✔	W3C HTML 3.2 ✔
HTML 4.0	W3C HTML 4.0 ✔	W3C HTML 4.0 ✔
HTML 4.01	W3C HTML 4.01 ✔	W3C HTML 4.01 ✔

Document type	"Gold"	Blue
XHTML 1.0	W3C XHTML 1.0 ✔	W3C XHTML 1.0 ✔
XHTML 1.1	W3C XHTML 1.1 ✔	W3C XHTML 1.1 ✔
XHTML Basic 1.0	W3C XHTML basic 1.0 ✔	W3C XHTML basic 1.0 ✔
XHTML-Print 1.0	W3C XHTML print 1.0 ✔	W3C XHTML print 1.0 ✔

FIGURE 2-13 · W3C's validation buttons

from browser to browser. Second, validating your pages is a sign of professionalism. Finally, validated pages get to display the snazzy W3C button. Figure 2-13 shows some of the possible buttons.

Summary

This chapter introduced how to create web pages. You learned the basic components of a web page. You created a template for future reuse. The most common HTML tags were introduced and used. Finally, you learned how to apply CSS to common HTML tags.

QUIZ

1. Deprecated tags and attributes have been replaced with _____.
   A. CSS properties
   B. newer HTML
   C. a strict DTD
   D. JavaScript

2. The _____ element of the head displays the name of the page in the caption bar of your browser.
   A. <meta>
   B. <style>
   C. <title>
   D. <link>

3. CSS rules are set using this format.
   A. property = value
   B. property:value;
   C. property = value;
   D. property:value

4. To display a horizontal rule on the page, use the _____ tag.
   A. <h1>
   B. <p>
   C.
   D. <hr />

5. Tags that self-close are known as _____ tags.
   A. deprecated
   B. empty
   C. handy
   D. property

6. Which of the following is the correct syntax for an attribute set on the <p> tag?
   A. <p>id="para1"</p>
   B. <p id=para1></p>
   C. <p id="para1"></p>
   D. <p id='para1'></p>

7. To create a paragraph, use the _____ tag.
   A.
   B. <p>
   C. <h1>
   D. <!-- -->

8. **The name of the first page loaded in web sites is _____ .**
   A. head.html
   B. first.html
   C. index.html
   D. begin.html

9. **The _____ tag is used to create the first set of subheaders on a page.**
   A. <h1>
   B. <h2>
   C. <h3>
   D. <h4>

10. **An embedded style sheet is created by _____ .**
    A. using the style attribute
    B. using the style tag
    C. using the link tag
    D. using the head tag

chapter **3**

Color and Graphics

You will learn how to use color and images on your web page. In addition to learning how to place images on your site, you will learn how to format the images so that all users can understand their content.

CHAPTER OBJECTIVES

In this chapter, you will

- Apply color to a web page
- Add images to a web site
- Acquire web graphics

The original HTML specification allowed only black-and-white text with no images. HTML 2 thankfully added color and images. Imagine how boring the Web would be without pictures and color!

The Internet is now a very colorful place. Sites use color and images to great effect. Stores use colors designed to stimulate your purchasing urges. Modified images provide humor on several sites.

Coloring Your Page

My favorite activity in grade school was coloring. Not that I was a great artist, I liked the big box of crayons my mother bought at the beginning of every school year. I liked both the smell and the myriad of colors. I opened a new box of crayons and felt like nothing could hold me back.

HTML colors are a bit like the big box of crayons. However, instead of 64 crayons, there are 16,777,216 possible color combinations. We will now list them all. Just kidding! You, however, need to learn how to build the colors.

HTML Color Codes

Colors on computer monitors are combinations of the colors red, green, and blue. Most developers call them RGB colors. By combining these colors, one can create nearly any color. For example combining red and blue will get you purple, while mixing red and green provides yellow. Combining all three colors yields white.

TIP *HTML colors are additive colors. Combining red and green produces yellow because of the manner their light waves interact. Wikipedia has a good article on additive colors.*

RGB colors are composed of three sets of values: one red, one green, and one blue. Each value can range from 0 to 255. Unfortunately, the values are not written in decimal numbers like humans use. RGB values use hexadecimal. Thus, the values range from 0 to FF.

Hexadecimal Primer

It is not overly important that you be able to read hexadecimal fluently. It is important that you have a basic understanding of how the numbers work. Humans usually deal with 10 single-digit numbers (0–9). The hexadecimal number system, or hex, contains 16 single-digit numbers (0–F). Table 3-1 contains a sampling of

TABLE 3-1 A Sampling of Hexadecimal Values and Their Decimal Equivalents

Hex	Decimal
0	0
1	1
9	9
A	10
B	11
C	12
D	13
E	14
F	15
10	16
1A	26
A5	165
BB	187
FF	255

hex values and their decimal equivalent. Notice that after 9 in hex, the digit A is presented. A through F are the additional six digits that, when combined with 0 through 9, make up the hexadecimal number system.

RGB Color Codes

RBG colors contain a pound (#) sign and six hexadecimal numbers. The first two positions indicate the amount of red in the color. The next two positions indicate the amount of green, and the last two positions the amount of blue. An RGB color code for fuchsia is #FF00FF. This reads as all of the red, no green, and all of the blue. Different colors result by varying the colors. A deep plum is #660099. The definition of black is the absence of colors, which is represented simply as #000000. White combines all colors as #FFFFFF.

TIP *To convert between Hexadecimal and English, use the calculator in Windows. Switch to scientific mode in Vista or earlier and the Programmers mode in Windows 7.*

As mentioned previously, there are over 16 million color combinations. Dozens of web sites provide examples of HTML color codes. One of the best is Webmonkey's color charts at www.webmonkey.com/reference/Color_Charts.

Still Struggling

RGB colors can seem difficult. All you need to do is learn how to use the colors. Any of the online color charts will provide the RGB code for a desired color. Copy and paste the desired color into your code.

You may see HTML colors in English names rather than RGB. This is acceptable, though not recommended. Some names are rather obvious. The name red is equivalent to #FF0000. The problem lies with the not-so-obvious ones. Cornflower Blue (#151B8D) is one example of a not-so-obvious color name. I did not know that corn produced flowers, let alone blue ones. I thought corn was white or yellow.

TIP   *Computerhope.com has a comprehensive page listing the color names and their equivalent RGB codes. Visit www.computerhope.com/htmcolor.htm to see the list.*

While it might be tempting to use the color names, the W3C recommends using the RGB values. The RGB values are consistent across browser and graphic programs.

TIP   *The HTML color codes are case insensitive. Thus, #FFFFFF works just as well as #ffffff.*

Coloring HTML Elements

Now that you know how HTML color works, it is time to color your page. We will apply color to both the background and text elements of the page. We will use CSS to perform this task.

The CSS property to change the background color is background-color. Background-color applies to many HTML tags, including the body, p tags, and header tags. Our first experiment with color will be a play document, just experimenting with color. To change the color of text, the proper CSS attribute is color. All CSS color elements are written in the same manner. Property:#colorCode;. Work through the following example to practice with colors.

Practice with HTML Background Colors

You will create a page called colorPlay.html that will demonstrate the use of colors in HTML.

1. Create a folder called **chapter3**.

2. In your editor, open the template you created in Chapter 2.

3. Save this template as **colorPlay.html** into your chapter3 folder.

4. Change the title tag contents to **Color Play**.

5. In the body tag, enter this tag:

   ```
   <h1>Color Play</h1>
   ```

6. After the <h1>, create a paragraph.

   ```
   <p>HTML has over 16 million colors.</p>
   ```

7. Code Block 3-1 shows the finished HTML document. Changed items are bolded. Switch to your browser and open the document using File | Open. Make sure it looks like the following illustration before going on.

CODE BLOCK 3-1

```
<!DOCTYPE html PUBLIC "-//W3C//DTD XHTML 1.1//EN"
"http://www.w3.org/TR/xhtml11/DTD/xhtml11.dtd">
<html xmlns="http://www.w3.org/1999/xhtml" xml:lang="en">
     <head>
          <title>Color Play</title>
          <meta name="description" _
          content="Experimenting with color"/>
          <meta name="author" content="Lee M. Cottrell" />
     </head>
     <body>
     <h1>Color Play</h1>
   <p>HTML has over 16 million colors.</p>
     </body>
</html>
```

8. Now scroll to the head tag. After the last meta tag and before the </head>, create an embedded style using the following code:

```
<style type="text/css">

</style>
```

9. Press ENTER a few times above the </style>. All of the CSS entries will be between the style tags.

10. Start by coloring the background of the HTML document itself. You will add the background-color property to the body. Make your style document look like the following code. I chose purple for my background. Choose whatever color you like.

```
<style type="text/css">
     body
     {
            background-color:#9999ff;
     }
</style>
```

11. Save your document and then re-fresh your page by clicking on the refresh button in your browser. The background color should change. Do not panic if it fails. Revisit each line of the code in Step 10. Be sure the color has six digits. Make sure there is a colon after color and a semicolon after the number. Most often, the error is quite small. This illustration shows my background has changed.

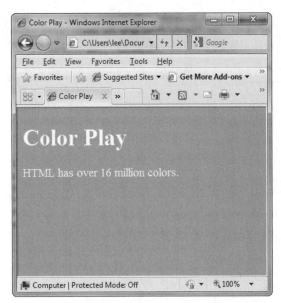

12. Now you will color the text on the document. Add the following line of code to the body css. I chose to use white. Again, choose any color you like. It does not matter if it is above or below the background-color.

```
color:#ffffff;
```

13. Save your document and then re-fresh your page. The foreground color should change. Again, if it fails, systematically ensure that your code looks like mine. Never panic. This illustration shows the change in text color.

14. Now, just because we can, we will change the coloring of our h1. We will flip the colors. Use the fore-ground color of the body as the background color of the h1, and vice versa. Enter the code shown here, after the closing brace, }, for the body and above the </style>.

```
h1
      {
            background-color:#ffffff;
            color:#9999ff;
      }
```

15. Your page should now look similar to the following illustration. The final
code is contained in Code Block 3-2.

CODE BLOCK 3-2

```
<!DOCTYPE html PUBLIC "-//W3C//DTD XHTML 1.1//EN"
"http://www.w3.org/TR/xhtml11/DTD/xhtml11.dtd">
<html xmlns="http://www.w3.org/1999/xhtml" xml:lang="en">
     <head>
          <title>Color Play</title>
          <meta name="description" _
          content="Experimenting with color"/>
          <meta name="author" content="Lee M. Cottrell" />
     <style type="text/css">
          body
          {
               background-color:#9999ff;
               color:#ffffff;
          }
          h1
          {
               background-color:#ffffff;
               color:#9999ff;
          }
     </style>
     </head>
     <body>
     <h1>Color Play</h1>
     <p>HTML has over 16 million colors.</p>
     </body>
</html>
```

Images on Your Web Site

Images have many uses on a web site. Images can be backgrounds, menu entries, navigation aids, or simply pictures illustrating the page. Each of these uses is valid and, when used properly, quite effective.

Inserting Inline Images

Inserting images directly onto your web site is accomplished with the <img /> tag. Like <br /> and <hr />, it is an empty tag. However, img requires several attributes before it performs properly.

The first and most important attribute of the img tag is the src attribute. This attribute describes to the browser where the image is. It can be a URL to a web picture or a picture in the same folder as the web page. Code Block 3-3 shows two images. The first src is a file in the same folder as the web page. The second src is a URL on the Web.

TIP *Unless you have a picture of my dog walking in the snow, the first image will not work. The second image will load. However, the code is correct to load an image from the same folder.*

CODE BLOCK 3-3

```
<img src="alexInSnow.jpg"/><br />
<img src="http://i480.photobucket.com/albums/_
rr163/leecottrell/snowman.jpg"/>
```

Notice that the <br /> tag is used after the first image. Images inserted with the img tag are inline images. Inline elements will not have a newline immediately after them. Since images are inline, text can be drawn around them. The code in Code Block 3-3 will successfully place an image onto your page. However, it is not complete. You need to use four additional attributes. These are height, width, alt, and title.

TIP *Using the height and width properties will speed the loading of your page a little. Browsers will reserve the space needed for the image and continue loading the page while the image downloads.*

The height and width attributes reserve space on the page for the image. They should be set to the exact size of the image. There are several ways to get the size of an image. You can open it in an image editor like Photoshop or

MS Paint. A simpler method is to open the image in Internet Explorer. Right-click the image in IE, and read the properties. The height and width are given. This illustration shows the width and height of an image in IE.

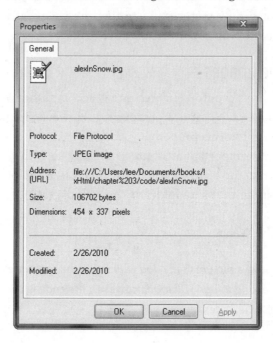

CAUTION *Do not use the height and width tags to resize your images. If the image needs to be resized, use an editor. Photoshop, MS Paint, and GIMP are all valid editors. Paint and the GIMP are free.*

The alt and title attributes are a little more complex. Alt is short for alternative information. Browsers display the alt tag when users have disabled images or when the image fails to load. Additionally, browsers for the visually impaired use it. The system reads the alt text to the user. Google images read the alt text to help categorize the image. You should include a description of the image and any copyright information in the alt attribute.

The title attribute names the picture. You should place a catchy phrase into the title. The contents of the title attribute become the tooltip in modern browsers. Hover over an image to see the title. Code Block 3-4 shows the complete code for inserting images. The order of the attributes has no effect on the outcome. Recall that your browser will ignore the newlines. Include them only for readability.

CAUTION *This code as typed will not pass validation. The img tags should be contained within another tag.*

CODE BLOCK 3-4

```
<img src="alexInSnow.jpg"
alt="Alex in the snow. 2-6-2010 taken in the backyard."
title="Alex in the snow"
height="454" width="357" />
<br />
<img src="http://i480.photobucket.com/albums/_
rr163/leecottrell/snowman.jpg"
height="1024" width="768"
alt="Lizzie's snowman made from the first big snowfall of 2010."
title="Lizzie's snowman" />
```

TIP *The Americans with Disabilities Act requires that all technology be usable by all Americans, regardless of physical ability. The alt and title tags help ensure your page is accessible to all.*

Images Should Be Local

Recall in Chapter 2, when we set up the first web site, I recommended that you create a folder for each project. The rationale was to help you organize your projects. The same holds true for images. Each project should have an images folder.

Create an image folder under the project folder for each of your web sites. Once this folder exists, place all images associated with your site into this folder. Your image code will change slightly to include the name of the folder. The bolded code in Code Block 3-5 shows the adjustment with the images folder in use.

CAUTION *Avoid using spaces in your folder names or your image names.*

CODE BLOCK 3-5

```
<img src="images/alexInSnow.jpg"
alt="Alex in the snow. 2-6-2010 taken in the backyard."
title="Alex in the snow"
height="454" width="357" />
```

For professional pages, you should avoid referring to images on another web site. Referring to images on other sites has several problems. First, it slows the loading of your pages. The Photobucket image in Code Block 3-4 takes nearly two seconds to load on my home system. In contrast, the local image loads immediately. A second problem is the legality of using other people's images. You do not own the right to those images. Finally, it is rude to embed other web sites' pictures onto yours. It eats up those web sites' speed.

Practice with Inline Images

For the next example, we will create a page with two inline images. If you wish to use my images, they are available from www.mhprofessional.com/ computingdownload. Feel free to use any images you choose.

1. Open your chapter3 folder.

2. Create a folder named images.

3. Place the two images you wish to use into the images folder. Be sure you know the full names of the images.

4. Open the template you created in Chapter 2.

5. Save it into the chapter3 folder as **auction.html**.

6. Change the title and first meta tags appropriately.

7. Create an h1 tag as follows.

   ```
   <h1>Winter Auction Items</h1>
   ```

8. Create two paragraph tags briefly describing each item and its price.

   ```
   <p>The first item is a brand new pink sweater jacket. Starting
   bid is $4.99.</p>
   <p>The second item are gently used blue snow pants. Starting
   bid is $2.99.</p>
   ```

9. Save your document and preview it in a browser.

10. Now we will insert the images into the paragraph tags. After the price in the first paragraph but before the </p> tag, press ENTER. Enter this code for the sweater:

    ```
    <img src="images/sweater.jpg" height="219" width="365"
    alt="Brand new pink sweater jacket" title="Pink sweater
    jacket" />
    ```

11. After the price in the second paragraph but before the </p>, press ENTER. Enter this code for the pants:

    ```
    <img src="images/pants.jpg" height="178" width="267"
    alt="Blue snow pants" title="Blue snow pants" />
    ```

12. Save your file and preview in a browser. The following illustration shows the output.

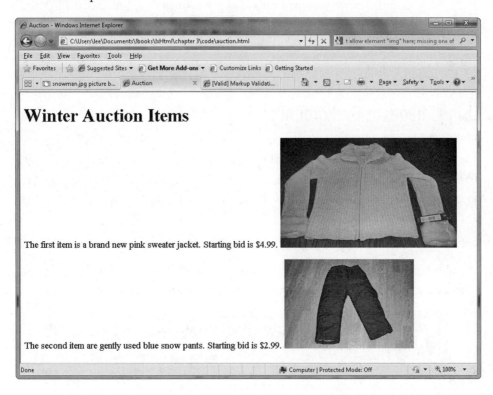

13. If desired, you may validate this page at W3's validator. The final version is in Code Block 3-6.

CODE BLOCK 3-6

```
<!DOCTYPE html PUBLIC "-//W3C//DTD XHTML 1.1//EN"
"http://www.w3.org/TR/xhtml11/DTD/xhtml11.dtd">
<html xmlns="http://www.w3.org/1999/xhtml" xml:lang="en">
     <head>
          <title>Auction</title>
          <meta name="description" _
          content="Winter Auction Items"/>
          <meta name="author" content="Lee M. Cottrell" />

     </head>
     <body>
     <h1>Winter Auction Items</h1>
     <p>The first item is a brand new pink sweater jacket.
      Starting bid is $4.99.
     <img src="images/sweater.jpg" height="219" width="365"
     alt="Blue snow pants" title="Blue snow pants" /></p>
```

```
<p>The second item are gently used blue snow pants.
 Starting bid is $2.99.
<img src="images/pants.jpg" height="178" width="267"
alt="Brand new pink sweater jacket" _
title="Pink sweater jacket" />
</p>
</body>
</html>
```

Using Images as Backgrounds

Setting images as backgrounds requires the use of CSS. The CSS property background-image can set the background of the page, or several other tags. Background-property requires the use of the CSS function url. Url provides the location of a file. The location of the file is enclosed inside of a set of parenthesis and again inside of double quotes.

```
background-image:url("images/grayback.gif");
```

When picking background images, you want to pick images that enhance the page but do not distract the reader. Figure 3-1 shows a good background choice.

FIGURE 3-1 · A good background choice

Figure 3-2 shows a horrible choice. Typically, the images are small and tile across the page. To *tile* means to completely fill the screen with small images, yet not be able to see the seams between the images. Good background images have similar characteristics.

CAUTION *Select your background image well. Make sure it does not distract the reader from the page!*

- A good background image will have a small number of colors.
- None of the colors in the image matches a color in the HTML document.
- The pattern is muted, and consistent.
- There is no text in the background image.
- The background image has a small file size.
- The image tiles well.

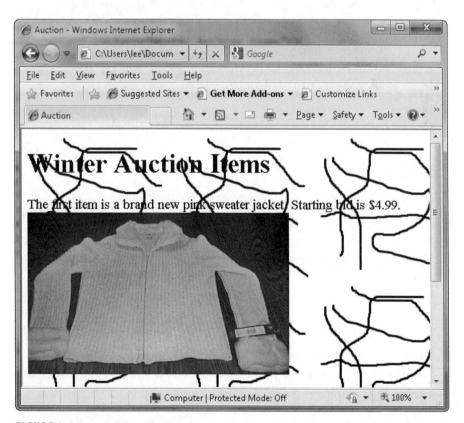

FIGURE 3-2 • A bad background choice

TIP   *There are several web sites devoted to good background images. I often use www.webpagebackground.com/ in my classes.*

When setting background images, you should also set a background color. You should choose a background color that matches the predominate color in your background image. In Figure 3-1, I would choose a dark gray color. In Figure 3-2, if you insisted on using it, white would be the correct choice. Choosing a background color that matches the image ensures your page will still look good if your background image fails to load.

TIP   *To get the RGB color of your image, you need to use the eyedropper tool in MS Paint or a similar program. Click the eyedropper on the color, and then edit the color. The RGB values will be in English. Use the calculator to convert.*

Practice Setting a Background Image

In this practice, you will place a background image onto a web page.

1. Find or create an image that you like for a background image. If you wish to use the one I used, you can download it from www.mhprofessional .com/computingdownload.

2. Save your background image into the chapter3/images folder.

3. Open the auction.html file you created earlier in the chapter.

4. In the head create a style tag like this one:

```
<style type="text/css">
</style>
```

5. Inside of the style section, create a body element.

6. In the body element, enter the background-image property with the URL value pointing to your image. Use my example to guide you. Replace bg20.jpg with your filename.

```
body{
        background-image:url("images/bg20.jpg");
}
```

7. Save and open the page in the browser. Your background will be visible.

8. Now get a color that matches the main color in your background image. Add the background-color property to the body. The final body formatting section is shown here with the change bolded.

```
body{
        background-image:url("images/bg20.jpg");
```

```
                background-color:#AAAAAA;
        }
```

9. Save and refresh the page in the browser. No changes will be visible. This version of the auction is displayed in Code Block 3-7.

CODE BLOCK 3-7

```
<!DOCTYPE html PUBLIC "-//W3C//DTD XHTML 1.1//EN"
"http://www.w3.org/TR/xhtml11/DTD/xhtml11.dtd">
<html xmlns="http://www.w3.org/1999/xhtml" xml:lang="en">
        <head>
                <title>Auction</title>
                <meta name="description" _
                content="Winter Auction Items"/>
                <meta name="author" content="Lee M. Cottrell" />
        <style type="text/css">
                body{
                        background-image:url("images/bg20.jpg");
                        background-color:#AAAAAA;
                }
        </style>
        </head>
        <body>
        <h1>Winter Auction Items</h1>
        <p>The first item is a brand new pink sweater jacket.
         Starting bid is $4.99.
        <img src="images/sweater.jpg" height="219" width="365"
        alt="Brand new pink sweater jacket" _
        title="Pink sweater jacket" /></p>
        <p>The second item are gently used blue snow pants.
         Starting bid is $2.99.
        <img src="images/pants.jpg" height="178" width="267"
        alt="Blue snow pants" title="Blue snow pants" />
        </p>
        </body>
</html>
```

Background Image Formatting

By default, background images will tile to fill the page. Usually, this is what you want to occur on your page. However, CSS provides several ways to change the default behavior of background images. Table 3-2 describes the CSS style properties associated with background images.

TABLE 3-2 CSS Background Properties

Property	Description	Common Values
background–attachment	Determines whether the background moves when the page is scrolled. Fixed will keep the background from moving.	Scroll, fixed
background–color	Sets the background color of the element.	Any RGB value
background–image	Loads the background image from the provided URL. If none is provided, the background image is not loaded.	URL("filename"), none
background–position	Provides x–y coordinates placing the background image.	Top, center, bottom, left, center, right, %, length.
background–repeat	Determines how background images repeat. They can be set to repeat horizontally, vertically, both or neither.	Repeat, repeat–x, repeat–y, no–repeat

Practice Using Background Properties

We are going to modify the auction.html file created earlier in the chapter. Instead of a gray background, we will create a background color of a dollar sign on the left of the page.

1. Download the dollarsign.png file from www.mhprofessional.com/computingdownload. Save it into the chapter3/images folder.

2. Open the auction.html file from the chapter3 folder.

3. Save the auction.html file as **auctionBackground.html**.

4. Change the CSS properties for the background-image and color in the body section. Values changed are indicated in bold.

```
body{
        background-image:url("images/dollarsign.png");
        background-color:#000000;
}
```

5. Save and open the page in a browser. You should look like the illustration. This is terrible. The background is too busy and conflicts with the foreground text.

6. Now we will change the background repeat pattern. Add this to the body section of your style element. Your page will now look like the following illustration.

```
background-repeat:repeat-y;
```

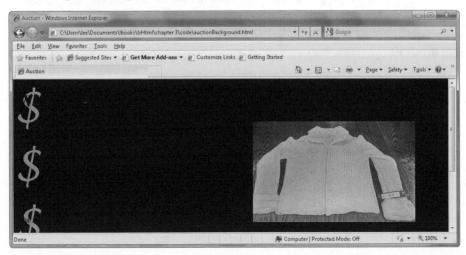

7. Now, however, the text is unreadable. We will move the text to the right and change the text color. Add the following lines to the body section in CSS to complete the page as shown in this illustration. Code Block 3-8 shows the complete code listing.

```
margin-left:80px;
color:#22b14c;
```

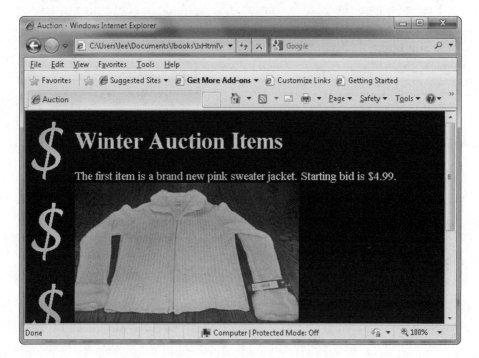

TIP   *The margin-left property tells the browser where to start the content. I chose 80 pixels because my dollar sign is 73 pixels wide.*

CODE BLOCK 3-8

```
<!DOCTYPE html PUBLIC "-//W3C//DTD XHTML 1.1//EN"
"http://www.w3.org/TR/xhtml11/DTD/xhtml11.dtd">
<html xmlns="http://www.w3.org/1999/xhtml" xml:lang="en">
    <head>
        <title>Auction</title>
        <meta name="description" _
        content="Winter Auction Items"/>
        <meta name="author" content="Lee M. Cottrell" />
    <style type="text/css">
        body{
            background-image:url("images/dollarsign.png");
            background-color:#000000;
```

```
            background-repeat:repeat-y;
            margin-left:80px;
            color:#22b14c;
        }
    </style>
    </head>
    <body>
    <h1>Winter Auction Items</h1>
    <p>The first item is a brand new pink sweater jacket.
     Starting bid is $4.99.
    <img src="images/sweater.jpg" height="219" width="365"
    alt="Brand new pink sweater jacket" _
    title="Pink sweater jacket" /></p>
    <p>The second item are gently used blue snow pants.
     Starting bid is $2.99.
    <img src="images/pants.jpg" height="178" width="267"
    alt="Blue snow pants" title="Blue snow pants" />
    </p>
    </body>
</html>
```

Acquiring Web Graphics

You will have images on your web site. You may create a vanity site for your children or a product page for an employer. While building your site, you will need to acquire images.

Several sites on the Web offer images. The obvious places are www.google .com and www.bing.com. These sites are fine if you are acquiring images for practice. However, you need to be very careful with images from these and other search engines. You may not have the proper license to use the image on your site. In general, unless you or your company created the image, you probably do not have the permission to use the image on a web site.

In order to use an image on a web site, you need to get legal permission to use the image. Several sites offer inexpensive images for use on your web site. For instance, www.corbis.com and www.istockphoto.com offer very inexpensive, professional-quality images. Many sites exist that offer free images. You "pay" for the image by citing the source of the image. www.freedigitalphotos .net and www.freefoto.com are two examples of these types of sites.

Sites exist for prebuilt or custom GIF or PNG images. The site www .free-graphics.com has over seven million images free for your use. As with freefoto.com, all you need to do is provide a reference to the site. If you need custom images, www.flamingtext.com can create custom banners and buttons for your site.

Web Image Formats

Images are very important to your web site. They must both be inserted properly and of the correct format. Currently the Web supports three image formats. These are JPG, GIF, and PNG files.

JPG is an acronym for Joint Photographic Experts Group. As the acronym suggests, JPGs are most suited for photographs. Despite the strange name, JPG files are everywhere. It is quite likely that your digital camera stores its pictures in JPG format.

The JPG format allows an image to be stored using a lossy compression algorithm. The algorithm loses minor details of the photograph to decrease its file size. The smaller the image's file size, the faster it loads.

While JPG files store pictures, there is a need for nonphotographic images. Logos, maps, and hand-drawn diagrams may need to be displayed. GIF and PNG files solve this need. GIF is an acronym for Graphics Interchange Format. CompuServe developed the GIF format to distribute graphics across its network in the early 1990s.

In addition to supporting hand-drawn images, GIF supports simple animation. Animated GIFs are one image file with several pictures embedded within them. The images inside of the GIF change every few seconds. The effect can enhance a web site, if properly used.

TIP   *While you can include animations in a web site, use them very sparingly. Too many animations will make your page seem unprofessional.*

GIF had a few legal and technical limitations that are beyond the scope of this book. The PNG file format addresses these limitations. PNG files can be used everywhere GIF files can. In practice, PNG files look a little better than GIF files, but PNG files are never animated.

Summary

In this chapter you learned how to add pizzazz to a web site. You learned how HTML describes colors and how to build custom color codes. Additionally, you learned how to place images inline with text on your page. Background images and colors through CSS were presented as well.

QUIZ

1. **Choose the HTML tag to insert an inline image.**
   A. <p>
   B. <img>
   C. <pic>
   D. <src>

2. **The CSS property used to set a background-color is _____ .**
   A. background-color
   B. bgcolor
   C. back-color
   D. color

3. **This HTML color code is green.**
   A. #ff0000
   B. #00ff00
   C. #0000ff
   D. #000000

4. **For images, the _____ property describes the images.**
   A. alt
   B. title
   C. src
   D. tip

5. **When setting a background image, you should also set a background color that _____ .**
   A. complements the background image
   B. overrides the background image
   C. matches the foreground color
   D. matches the predominate color in the background image

6. **This image type is best suited for photographs.**
   A. PNG
   B. GIF
   C. JPG
   D. BMP

7. **To reserve space on the page for the image, you need to use the _____ and _____ attributes.**
   A. length
   B. height
   C. width
   D. size

8. The _____ attribute of the img tag specifies the location of the image.
   A. alt
   B. title
   C. src
   D. tip

9. A small background image will repeat to fill the screen. This is the definition of _____ .
   A. tiling
   B. scaling
   C. stretching
   D. filling

10. In CSS, the _____ function describes the location of the file.
    A. file
    B. location
    C. url
    D. place

chapter 4

Using Hyperlinks

You will learn to link to external pages, create navigation systems, and use external style sheets. Additionally, you will learn how to format links for usability.

CHAPTER OBJECTIVES

In this chapter, you will

- Create a hyperlink
- Create links to pages on your site
- Create effective site navigation
- Build intra-page links
- Format links
- Create a style document

As early as 1945, computer scientists were envisioning an easier method of working with computers. Vannevar Bush theorized about a library system called the Memex that had documents linked to each other. This article so inspired Douglas Englebart, the inventor of the mouse, that he built the first working hypertext system, called the NLS. The NLS was the second machine placed on the ARPANET.

Flash forward to the mid-eighties. Apple releases first the Lisa and then the Macintosh computer, designed with a mouse interface rather than just a typing interface. During this time, users navigated the Internet by typing arcane commands.

Tim Berners-Lee, in wanting to share his research papers, developed a hypertext system to make it easy to retrieve other papers and create active links within documents. This hypertext system, when combined with HTML and the protocol to deliver papers, made the Web as we know it today.

Today, these hyperlinks are everywhere on the Internet. Web search engines result in pages of links that might hold the answer to your questions. Web sites have complex navigation systems, based on links, which provide breadcrumbs that tell you both what page you are on, and what pages you followed to reach the current page You need to learn how to harness the power of hyperlinks.

Creating Hyperlinks

A *hyperlink* is like a shortcut to a file on the Internet. The link holds the URL to a page on the Web. When clicked, the URL is opened in your browser. The tag that creates the hyperlinks is the <a> tag.

External Links

An *external* link is a hyperlink that leads to a page that is not in your web site. For example, a link on your site to www.google.com is an external link. To build a link, you need to start an <a> tag, provide the URL to the site, and give the users something to click on. Consider the code shown next. Notice that the <br /> tag is used to separate the lines. Like the <img> tag, <a> is an inline tag. This feature allows hyperlinks in any portion of the page.

```
<a href="http://www.google.com">Google.com</a><br />
<a href="http://www.youtube.com/mrcottrellbradford">_
My YouTube Channel</a><br />
```

The code has a few components that need to be explained. Href is an acronym for hypertext reference. The href attribute of the <a> tag holds the exact URL of the site. Remember to include the http:// in the URL. Contained within the <a> </a> element are words that the user can click on. Words within the element are underlined in the browser. The underlined words are something to click.

TIP *Always provide your users with something to click. Make sure the link tells users where they are heading by following the link.*

The code shown previously will provide a working link. However, there are a few problems with the tag. First, the link will open in the current window, replacing the current web page. This is quite bad. Imagine that your page is selling a product, and you provide a link to the manufacturer's site. If this link overwrites your page, you may potentially lose a customer. By opening a new window, you enable the customer to see the related information on the other page, and still have your page on the screen.

TIP *Before typing the href attribute, open the page in the browser. Then copy and paste the URL into the href attribute.*

Opening links in a new window requires the use of the target attribute. The target will create a new browser window. The value you give target will change how your link works. XHTML has a few built-in targets. The most commonly used one is _blank. Setting this target will result in a new browser window to open upon every click.

TIP *The target attribute is deprecated in HTML 4.01 and XHTML 1.1. However, it is not deprecated in HTML 5. I recommend using the target attribute, even though you will not pass validation.*

I do not like using _blank. It tends to open too many windows on my client's machines. Figure 4-1 shows what happens when _blank links are clicked multiple times. Instead, I choose a different value for the target. I use the word "new," although you can use whatever word you like. Using a word you specify for the target will result in only one window opened on every click. The following code block shows the use of both _blank and new.

```
<a href="http://w3.org" target="_blank">W3.org</a><br />
<a href="http://www.webstandards.org" target="new">Webstandards</a>
```

FIGURE 4-1 · Clicking the w3.org link five times

When building links, you should also use the title attribute. Like the title attribute of images, the title attribute will create a tooltip for your links. The tooltip is visible when a user hovers over the site. As discussed in Chapter 3, your page needs to be accessible by all. The title attribute makes your page accessible. Browsers that read aloud to their users will read the title text to the user. For full accessibility, this attribute should communicate the name of the web site that the link opens and alert the user if the link will open in a new window. The following code demonstrates the title attributes for three links. The last link opens in the current window.

```
<a href="http://w3.org" target="_blank"

title="Link to www.w3.org, opens in a new window">W3.org</a><br />
<a href="http://www.webstandards.org" target="window"
```

```
title="Link to www.webstandards.org, opens in a new
window">Webstandards</a><br />
<a href="http://www.w3schools.com"

title="Link to www.webstandards.org, opens in the current
window">Webstandards</a><br />
```

Practice Building External Links

You are going to build a page listing search engines. You will see how the target and title attributes work.

1. Create a chapter4 folder.

2. Open your !template.html and save it as **externallink.html**.

3. Change the title tag to read **Search Engines**.

4. In the body element, create a heading similar to mine.

```
<h1>Search Engines</h1>
```

5. Under the <h1>, create this paragraph.

```
<p>There are hundreds of search engines. One of the most
popular is Google. Newcomer Microsoft's Bing has gained in
popularity. Finally, the original Yahoo is still going
strong.</p>
```

6. You are going to make the words Google, Bing, and Yahoo link out each to the appropriate site. Start with the Google link.

   a. In a browser, type **http://www.google.com**. Once the page loads, copy the address from the address box.

   b. Click into the paragraph tag, in front of Google. Type the following code. Paste the address into the href attribute.

   ```
   <a href="http://www.google.com">
   ```

   c. After Google, close the <a> tag with </a>. As a reminder, Programmer's Notepad will automatically close your tags for you.

   d. Repeat Steps a through c for www.bing.com and www.yahoo.com.

7. Save and open the page in a browser. Google should be underlined. If it is not underlined, revisit your code and find the error. The following illustration shows the output in Internet Explorer.

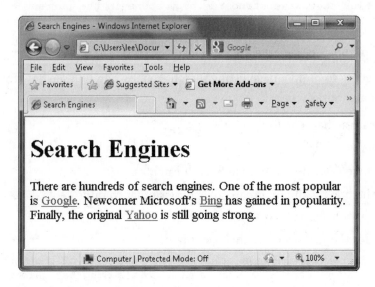

TIP   *If the entire page is underlined, you failed to close your <a> tag.*

8. Click the Google link. Notice how Google replaces your page. External links should always open in a new window. You will change the link to act in this manner.

9. Click into the attribute space inside of the link to Google. Enter the following target and title attributes.

```
target="_blank" title="Link to www.google.com opens in a new
window."
```

10. Save and refresh the page in your browser. Click the link several times. One window to Google should appear for every click.

11. Change the target value to **"window"**. Save your document.

```
target="window" title="Link to www.google.com opens in a new
window."
```

12. Close all browser windows. Reopen your browser and open this page. Click the Google link several times. Only one additional window should appear.

13. Apply the target and title for the www.bing.com and www.yahoo.com links.

14. The finished code appears in Code Block 4-1. The output is shown in the illustration with Step 7.

CODE BLOCK 4-1

```
<!DOCTYPE html PUBLIC "-//W3C//DTD XHTML 1.1//EN"
"http://www.w3.org/TR/xhtml11/DTD/xhtml11.dtd">
<html xmlns="http://www.w3.org/1999/xhtml" xml:lang="en">
    <head>
        <title>Search Engines</title>
        <meta name="description"
         content="Search engines"/>
        <meta name="author" content="Lee M. Cottrell" />
    </head>
    <body>
    <h1>Search Engine</h1>
    <p>There are hundreds of search engines. One of the most
    popular is <a href="http://www.google.com"
    target="window" title="Link to www.google.com opens in a
    new window.">Google</a>. Newcomer Microsoft's
    <a href="http://www.bing.com" target="window"
    title="Link to www.bing.com opens in a new window.">
    Bing</a> has gained in popularity. Finally, the original
    <a href="http://www.yahoo.com" target="window"
    title="Link to www.yahoo.com opens in a new window.">
    Yahoo</a> is still going strong.</p>
    </body>
</html>
```

TIP   *If external links do not work, ensure you spelled the link correctly. Be sure to correctly type http:// in front of the URL.*

Links to Pages on Your Site

Linking to external pages is an important skill. It allows web users easy access to nearly any content on the Web. Linking to pages on your web site, or *internal* linking, is actually easier than linking to external sites.

Building an internal link is very similar to creating an external link. There are two differences. First, the href no longer uses a URL to a page. Second, there is no need to use the target attribute. You want your page to appear in the same browser window. Code Block 4-2 shows two internal links. One link is to a web page; the other is to an image.

CODE BLOCK 4-2

```
<a href="family.html" _
title="Link to family.html in the same window">Family</a><br />
<a href="images/lizzieHomeRun.jpg" _
title="Link to a picture of Lizzie's first home run!">Home run Picture</a>
```

Code Block 4-2 illustrates how an internal link works. The href to family .html only lists the page itself. The pages will most likely be in the same folder, so the href family.html will find the page. Remember that images should be in their own folder. This is reflected in the second href. The path images/ lizzieHomeRun.jpg should find the image.

Site Navigation

Site navigation is the most common use for internal linking. You want the visitors to your site to find the information. To get around, users need navigation aids. You provide the aids through links on each page.

There are many different strategies for creating navigation aids. The original method was to have one main page that links to the other pages. This method, called *hierarchical*, works well for smaller sites. The user lands initially on the home page. The home page has a link to each of the other pages on the site. Each other page has a link back to the main page. Occasionally a page has links to subpages below it. Figure 4-2 shows a hierarchical layout for a sports page.

Figure 4-2 shows a reasonably complex page. The main page, index.html contains links to the baseball.html, football.html, hockey.html, and soccer.html pages. Football.html contains links to subpages named flag.html and tackle.html and back to index.html. Similarly, hockey.html contains links to deck.html, ice.html, and index.html. Soccer.html has one subpage titled worldcup.html. Baseball.html has no subpages but does link back to index.html.

The hierarchical layout works well for a small web site. However, the meshed layout has replaced the hierarchical layout. In the meshed layout, most pages link to other pages. Modern implementations use menu bars to build meshed layouts. You will create a meshed layout in the next section.

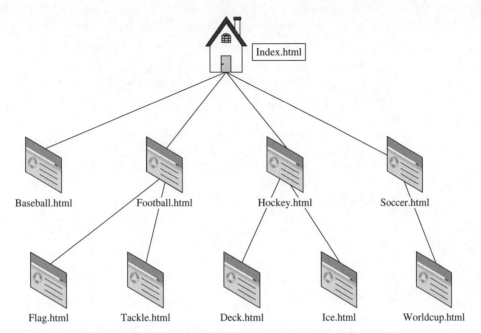

Baseball.html   Football.html   Hockey.html   Soccer.html

Flag.html   Tackle.html   Deck.html   Ice.html   Worldcup.html

FIGURE 4-2 · A hierarchical layout for a sports page

Practice Creating a Meshed Layout

You are going to build the site shown in Figure 4-2. You will build the index.html and the first level of pages containing baseball.html. Each page will simply be a shell containing an <h1> tag and several links.

1. Open the !template.html file created in Chapter 2.

2. Save this file as index.html in a new folder titled **sports**.

3. Change the title tag of index.html to **Sports Page**. Adjust the meta tag appropriately.

4. In the body section add the following <h1> element. Save your document.

```
<h1>Sports Pages</h1>
```

5. You are now going to create the baseball.html page. The trick is to save index.html as baseball.html and then change it.

   a. Save the index.html file as **baseball.html**.

   b. Change the title to **Baseball Page**.

   c. Change the meta tag appropriately.

   d. Change the h1 to read **Baseball Page**.

   e. Save the document.

6. Open the page in your browser to ensure it looks right. The following illustration shows what it should look like in Internet Explorer.

7. Repeat Step 5 for football.html, hockey.html, and soccer.html.

TIP *Changing the Baseball to Football can be done with the search and replace feature of your editor.*

8. Open all pages in your editor. To open them all at once, in the File Open screen, use the mouse to draw a selection box around all of the filenames.

9. Switch to index.html.

10. Now you are going to create the links to the individual sports pages.

11. Start by creating a link to baseball.html. Enter the code under the <h1> tag.

```
<p>
<a href="baseball.html" title="Link to baseball.html. The
link opens in the same window">Baseball</a><br />
</p>
```

CAUTION *The <p> tag is included to ensure that the page passes a validation check. Failing to include the <p> tag will still allow the page to work, just not pass validation.*

12. Verify that the link works in a browser.

13. Repeat the links for the remaining pages inside of the <p> tag after the <br />. Be sure to build the page links in alphabetic order.

```
<a href="football.html" title="Link to football.html. The
link opens in the same window">Football</a><br />
<a href="hockey.html" title="Link to hockey.html. The link
opens in the same window">Hockey</a><br />
<a href="soccer.html" title="Link to soccer.html. The link
opens in the same window">Soccer</a><br />
```

14. Add a link to the index.html page above the baseball link. Use the text "home" for the link text.

```
<a href="index.html" title="Link to the home page. The link
opens in the same window">Home</a><br />
```

15. Open a page in a browser and ensure that all links work.

Still Struggling

The index page link is included for two reasons. First, the link provides a way back to the home page from baseball.html and the other pages. Second, once you start building menu bars, they always include a manner to go home.

16. Copy and paste the paragraph tag and all five links to the other pages in your site. Your page should resemble the following illustration.

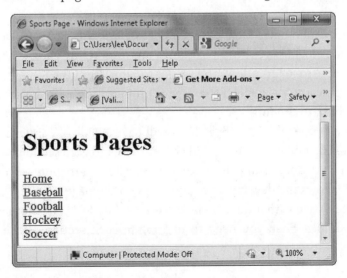

17. The final code for index.html appears in Code Block 4-3.

CODE BLOCK 4-3

```
<!DOCTYPE html PUBLIC "-//W3C//DTD XHTML 1.1//EN"
"http://www.w3.org/TR/xhtml11/DTD/xhtml11.dtd">
<html xmlns="http://www.w3.org/1999/xhtml" xml:lang="en">
     <head>
          <title>Sports Page</title>
          <meta name="description" content="Sports pages"/>
          <meta name="author" content="Lee M. Cottrell" />

     </head>
     <body>
     <h1>Sports Pages</h1>
     <p>
     <a href="index.html" title="Link to the home page
     opens in the same window">Home</a><br />
     <a href="baseball.html" title="Link to baseball.html
     opens in the same window">Baseball</a><br />
     <a href="football.html" title="Link to football.html
     opens in the same window">Football</a><br />
     <a href="hockey.html" title="Link to hockey.html
     opens in the same window">Hockey</a><br />
     <a href="soccer.html" title="Link to soccer.html
     opens in the same window">Soccer</a>
<br />
     </p>
     </body>
</html>
```

Intra-Page Links

Internal links build navigation between pages. *Intra-page* links provide navigation within a single page. Intra-page links are important when a page is very large. The intra-page link allows the reader to jump from the top of the page to a topic far down on the page. If the page is properly configured, the reader can also jump back to the top.

Typically, a page with intra-page links will have a table of contents at the top of the page. The table of contents will contain a link to each section on the page. You identify sections using the id attribute. The id attribute, as defined in Chapter 2, allows the developer to name tags on the page.

To create a page with intra-page links, you need to do a little more work than for internal links. First, you need to id a tag in each section of the page. Ids should be short words that describe the section. Use all lowercase letters and no spaces. I recommend using the id attribute in a header element. The end of the section will include a link back to the table of contents.

```
<h2 id="pony">Pittsburgh Pony Baseball</h2>
```

Once the sections are id'ed, the table of contents needs to be built. The table of contents will be links that jump to the ids of the section. The link is a little different. Instead of a page or a URL, the href will point to the id. The correct syntax includes # in front of the id.

```
<a href="#pony" title="Link to Pony Baseball section.">Pony</a>
```

TIP *HTML provides two IDs on the page. #top refers to the top of the page, and #bottom refers to the bottom of the page.*

Build an Intra-Page Link

You are going to build a page with intra-page links. Rather than type the large amount of text that typically accompanies these types of pages, you are going to simulate the effect by using placeholder text. You will create a number of fictitious youth baseball teams for practice.

1. Open the baseball.html page created earlier. If you did not create this page, create a new page from your template.

2. Under the links, create a header for the Allentown Alligators. Set the id attribute to be **alligators**.

   ```
   <h2 id="alligators">Allentown Alligators</h2>
   ```

3. Create three additional headers for the Elliott Eagles, Mt. Washington Presidents, and Sheraden Sluggers. Set the ids appropriately.

   ```
   <h2 id="eagles">Elliott Eagles</h2>
   <h2 id="presidents">Mt. Washington Presidents</h2>
   <h2 id="sluggers">Sheraden Sluggers</h2>
   ```

4. Now you need to generate text. To see the effect properly, you need many paragraphs between each header. Enter a <p> tag similar to mine and copy it at least ten times after each header. I used the standard Latin dummy text of "Lorem ipsum dolor sit amet." Feel free to use text of your own devising.

TIP *The dummy text used here is not intended for meaning. It is a standard used in the publishing industry when text is needed to show formatting.*

```
<h2 id="alligators">Allentown Alligators</h2>
<p>Lorem ipsum dolor sit amet. </p>
<p>Lorem ipsum dolor sit amet. </p>
<p>Lorem ipsum dolor sit amet. </p>
<p>Lorem ipsum dolor sit amet. </p>
<p>Lorem ipsum dolor sit amet. </p>
<p>Lorem ipsum dolor sit amet. </p>
<p>Lorem ipsum dolor sit amet. </p>
<p>Lorem ipsum dolor sit amet. </p>
<p>Lorem ipsum dolor sit amet. </p>
<p>Lorem ipsum dolor sit amet. </p>
```

5. View your page in the browser. Ensure it looks similar to the image shown here:

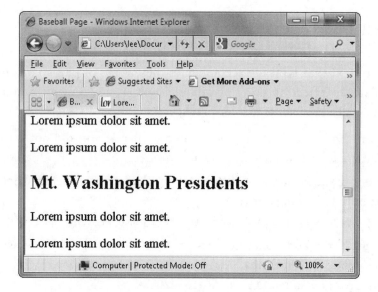

6. Scroll to above the <h2> for the Allentown Alligators.

7. Create an <h2> for League Baseball Teams. Id the header as **teams**.

```
<h2 id="teams">League Baseball Teams</h2>
```

8. Under the <h2>, create a paragraph. Inside of the paragraph, create a link to the alligators using the id for the href.

```
<a href="#alligators"

title="Intra page link to lower on the page">Allentown
Alligators</a><br />
```

9. Save the file and view it in the browser. Ensure that the link jumps to the Alligators. If you do not see the effect, shrink your browser to simulate more text on the page.

TIP   *The Sheraden Sluggers may not jump to the top of the page as the other teams did. This is normal, as there is nothing after this team to fill the page.*

10. Repeat the link inside of the paragraph for the other three teams.

```
<a href="#eagles" title="Intra page link to lower on the
page">Elliott Eagles</a><br />
<a href="#presidents" _
title="Intra page link to lower on the page">Mt. Washington
Presidents</a><br />
<a href="#sluggers" title="Intra page link to lower on the
page">Sheraden Sluggers</a><br />
```

11. Verify that the links work for each team.

12. Now you need to create a link back to the team list. Scroll to your code immediately above the header for the Elliott Eagles.

13. Add a link back to the team list.

```
<a href="#teams" title="Intra page link to higher on the
page">Back to the team list</a>
```

14. Save the file and view the page in the browser. Click the link to jump to the Eagles. Scroll to the end of this section and click the link back to the team list. Your team list should appear.

15. Repeat for each of the other sections.

16. The complete code listing appears in Code Block 4-4.

CODE BLOCK 4-4

```
<!DOCTYPE html PUBLIC "-//W3C//DTD XHTML 1.1//EN"
"http://www.w3.org/TR/xhtml11/DTD/xhtml11.dtd">
<html xmlns="http://www.w3.org/1999/xhtml" xml:lang="en">
    <head>
        <title>Baseball Page</title>
        <meta name="description" content="Baseball
        pages"/>
        <meta name="author" content="Lee M. Cottrell" />

    </head>
    <body>
    <h1>Baseball</h1>
```

```
        <p>
<a href="index.html" title="Link to the home page. The
 link opens in the same window">Home</a><br />
<a href="baseball.html" title="Link to baseball.html.
 The link opens in the same window">Baseball</a><br />
<a href="football.html" title="Link to football.html.
 The link opens in the same window">Football</a><br />
<a href="hockey.html" title="Link to hockey.html. The
 link opens in the same window">Hockey</a><br />
<a href="soccer.html" title="Link to soccer.html. The
 link opens in the same window">Soccer</a><br />
</p>
<h2 id="teams">League Baseball Teams</h2>
<p>
<a href="#alligators" title="Intra page link to lower
 on the page">Allentown Alligators</a><br />
<a href="#eagles" title="Intra page link to lower on
 the page">Elliott Eagles</a><br />
<a href="#presidents" title="Intra page link to lower
 on the page">Mt. Washington Presidents</a><br />
<a href="#sluggers" title="Intra page link to lower on
 the page">Sheraden Sluggers</a><br />
</p>
<h2 id="alligators">Allentown Alligators</h2>
<p>Lorem ipsum dolor sit amet. </p>
<p>Lorem ipsum dolor sit amet. </p>
<p>Lorem ipsum dolor sit amet. </p>
<p>Lorem ipsum dolor sit amet. </p>
<p>Lorem ipsum dolor sit amet. </p>
<p>Lorem ipsum dolor sit amet. </p>
<p>Lorem ipsum dolor sit amet. </p>
<p>Lorem ipsum dolor sit amet. </p>
<p>Lorem ipsum dolor sit amet. </p>
<p>Lorem ipsum dolor sit amet. </p>

<a href="#teams" title="Intra page link to higher on
 the page">Back to the team list</a>

<h2 id="eagles">Elliott Eagles</h2>
<p>Lorem ipsum dolor sit amet. </p>
<p>Lorem ipsum dolor sit amet. </p>
<p>Lorem ipsum dolor sit amet. </p>
<p>Lorem ipsum dolor sit amet. </p>
<p>Lorem ipsum dolor sit amet. </p>
<p>Lorem ipsum dolor sit amet. </p>
<p>Lorem ipsum dolor sit amet. </p>
<p>Lorem ipsum dolor sit amet. </p>
<p>Lorem ipsum dolor sit amet. </p>
<p>Lorem ipsum dolor sit amet. </p>
```

```
<a href="#teams" title="Intra page link to higher on
  the page">Back to the team list</a>

<h2 id="presidents">Mt. Washington Presidents</h2>
<p>Lorem ipsum dolor sit amet. </p>
<p>Lorem ipsum dolor sit amet. </p>
<p>Lorem ipsum dolor sit amet. </p>
<p>Lorem ipsum dolor sit amet. </p>
<p>Lorem ipsum dolor sit amet. </p>
<p>Lorem ipsum dolor sit amet. </p>
<p>Lorem ipsum dolor sit amet. </p>
<p>Lorem ipsum dolor sit amet. </p>
<p>Lorem ipsum dolor sit amet. </p>
<p>Lorem ipsum dolor sit amet. </p>

<a href="#teams" title="Intra page link to higher on
  the page">Back to the team list</a>
<h2 id="sluggers">Sheraden Sluggers</h2>
<p>Lorem ipsum dolor sit amet. </p>
<p>Lorem ipsum dolor sit amet. </p>
<p>Lorem ipsum dolor sit amet. </p>
<p>Lorem ipsum dolor sit amet. </p>
<p>Lorem ipsum dolor sit amet. </p>
<p>Lorem ipsum dolor sit amet. </p>
<p>Lorem ipsum dolor sit amet. </p>
<p>Lorem ipsum dolor sit amet. </p>
<p>Lorem ipsum dolor sit amet. </p>
<p>Lorem ipsum dolor sit amet. </p>

<a href="#teams" title="Intra page link to higher on
  the page">Back to the team list</a>
</body>
</html>
```

Accessing Intra-Page Links from Other Pages

The intra-page ids can be accessed from other pages. The href code for the <a> tag is merged together. To link from the soccer.html page to the Elliott Eagles, the following code is used.

```
<a href="baseball.html#eagles" _
title="Link to eagles on baseball.html The link opens in the
window">Eagles Baseball</a><br />
```

Formatting Links

The <a> tag, like nearly every other HTML tag, can be formatted to match your pages design. Using CSS, the color, font, and font decoration can be changed. Using a CSS pseudo-class, simple animation is possible.

Styling Links

By default, Internet Explorer colors links blue. Once you have visited the page, the color changes to purple. The color change is helpful to viewers. It allows them to know what pages they have already visited. Unfortunately, the color choices do not work on all pages.

You start formatting links using CSS. Create an "a" element in your style section. Then set the color and font properties as we have done earlier. With this done, both visited and nonvisited links are the same color.

TIP   *Web design convention is to change the color of visited links. However, many sites break this rule and keep visited and nonvisited links the same color. It is your preference how you format your site.*

To change the visited link, a pseudo-class is necessary. A good analogy to the pseudo-class is the states an object can be in. Consider the traffic light. A working traffic light can be in three possible states: green, yellow, or red. Each of these states is a class of the light, and appropriate rules are assigned to each class.

The pseudo-class applies this to HTML tags. Several pseudo-classes for links exist. Table 4-1 lists the more commonly used pseudo-classes for the a tag.

Practice Formatting Links with CSS

You are going to modify the baseball.html page to have nicely formatted links. You will also apply a different format for the links. Rather than have the links

TABLE 4-1 Common Pseudo-Classes for the a Tag	
Pseudo class	**Description**
a:active	Used to format links that are currently being used.
a:link	Used to format nonvisited links.
a:hover	Applies rules when the mouse is over a link.
a:visited	Sets rules for visited links.

underlined, you will configure the page to underline the links when the mouse is over the link.

1. Open the baseball.html page in your editor.

2. Scroll to the head section, after the </title> tag.

3. Create a style element.

```
<style type="text/css">

</style>
```

4. Inside of the <style> element, create rules for the body. You will set the background color to #610b0b and a foreground color to #ffffff. Save your page.

```
body{
            background-color:#610b0b;
            color:#ffffff;
}
```

5. Open your page in a browser and verify that the page has a dark red background with white text.

6. Create a rule for the <a> tag. You will set the foreground color to #fe2e2e and turn off the underlining by setting the text-decoration property to none.

```
a{
      color:#fe2e2e;
      text-decoration:none;
}
```

7. Save and refresh your page. Verify that your links have changed to a bright red and are not underlined.

8. Create a rule for the a:visited pseudo-class. You will set the foreground color to #df0101.

```
a:visited{
      color:#df0101;
}
```

9. Save and refresh your page. Verify that the visited links are a darker red.

10. Now create a rule for the a:hover pseudo-class. You will underline the link using the text-decoration property.

```
a:hover{
      text-decoration:underline;
}
```

11. Save and refresh your page. Hover over any link in the browser. Verify that the underline appears under your mouse, similar to this illustration:

12. The complete style tag appears in Code Block 4-5.

CODE BLOCK 4-5

```
<style type="text/css">
body{
        background-color:#610B0B;
        color:#ffffff;
}
a{
        color:#FE2E2E;
        text-decoration:none;
}
a:visited{
color:#df0101;
}
a:hover{
        text-decoration:underline;
}
</style>
```

Using Images for Links

When creating hyperlinks, users need something to click on. The earlier examples used text. Images can be used in place of text. To use an image as a link, you simply need to use the <img> tag inside of the <a> tags. The img tag should still use the height and width properties. The alt image attribute is needed. However, there is no need to use the title attribute. The title attribute of the link will override the image attributes.

The link image will appear as any other image, except the browser will place a border around the image. The border is HTML's attempt to identify the image as a link. The CSS border property will allow you to format the border as you see fit.

Practice Using Images for Links

You are going to create a menu bar for the index page that is drawn across the top or the side of the page. The menu contains a link to each of the main pages in your site. Menu bars are the most common method of creating navigation for web sites.

I created five gif images on Flamingtext.com for the menu bar. Each image is 150 pixels wide and 35 pixels tall. Their names represent their sport, as shown by the example soccer.gif file here. These images may be downloaded from www.mhprofessional.com/computingdownload.

Soccer

1. Create an images folder under your sports folder.
2. Download the images from www.mhprofessional.com/computingdownload into the images folder.
3. Open the index.html file from the sports folder into your editor and browser.
4. In your editor, move the <h1>Sports Pages</h1> to be after the links.
5. Find the first <a> tag in your document. This should be the Home link.
6. Delete the linking text "home". Replace it with the <img> tag that displays the home.gif file. Remember to set the width, height, and alt properties. Be sure the <img> tag is between the open and close <a> tags.

```
<img src="images/home.gif" width="150" height="35"
title="home navigation"/>
```

7. Save and refresh the page. Your page will have one image with a border around it. It should be similar to the following illustration.

8. You now will change the remaining links. As in Step 6, delete the linking text and replace with the img tag. The image code for the rest of the pictures follows.

```
<img src="images/baseball.gif" width="150" height="35" _
title="baseball navigation"/>
<img src="images/football.gif" width="150" height="35" _
title="football navigation"/>
<img src="images/hockey.gif" width="150" height="35" _
title="hockey navigation"/>
<img src="images/soccer.gif" width="150" height="35" _
title="soccer navigation"/>
```

9. Save and refresh your page. You should have one image per line, each with a border around it. Compare your document with the image shown here:

10. Remove the <br /> tags at the end of each link. This will cause our menu bar to render across the top of the page. Click any of the pictures; the link should work.

11. Menu bars are quite common on the Web. You do not need the boxes around the images. Create a style element in the head of the page.

```
<style type="text/css">
</style>
```

12. Add an img section to the style. Set the border property to 0.

```
img{
      border:0;
}
```

13. Save and refresh your page. Your document should now have images across the top of the page. The borders are gone. The illustration shows the completed project. Code Block 4-6 has the complete code. For consistency, you should copy the modified links to the remaining sports pages.

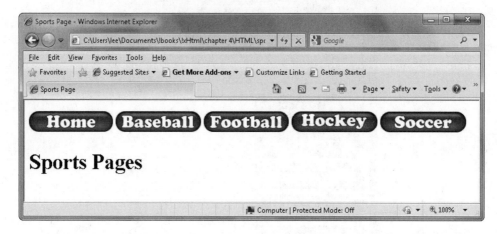

CODE BLOCK 4-6

```
<!DOCTYPE html PUBLIC "-//W3C//DTD XHTML 1.1//EN"
"http://www.w3.org/TR/xhtml11/DTD/xhtml11.dtd">
<html xmlns="http://www.w3.org/1999/xhtml" xml:lang="en">
     <head>
          <title>Sports Page</title>
          <meta name="description" content="Sports pages"/>
          <meta name="author" content="Lee M. Cottrell" />
          <style type="text/css">
               img{
                    border:0;
               }
          </style>
     </head>
     <body>

     <p>
     <a href="index.html" title="Link to the home page.
     The link opens in the same window"> <img src="images/
     home.gif" width="150" height="35"
     title="home navigation"/></a>
     <a href="baseball.html" title="Link to baseball.html.
     The link opens in the same window"><img src="images/
     baseball.gif" width="150" height="35"
     title="baseball navigation"/></a>
     <a href="football.html" title="Link to football.html.
     The link opens in the same window"><img src="images/
     football.gif" width="150" height="35"
     title="football navigation"/></a>
```

```
<a href="hockey.html" title="Link to hockey.html.
The link opens in the same window"><img src="images/
hockey.gif" width="150" height="35"
title="hockey navigation"/></a>
<a href="soccer.html" title="Link to soccer.html.
The link opens in the same window"><img src="images/
soccer.gif" width="150" height="35"
title="soccer navigation"/></a>
</p>
<h1>Sports Pages</h1>
</body>
</html>
```

Creating a Style Document

You have just spent a lot of time formatting your web site. Unfortunately, there are style elements on each page. This can cause a problem as web pages grow larger. With the style information embedded on each page, change becomes very difficult. On your sports site, changing the color of a link on all pages would require modifying five pages. This is clearly not practical.

CSS allows the developer to separate formatting from content. Create a CSS document containing all of the rules for the web site. Cut and paste any CSS from the HTML pages into the CSS document. Finally, link the CSS document to the web page through the <link> tag in the <head> section. The rel attribute tells the browser that a style sheet document will be inserted. The href is the location of the document.

```
<link rel="stylesheet" href="sports.css" />
```

TIP *The href does not have to be on your site. You may link to a CSS document on another site. Be sure you get permission to do so if you are using a commercial site.*

Practice Creating a Style Document

You will move the CSS elements from your sports pages to a new, external CSS page.

1. Open all of the HTML files from the sports folder in your editor.

2. Create a new file. Save it in the sports folder as sports.css.

3. Switch to the index.html file. Cut the img rule from the style section. Paste it into the CSS document.

4. Switch to the baseball.html file. Cut all of the code within the style section and paste it into the CSS document after the img rule. Do not include the <style type="text/css"> in your cut.

5. Remove the <style type="text/css"></style> from the index.html and baseball.html files.

6. Save all files.

7. Switch to the index.html file. In the head section immediately after the </title>, enter the code to link to the CSS page.

8. Save the index file and open it in the browser. Ensure your page has a dark red background and the images do not have a border.

9. Copy the <link> tag to the other pages. Be sure to place it after the </title> tag.

10. Save all pages. Open any page in the browser. Each will have the same formatting. Code Block 4-7 contains the finished CSS code.

CODE BLOCK 4-7

```
body{
        background-color:#610B0B;
        color:#ffffff;
}

a{
        color:#FE2E2E;
        text-decoration:none;
}

a:visited{

        color:#df0101;
}

a:hover{
        text-decoration:underline;
}
img{
        border:0;
}
```

Still Struggling

My students often fail to see the need for an external document. To demonstrate its validity, change the background-color code in the CSS document from #610b0b to #000000. Once you refresh, all pages now have a black background. Without the external CSS document, you would have needed to edit every page.

Summary

This chapter was all about links. You learned how to link to pages both inside and outside of your web site. In addition, you learned how to control where the links open. Extensive site navigation techniques were contrasted. You used CSS to format the links. Finally, you learned how to create an external style sheet.

QUIZ

1. This attribute of the <a> tag specifies the URL of the desired document.
   A. href
   B. title
   C. alt
   D. link

2. To access an external style sheet, use the _____ tag.
   A. <a>
   B. <style>
   C. <link>
   D. <head>

3. Intra-page links are identified with the _____ symbol.
   A. #
   B. $
   C. %
   D. !

4. This HTML target value creates a new window every time a link is clicked.
   A. new
   B. _popup
   C. _blank
   D. window

5. The terms a:visited and a:link are examples of CSS _____ .
   A. properties
   B. classes
   C. attributes
   D. pseudo-classes

6. A(n) _____ is a link to a page on a different site.
   A. internal link
   B. external link
   C. intra-page link
   D. targeted

7. A(n) _____ is a link to a page on the current web site.
   A. internal link
   B. external link
   C. intra-page link
   D. targeted link

8. **This attribute of the <a> tag creates a tooltip for the link.**
   A. href
   B. title
   C. alt
   D. link

9. **Style sheet documents should end with the _____ extension.**
   A. .css
   B. .format
   C. .html
   D. .fmt

10. **This CSS reacts when the mouse is over the link.**
    A. a:hover
    B. a:link
    C. a:mouse
    D. a:active

chapter 5

Using Lists

You are going to learn how to create the three types of lists currently supported by HTML. You will create an ordered list, an unordered list, and a definition list. Finally, you will learn how to format the lists using CSS.

CHAPTER OBJECTIVES

In this chapter, you will

- Define HTML lists
- Create ordered and unordered lists
- Create definition lists

Recall that HTML was intended to simplify the delivery of research materials. Research documents often require an outline. The HTML list feature provides this functionality.

In current practice, lists do much more than simple outlines. Lists generate directions, create bullet points, and even generate navigational aids. Lists are a very powerful addition to your HTML toolbox.

Lists

Lists are an ingrained part of our culture. We take lists to the store, read a list of directions when cooking, we might have a "honey-do" list, and we even just create wish lists at various times of the year.

Lists typically have short pieces of information, each on their own line. Directions have sequencing information at the beginning of the list. In recipes, these are typically numbered. The first list in Figure 5-1 shows an ordered list.

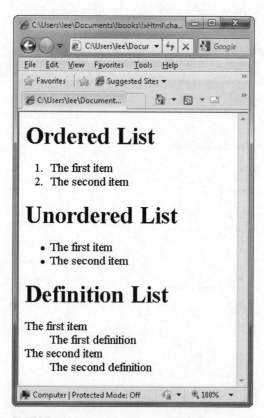

FIGURE 5-1 · The three types of HTML lists

Ingredient lists have no sequence but include a bullet or other small graphic before the information. The second list in Figure 5-1 shows the default bullet for unordered lists.

Definition lists are a little different. The definition list includes at least two pieces of information, each on their own line. The defined word renders at the margin of the page. The definition indents about ½ inch under the word. The last list in Figure 5-1 shows the relationship between the defined term and the definition. Code Block 5-1 shows the code that created Figure 5-1.

CODE BLOCK 5-1

```
<h1>Ordered List</h1>
<ol>
      <li>The first item</li>
      <li>The second item</li>
</ol>
<h1>Unordered List</h1>
<ul>
      <li>The first item</li>
      <li>The second item</li>
</ul>
<h1>Definition List</h1>
<dl>
      <dt>The first item</dt>
      <dd>The first definition</dd>
      <dt>The second item</dt>
      <dd>The second definition</dd>
</dl>
```

Ordered Lists

The first list in Figure 5-1 is an ordered list. You will use an ordered list whenever you have a list that follows a particular sequence. Examples include recipes, directions to solve a problem, or chapter titles. By default, HTML will render an ordered list using Arabic numbers (1, 2, 3, . . .)

The <ol> tag starts the ordered list. This tag tells the browser that list items will follow, and to render them using a sequenced value. Inside of the <ol>, a <li> tag describes each list item. <li> tags are container tags like the <p> tag. As such, they can hold other HTML tags. Like all HTML tags, both the <li> and the <ol> tag need to be closed. Close the <li> tag after the list item and the <ol> tag after the last list item. Code Block 5-2 shows an ordered list providing directions to make a peanut butter and jelly sandwich.

CODE BLOCK 5-2

```
<ol>
<li>Open the peanut butter and jelly jars</li>
<li>Place 2 pieces of bread on the table</li>
<li>Spread some peanut butter on one slice of bread</li>
<li>Spread some jelly on the other slice of bread</li>
<li>Place the peanut buttered side on top of the jelly</li>
<li>Eat and enjoy</li>
</ol>
```

As mentioned earlier, the <ol> tag will automatically render each list item using a number. However, there are several different styles available. To change the style for the list item, apply the list-style-type to the ol tag. Table 5-1 lists the currently supported values for the <ol> tag.

TIP *Internet research will lead you to find exotic values for the list-style-type property. As of publication, only the values listed in Table 5-1 are supported in browsers.*

Practice Using Ordered Lists

The example for this chapter will create a page of lists for bicycling. The first portion of the page will create the steps to adjust the derailleur and brakes on a bicycle.

1. Use your template to create a new file called bicycle.html. Save it in the chapter5 folder.

2. Set the title of the page to read **A guide to bicycling**. Create appropriate meta information.

TABLE 5-1 List-Style-Type Values Supported for the <ol> Tag

Value	Example
upper–roman	I. Item 1 II. Item 2
lower–roman	i. Item 1 ii. Item 2
upper–alpha	A. Item 1 B. Item 2
lower–alpha	a. Item 1 b. Item 2
decimal	1. Item 1 2. Item 2

3. Create the <h1> tag and introductory paragraph.

```
<h1>Bicycling</h1>
<p>Bicycling is more than a kid's pastime. Across the world,
bikes are used for pleasure, transportation, and competition.
This page holds a variety of resources for the cyclist.</p>
```

4. Save the file and view it in a browser.

5. Create an <h2> for adjusting the rear derailleur.

```
<h2>Adjusting the Rear Derailleur</h2>
```

6. Create a paragraph describing the derailleur and an ordered list detailing the steps to adjust the derailleur.

```
<p>The derailleur changes the gears on the bike. Most
derailleurs are set properly and only need tweaks. Consult
your bike store for a complete adjustment.</p>
<ol>
<li>Shift to the smallest cog on the rear wheel.</li>
<li>Twist the barrel connector on the cable until the cable
is loose.</li>
<li>Shift to the highest cog on the rear wheel.</li>
<li>Look at the chain. If it is not centered on the cog, or
looks like it will fall off the top, adjust the H screw on
the derailleur. <br/>As you turn the screw, the derailleur
will shift with the turn.</li>
<li>Tighten the barrel connector until the cable becomes
tight.</li>
<li>Shift down to the smallest cog on the rear wheel.</li>
<li>Look at the chain. If it is not centered on the cog, or
looks like it will fall off the bottom, adjust the L screw on
the derailleur. <br/>As you turn the screw, the derailleur
will shift with the turn.</li>
<li>Now try shifting up and down. If the cable sticks while
going to larger gears, increase the tension. If the shift
does not want to go to smaller gears, decrease the tension.
Continue until each gear is easily accessible. </li>
</ol>
```

7. Save the file and view it in the browser. Your list should resemble the image shown here:

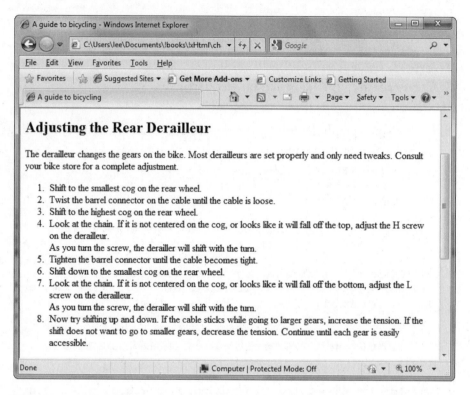

TIP *If you have an extra number, it means that you added an extra <li> instead of a </li> above the extra number.*

8. Create an <h2> for checking the seat height.

```
<h2>Checking Seat Height</h2>
```

9. Create a paragraph and an ordered list detailing how to determine proper seat height.

```
<p>Proper seat height is crucial for best performance and the
health of your knees. When purchasing a new bike have the
bike store do a proper fitting. The following steps work when
a bike professional is not nearby.</p>
    <ol>
    <li>Ensure the seat is level.</li>
    <li>Sit on the seat.</li>
    <li>Pedal backwards. If your knee is fully extended at
      the bottom of the stroke, your seat is at the proper
      height.</li>
    </ol>
```

10. Save the file and view it in the browser. Your second list should resemble the following illustration.

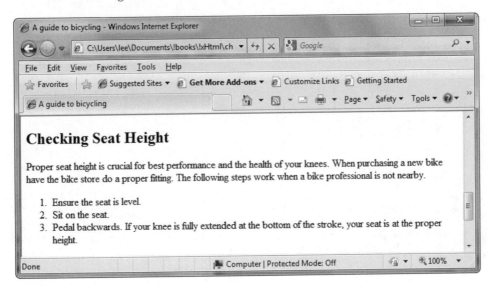

11. The complete code is shown in Code Block 5-3.

TIP *If your second <h2> and list are indented, it means that you failed to close your first <ol> tag.*

CODE BLOCK 5-3

```
<!DOCTYPE html PUBLIC "-//W3C//DTD XHTML 1.1//EN"
"http://www.w3.org/TR/xhtml11/DTD/xhtml11.dtd">
<html xmlns="http://www.w3.org/1999/xhtml" xml:lang="en">
    <head>
        <title>A guide to bicycling</title>
        <meta name="description"
        content="A site dedicated to bicycling"/>
        <meta name="author" content="Lee M. Cottrell" />

    </head>
    <body>
    <h1>Bicycling</h1>
    <p>Bicycling is more than a kid's pastime. Across the
    world, bikes are used for pleasure, transportation,
    and competition. This page holds a variety of
    resources for the cyclist.</p>
```

```
<h2>Adjusting the Rear Derailleur</h2>
<p>The derailleur changes the gears on the bike. Most
derailleurs are set properly and only need tweaks. Consult
your bike store for a complete adjustment.</p>
<ol>
<li>Shift to the smallest cog on the rear wheel.</li>
<li>Twist the barrel connector on the cable until the
cable is loose.</li>
<li>Shift to the highest cog on the rear wheel.</li>
<li>Look at the chain. If it is not centered on the cog,
or looks like it will fall off the top, adjust the H screw on
the derailleur. <br/>As you turn the screw, the derailleur
will shift with the turn.</li>
<li>Tighten the barrel connector until the cable becomes
tight.</li>
<li>Shift down to the smallest cog on the rear wheel.
</li>
<li>Look at the chain. If it is not centered on the cog,
or looks like it will fall off the bottom, adjust the L screw
on the derailleur. <br/>As you turn the screw, the derailleur
will shift with the turn.</li>
<li>Now try shifting up and down. If the cable sticks
while going to larger gears, increase the tension. If the
shift does not want to go to smaller gears, decrease the
tension. Continue until each gear is easily accessible. </li>
</ol>
<h2>Checking Seat Height</h2>
<p>Proper seat height is crucial for best performance
and the health of your knees. When purchasing a new bike have
the bike store do a proper fitting. The following steps work
when a bike professional is not nearby.</p>
<ol>
<li>Ensure the seat is level.</li>
<li>Sit on the seat.</li>
<li>Pedal backwards. If your knee is fully extended at
the bottom of the stroke, your seat is at the proper height.
</li>
</ol>
</body>
</html>
```

Unordered Lists

The second list in Figure 5-1 is an unordered list. Use unordered lists whenever you have a list of items that is in no particular order. Good examples of unordered lists include ingredient lists and shopping lists. By default, HTML will render the unordered list with the disc, a solid circle.

TIP *Alphabetizing unordered lists is a good way to make your pages appear organized.*

The <ul> tag starts the unordered list. This tag tells the browser that list items will follow, and to render them as a bulleted list. Like the <ol> tag, the <li> tag describes each list item. An unordered list listing the ingredients for a peanut butter and jelly sandwich is shown in Code Block 5-4.

CODE BLOCK 5-4

```
<ul>
<li>A jar of peanut butter</li>
<li>A jar of jelly</li>
<li>Two slices of bread</li>
<li>A butter knife</li>
</ul>
```

By default, the <ul> renders using the disc. However, the CSS property list-style-type changes how the browser renders the list items. The values of circle, disc, and square are supported on all browsers. The following illustration displays the circle, disc, and square rendered in Internet Explorer and Firefox. Notice that the circles render a little differently between the two browsers.

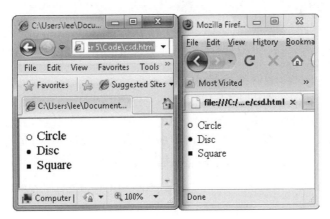

In addition to the list-style-type, the ul tag can use images as bullets. Using image files for bullets allows a great deal of customization for your pages. However, the images must be .gif files and should be small, around 32 × 32 pixels or smaller.

CAUTION   *Do not use animated GIFs for bullets! It is very distracting.*

To place images in your lists, you will use the list-style-image property. List-style-image requires the use of the URL function passing the location of the image. In addition to setting an image, you should also set a list-style-type. The list-style-type value will apply if the bullet image fails to load. Code Block 5-5 shows the correct syntax to use bullet.gif as a bullet image.

CODE BLOCK 5-5

```
ul{
        list-style-type:circle;
        list-style-image:URL("images/bullet.gif");
}
```

Still Struggling

Building lists can be difficult. Visit www.htmlbasix.com/list.shtml for an automated list builder.

Practice Using Unordered Lists

You are going to add an unordered list to the page you created earlier in the chapter. You will format the list using a custom image instead of the default values.

1. Create an images folder under the chapter5 folder.
2. Download the bicycle.gif file from www.mhprofessional.com/computingdownload. Save it into the chapter5/images folder.
3. Open the bicycle.html file created earlier in your editor and browser.
4. In the editor, scroll to the end of the document, right above the </body> tag.
5. Create an <h2> for Bicycling Links.

   ```
   <h2>Bicycling Links</h2>
   ```
6. Create a <ul> tag. Be sure to close the tag.

7. Inside of the <ul> tag, enter three <li> tags with links to bicycling references on the Web.

```
<ul>
<li><a href="http://www.bicycling.com"
title="link to bicycling.com opens in a new window"
target="new">Bicycling Magazine</a></li>
<li><a href="http://http://www.dirtragmag.com/"
title="link to dirtragmag.com opens in a new window"
target="new">DirtRag Magazine</a></li>
<li><a href="http://maps.google.com/biking"
title="link to Google's biking directions opens in a new
window" target="new">Google Biking Directions</a></li>
</ul>
```

8. Save your document. Refresh the browser. Your page should look like the image shown here:

9. Now you are going to change the bullet to a bicycle. Create a style section at the top of the page in the <head> section.

```
<style type="text/css">
</style>
```

10. Add a ul entry to the style section.

11. Create the rules to use the circle list-style-type and render the bicycle.gif file for the bullet.

```
ul{
      list-style-type:circle;
      list-style-image:URL("images/bicycle.gif");
}
```

12. Save your page. Refresh the browser. Your document should look like this illustration:

13. The complete code is contained within Code Block 5-6.

CODE BLOCK 5-6

```
<!DOCTYPE html PUBLIC "-//W3C//DTD XHTML 1.1//EN"
"http://www.w3.org/TR/xhtml11/DTD/xhtml11.dtd">
<html xmlns="http://www.w3.org/1999/xhtml" xml:lang="en">
     <head>
          <title>A guide to bicycling</title>
          <meta name="description" content="A site dedicated
           to bicycling"/>
          <meta name="author" content="Lee M. Cottrell" />
            <style type="text/css">
               ul{
                  list-style-type:circle;
                  list-style-image:URL("images/bicycle.gif");
                  }
            </style>
     </head>
     <body>
     <h1>Bicycling</h1>
     <p>Bicycling is more than a kid's pastime. Across the
     world, bikes are used for pleasure, transportation,
     and competition. This page holds a variety of
     resources for the cyclist.</p>
     <h2>Adjusting the Rear Derailleur</h2> <p>The derailleur
     changes the gears on the bike. Most derailleurs are set
     properly and only need tweaks.
     Consult your bike store for a complete adjustment.</p>
     <ol>
```

```
<li>Shift to the smallest cog on the rear wheel.</li>
<li>Twist the barrel connector on the cable until the
 cable is loose.</li>
<li>Shift to the highest cog on the rear wheel.</li>
<li>Look at the chain. If it is not centered on the cog,
or looks like it will fall off the top, adjust the H screw
on the derailleur. <br/>As you turn the screw,
the derailleur will shift with the turn.</li>
<li>Tighten the barrel connector until the cable becomes
 tight.</li>
<li>Shift down to the smallest cog on the rear wheel.
</li>
<li>Look at the chain. If it is not centered on the cog,
or looks like it will fall off the bottom, adjust the L
screw on the derailleur. <br/>As you turn the screw,
the derailleur will shift with the turn.</li>
<li>Now try shifting up and down. If the cable sticks
while going to larger gears, increase the tension. If the
shift does not want to go to smaller gears, decrease the
tension. Continue until each gear is easily accessible. </li>
</ol>
<h2>Checking Seat Height</h2>
<p>Proper seat height is crucial for best performance and
the health of your knees. When purchasing a new bike
have the bike store do a proper fitting. The following
steps work when a bike professional is not nearby.</p>
<ol>
<li>Ensure the seat is level.</li>
<li>Sit on the seat.</li>
<li>Pedal backwards. If your knee is fully extended at
 the bottom of the stroke, your seat is at the
 proper height.</li>
</ol>
<h2>Bicycling Links</h2>
<ul>
<li><a href="http://www.bicycling.com"
 title="link to bicycling.com opens in a new window"
 target="new">Bicycling Magazine</a></li>
<li><a href="http://http://www.dirtragmag.com/"
 title="link to dirtragmag.com opens in a new window"
 target="new">DirtRag Magazine</a></li>
<li><a href="http://maps.google.com/biking" title="link
 to Google's biking directions opens in a new window"
 target="new">Google Biking Directions</a></li>
</ul>
</body>
</html>
```

Definition Lists

The third list in Figure 5-1 is a definition list. Use definition lists whenever you have a list of words that need to be defined. By default, HTML will render the terms on the left margin and the definition indented about ½ inch under the word.

Definition lists require two additional tags. Unlike the <ol> and <ul> tags, the <li> tag is not used. Instead, the <dt> and <dd> replace the <li> tag. The <dt>, or data term, tag is used to render the term to define. Unlike the <ol> and <ul> tags, there are no dedicated CSS properties associated with the <dl>, <dt>, or <dd>. Code Block 5-7 defines some of the items used in a peanut butter and jelly sandwich.

TIP *Alphabetize the terms to make it easier for your users to find the terms.*

CODE BLOCK 5-7

```
<dl>
<dt>Butter knife</dt>
<dd>A dull knife used to spread food</dd>
<dt>Peanut butter</dt>
<dd>A food product containing crushed peanuts and vegetable oil</dd>
</dl>
```

Practice Using Definition Lists

For the last practice session, you are going to create a definition list. This list will define terms common to cycling.

1. Open the file bicycle.html in your browser and editor.

2. In your editor, scroll to the bottom of the page, immediately above the </body>.

3. Create an <h2> tag stating **Bicycling Terms**.
   ```
   <h2>Bicycling Terms</h2>
   ```

4. Open a <dl> tag. Be sure to close the tag.
   ```
   <dl>
   </dl>
   ```

5. Create a term and definition for the word "cog." Cog is the cycling term for the gear on the rear wheel.
   ```
   <dt>cog</dt>
   <dd>the gear on the rear wheel</dd>
   ```

6. Save and refresh your page in the browser.

7. Repeat for the following words and terms.

- derailleur—mechanism that moves the chain
- downtube—the tube that runs from the handlebars to the pedals
- seatstay—the tubes that run from the rear hub to the seatpost
- shifter—lever to move the derailleur

```
<dt>derailleur</dt>
<dd>mechanism that moves the chain</dd>
<dt>downtube</dt>
<dd>the tube that runs from the handlebars to the pedals
</dd>
<dt>seatstay </dt>
<dd>tubes that run from the rear hub to the seatpost</dd>
<dt>shifter</dt>
<dd>lever to move the derailleur</dd>
```

8. Save and refresh your browser. The page should look like the image shown here.

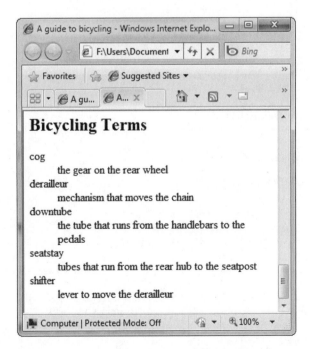

9. Now you will use CSS to format the list. Scroll up to the <style> section.

10. Create a dt entry. Inside of the braces, use the font-weight property to create a rule setting bold font for the dt.

```
dt{
        font-weight:bold;
}
```

11. Create a dd entry. Inside of the braces, use the font-style property to create a rule setting italic fonts for the dd.

```
dd{
        font-style:italic;
}
```

12. The final version of the definition list appears in the image shown next. The final code listing appears in Code Block 5-8.

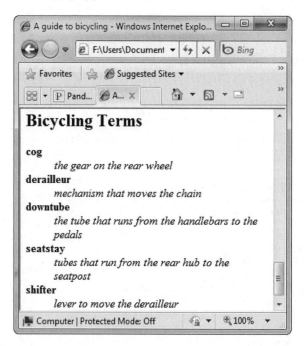

CODE BLOCK 5-8

```
<!DOCTYPE html PUBLIC "-//W3C//DTD XHTML 1.1//EN"
"http://www.w3.org/TR/xhtml11/DTD/xhtml11.dtd">
<html xmlns="http://www.w3.org/1999/xhtml" xml:lang="en">
        <head>
                <title>A guide to bicycling</title>
                <meta name="description"
                 content="A site dedicated to bicycling"/>
                <meta name="author" content="Lee M. Cottrell" />
                <style type="text/css">
```

```
        ul{
                list-style-type:circle;
                list-style-image:URL("images/bicycle.gif");
        }
        dt{
                font-weight:bold;
        }

        dd{
                font-style:italic;
        }
        </style>
</head>
<body>
<h1>Bicycling</h1>
<p>Bicycling is more than a kid's pastime. Across the
world, bikes are used for pleasure, transportation,
and competition. This page holds a variety of
resources for the cyclist.</p>
<h2>Adjusting the Rear Derailleur</h2> <p>The
derailleur changes the gears on the bike. Most
derailleurs are set properly and only need tweaks.
Consult your bike store for a complete adjustment.</p>
<ol>
<li>Shift to the smallest cog on the rear wheel.</li>
<li>Twist the barrel connector on the cable until
the cable is loose.</li>
<li>Shift to the highest cog on the rear wheel.</li>
<li>Look at the chain. If it is not centered on the cog,
or looks like it will fall off the top, adjust
the H screw on the derailleur.
<br/>As you turn the screw, the derailleur will shift
with the turn.</li>
<li>Tighten the barrel connector until the cable
becomes tight.</li>
<li>Shift down to the smallest cog on the rear
wheel.</li>
<li>Look at the chain. If it is not centered on the cog,
or looks like it will fall off the bottom, adjust
the L screw on the derailleur.
<br/>As you turn the screw, the derailleur will shift
with the turn.</li> <li>Now try shifting up and down.
If the cable sticks while going to larger gears,
increase the tension. If the shift does not want to go
to smaller gears, decrease the tension. Continue until
each gear is easily accessible. </li>
</ol>
<h2>Checking Seat Height</h2>
<p>Proper seat height is crucial for best performance and
the health of your knees. When purchasing a new bike have
```

```
                   the bike store do a proper fitting. The following steps
                   work when a bike professional is not nearby.</p>
                   <ol>
                   <li>Ensure the seat is level.</li>
                   <li>Sit on the seat.</li>
                   <li>Pedal backwards. If your knee is fully extended at
                    the bottom of the stroke, your seat is at the
                    proper height.
       </li>
                   </ol>
                   <h2>Bicycling Links</h2>
                   <ul>
                   <li><a href="http://www.bicycling.com" title="link to
                   bicycling.com opens in a new window" target="new">
                   Bicycling Magazine</a></li>
                   <li><a href=" http://www.dirtragmag.com/" title="link to
                   dirtragmag.com opens in a new window" target="new">
                   DirtRag Magazine</a></li>
                   <li><a href="http://maps.google.com/biking" title="link to
                   google's biking directions opens in a new window"
                   target="new">Google Biking Directions</a></li>
                   </ul>
                   <h2>Bicycling Terms</h2>
                   <dl>
                       <dt>cog</dt>
                       <dd>the gear on the rear wheel</dd>
                       <dt>derailleur</dt>
                       <dd>mechanism that moves the chain</dd>
                       <dt>downtube</dt>
                       <dd>the tube that runs from the handlebars to the
                        pedals</dd>
                       <dt>seatstay </dt>
                       <dd>tubes that run from the rear hub to the
                        seatpost</dd>

                       <dt>shifter</dt>
                       <dd>lever to move the derailleur</dd>
                   </dl>
                   </body>
       </html>
```

Summary

This chapter was about lists. You built three types of lists: ordered, unordered, and definition lists. As in other chapters, you formatted the lists using CSS.

QUIZ

1. **This tag is used by ordered and unordered lists to specify the list items.**
   A. <li>
   B. <ol>
   C. <ul>
   D. <dt>

2. **To create an ordered list, use the _____ tag.**
   A. <ul>
   B. <ol>
   C. <dl>
   D. <li>

3. **Which of the following items is the default bullet for an unordered list?**
   A. circle
   B. disc
   C. triangle
   D. square

4. **To change the numbering style for the ordered list, use the _____ property in a style section.**
   A. number-style
   B. list-type
   C. list-style-type
   D. counter-style

5. **The default style for the ordered list.**
   A. upper-alpha
   B. decimal
   C. upper-roman
   D. numeric

6. **To create a definition list, use the _____ tag.**
   A. <ul>
   B. <ol>
   C. <dl>
   D. <li>

7. **A list of items to take to school tomorrow is best rendered using a(n) _____.**
   A. ordered list
   B. unordered list
   C. paragraph
   D. definition list

8. To create an unordered list, use the _____ tag.
   A. <ul>
   B. <ol>
   C. <dl>
   D. <li>

9. The _____ tag defines a term in the definition list.
   A. <li>
   B. <dd>
   C. <dl>
   D. <dt>

10. A pirate's treasure map is best rendered using a(n) _____ .
    A. ordered list
    B. unordered list
    C. paragraph
    D. heading

chapter **6**

Building Tables

Tables have many uses. You are going to use tables to organize data, group information, and simplify page navigation. Common uses of tables include listing products, schedules, sales data, and simple page layout.

CHAPTER OBJECTIVES

In this chapter, you will

- Define and create tables
- Span rows and columns
- Format tables with CSS

The preceding chapters have focused on text as headings or inside of paragraphs. This works for the majority of the text elements on your pages. However, there is often a need to create structured data that exists in rows and columns. This is the job of the table tag.

The table tag allows you to create rows and columns of data. It does a very nice job of arranging your data on the screen. Without any guidance from you, the browser will render the text very well, creating a very readable layout.

Tables

Tables are a manner of arranging data into rows and columns. The information in each row relates to each other. Items in the same column are of the same category. Figure 6-1 shows a simple table. The table has four rows and four columns. The information in the first row all pertains to the 8:00 class. The third column describes the room number for the class. The intersection of a row and a column is a *cell*. Code Block 6-1 contains the HTML that created the table.

TIP *Tables in HTML are similar to worksheets in spreadsheet programs like Microsoft Excel.*

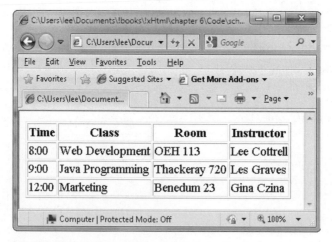

FIGURE 6-1 · A table created in HTML

CODE BLOCK 6-1

```
<table border="1">
<tr>
        <th>Time</th>
        <th>Class</th>
        <th>Room</th>
        <th>Instructor</th>
</tr>
<tr>
        <td>8:00</td>
        <td>Web Development</td>
        <td>OEH 113</td>
        <td>Lee Cottrell</td>
</tr>
<tr>
        <td>9:00</td>
        <td>Java Programming</td>
        <td>Thackeray 720</td>
        <td>Les Graves</td>
</tr>
<tr>
        <td>12:00</td>
        <td>Marketing</td>
        <td>Benedum 23</td>
        <td>Gina Czina</td>
</tr>
</table>
```

Like a list, a table requires several tags to build. The <table> tag creates the table. The <table> tag contains several additional tags that compose the table structure. The table in Figure 6-1 has a border surrounding it. The border is an attribute of the table tag.

TIP *Borders with values larger than five look really bad.*

The first line of Code Block 6-1 builds the table. Included is the border attribute. The border attribute expects a numeric value describing the width of the border. Larger border values result in thicker borders. This image shows the same table with a border attribute of 5. Tables have several additional attributes, defined in Table 6-1.

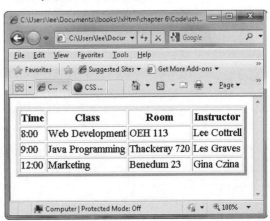

TABLE 6-1 Common Table Attributes

Attribute	Description	Values
border	Sets the number of pixels in the border.	0–1000 0 means no border
cellspacing	Distance in pixels between the cells in the table.	0–1000 0 means no space
cellpadding	Distance in pixels between the cell border and the cell data.	0–1000 0 means no space
frame	Describes where on the outside of the table borders appear. This attribute may contain multiple values.	above—Border on top only below—Border on bottom only box—All four borders hsides—The top and bottom borders only lhs—The left-hand border only rhs—The right-hand border only vsides—The right and left borders only
rules	Describes where on the outside of the cell borders appear. This attribute may contain multiple values.	all—Borders appear between all rows and columns cols—Borders appear between columns only groups—Borders appear between row groups and column groups rows—Borders appear between rows only
summary	Provides a summary of the table. Used by screen readers.	Text describing the table

TIP *The frame and rules attributes have a CSS equivalent.*

The table in Figure 6-1 has four rows. The <tr> tag creates the row. You will need to create one <tr> tag per row. Code Block 6-1 has four <tr> tags, one for each row. If my schedule had ten classes, I would need ten <tr> tags.

The first row contains the headers for the table. The <th> tag creates the column headers. Browsers render the <th> tag as centered in the column and in boldface font. The table in Figure 6-1 has four <th> tags, one for each column. If I had seven columns, I would need seven <th> tags.

TIP *Tables displaying tabular data should always have column headings.*

The second through fourth rows contain the data for the table. A <td> tag stores the data for the table. There is one <td> tag per column in the row. The data in the <td> tag is left aligned and in normal font face. The browser determines the width of the column. The browser will determine the longest value in each <th> or <td> tag. The width of the column will be set to the longest value in each column.

TIP *You can use CSS to adjust the widths of the table and columns.*

Figure 6-1 shows a common table. However, there is no indication as to what the table holds. Tables should have a caption describing what the table holds. The <caption> tag, placed within the <table>, will render a caption on the web page. Code Block 6-2 shows where to use the <caption> tag in a table. Figure 6-2 shows the output of the code.

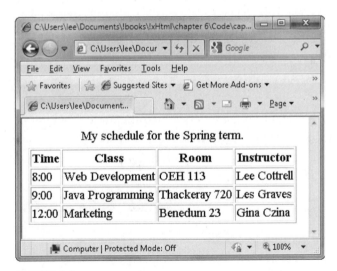

FIGURE 6-2 · A captioned table

CODE BLOCK 6-2

```
<table border="1">
<caption>My schedule for the Spring term.</caption>
<tr>
        <th>Time</th>
        <th>Class</th>
        <th>Room</th>
        <th>Instructor</th>
</tr>
<tr>
        <td>8:00</td>
        <td>Web Development</td>
        <td>OEH 113</td>
        <td>Lee Cottrell</td>
</tr>
<tr>
        <td>9:00</td>
        <td>Java Programming</td>
        <td>Thackeray 720</td>
        <td>Les Graves</td>
</tr>
<tr>
        <td>12:00</td>
        <td>Marketing</td>
        <td>Benedum 23</td>
        <td>Gina Czina</td>
</tr>
</table>
```

The caption in Figure 6-2 renders above the table. Using CSS, the caption will render to the top or bottom. The caption-side property is supposed to control the location. Code Block 6-3 modifies the <caption> tag to place the caption under the table, as shown here:

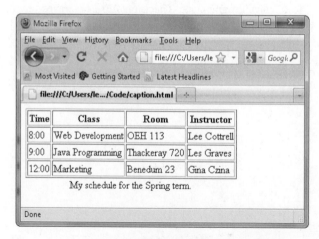

CODE BLOCK 6-3

```
<caption style="caption-side:bottom;">My schedule for the Spring
term.</caption>
```

Unfortunately, the caption-side property does not work in Internet Explorer 8. To achieve this effect, you need to use the deprecated align attribute of the <caption> tag. Assuming that this attribute remains deprecated, Explorer will eventually stop supporting the align attribute. To support both Firefox and Internet Explorer 8, you need to include both the align attribute and the style in your caption. Code Block 6-4 shows the caption with both alignments set.

CODE BLOCK 6-4

```
<caption style="caption-side:bottom;" align="bottom">My schedule
for the Spring term.</caption>
```

 Still Struggling

There are many inconsistencies between how Internet Explorer and Firefox render HTML. Remember from Chapter 1 that HTML is not a standard, it is a recommendation. It is up to the individual browser developers to decide how to handle HTML code. You will need to view your HTML in all browsers, and ensure that your code renders well in each.

Practice Creating Tables

You are going to create a table detailing the menu for a dinner party.

1. Use your template to create a new file titled **dinner.html**. Save it in the chapter6 folder.

2. Set the title of the page to read **Faculty dinner assignments**. Create appropriate meta information.

3. Create a table with a border and a caption.

   ```
   <table border="1">
   <caption>Faculty dinner assignments</caption>
   </table>
   ```

4. Immediately after the </caption>, create the column header row with two columns for "Recipe Name" and "Person Providing."

```
<tr>
      <th>Recipe Name</th>
      <th>Person Providing</th>
</tr>
```

5. Save the file. Open the file in your browser. It should resemble the following image:

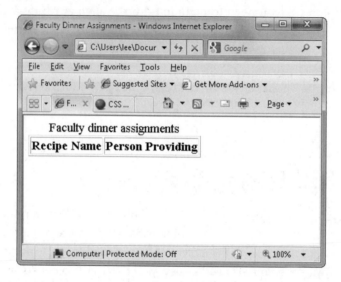

6. Create three rows with three appetizers and a faculty member name. For compatibility with a future exercise, please ensure the same faculty member brings all of the appetizers.

```
<tr>
      <td>Spicy Chicken Wings</td>
      <td>Gina Czina</td>
</tr>
<tr>
      <td>Chicken Dumplings</td>
      <td>Gina Czina</td>
</tr>
<tr>
      <td>Cheesy Nachos</td>
      <td>Gina Czina</td>
</tr>
```

7. Save and refresh the page in your browser. It should resemble the image shown here:

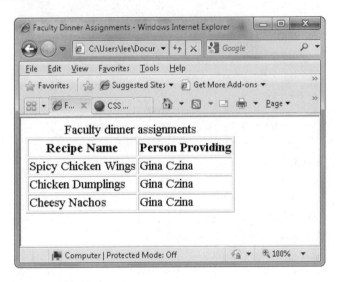

8. Create three more rows for entrees. Again, include the entrée name and a faculty member. For compatibility with a future exercise, have one faculty member bring two of the items.

```
<tr>
      <td>Chicken Cordon Bleu</td>
      <td>Lee Cottrell</td>
</tr>
<tr>
      <td>Spaghetti with Marinara</td>
      <td>Les Graves</td>
</tr>
<tr>
      <td>Bacon wrapped filet mignon</td>
      <td>Les Graves</td>
</tr>
```

9. Save and refresh the page in your browser. It should resemble this image:

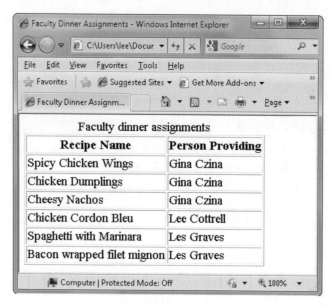

10. Create two dessert entrees. Assign the dessert entries to faculty members as you see fit.

```
<tr>
        <td>Cheesecake</td>
        <td>Les Graves</td>
</tr>
<tr>
        <td>Apple Pie</td>
        <td>Lee Cottrell</td>
</tr>
```

11. Save and refresh. Your document should look like the image shown next. The final code listing is contained in Code Block 6-5.

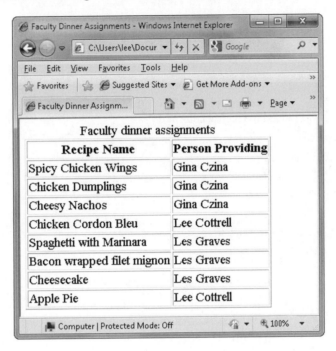

CODE BLOCK 6-5

```
<!DOCTYPE html PUBLIC "-//W3C//DTD XHTML 1.1//EN"
"http://www.w3.org/TR/xhtml11/DTD/xhtml11.dtd">
<html xmlns="http://www.w3.org/1999/xhtml" xml:lang="en">
    <head>
        <title>Faculty Dinner Assignments</title>
        <meta name="description" content="This month's
         faculty dinner assignments"/>
        <meta name="author" content="Lee M. Cottrell" />

    </head>
    <body>
    <table border="1">
    <caption>Faculty dinner assignments</caption>
    <tr>
        <th>Recipe Name</th>
        <th>Person Providing</th>
    </tr>
```

```
       <tr>
               <td>Spicy Chicken Wings</td>
               <td>Gina Czina</td>
       </tr>
       <tr>
               <td>Chicken Dumplings</td>
               <td>Gina Czina</td>
       </tr>
       <tr>
               <td>Cheesy Nachos</td>
               <td>Gina Czina</td>
       </tr>
               <tr>
               <td>Chicken Cordon Bleu</td>
               <td>Lee Cottrell</td>
       </tr>
       <tr>
               <td>Spaghetti with Marinara</td>
               <td>Les Graves</td>
       </tr>
       <tr>
               <td>Bacon wrapped filet mignon</td>
               <td>Les Graves</td>
       </tr>
       <tr>
               <td>Cheesecake</td>
               <td>Les Graves</td>
       </tr>
       <tr>
               <td>Apple Pie</td>
               <td>Lee Cottrell</td>
       </tr>
       </table>
       </body>
   </html>
```

Spanning Rows and Columns

The <td> tag contains the data for the table. Typically, one cell holds one piece of data. However, there might be times where multiple cells need to hold one piece of data. Another way to think of this is to merge multiple cells into one cell. In HTML, this is called *spanning*.

TIP *Spanning is very similar to cell merging in Microsoft Excel.*

There are two types of spanning. You can span across rows or span across columns. Both result in one <td> being used across the span. The rowspan attribute of the <td> tag creates a row span. Row spanning in effect will make a cell seem taller.

Consider the table shown in Figure 6-3. The table sells several products for a sports team. Three jerseys and two hats are for sale. Notice how the item repeats several times and the price repeats. These are good candidates for row spanning.

The code in Code Block 6-6 creates Figure 6-3.

CODE BLOCK 6-6

```
<table border="1">
<caption>Team products for sale</caption>
<tr>
      <th>Product</th>
      <th>Team</th>
      <th>Price</th>
</tr>
<tr>
      <td>Home Jersey</td>
      <td>Elliott Eagles</td>
      <td>$35.99</td>
</tr>
```

FIGURE 6-3 · A table of products before row spanning

```
<tr>
     <td>Home Jersey</td>
     <td>Allentown Alligators</td>
     <td>$35.99</td>
</tr>
<tr>
     <td>Home Jersey</td>
     <td>Mt. Washington Presidents</td>
     <td>$35.99</td>
</tr>
<tr>
     <td>Hat</td>
     <td>Elliott Eagles</td>
     <td>$19.99</td>
</tr>
<tr>
     <td>Hat</td>
     <td>Mt. Washington Presidents</td>
     <td>$19.99</td>
</tr>
</table>
```

Again, notice that there are three jerseys and two hats. These numbers become important when row spanning. The steps to span a series of rows are

1. Count the number of rows to span.

2. Add the attribute rowspan="row num" to the first <td> tag.

3. Remove the other <td> tags.

Code Block 6-7 and the following illustration show the row-spanned table. The jersey, hat, and prices have been merged into one cell respectively. This table is easier to read than the one in Figure 6-3.

CODE BLOCK 6-7

```
<table border="1">
<caption>Team products for sale</caption>
<tr>
        <th>Product</th>
        <th>Team</th>
        <th>Price</th>
</tr>
<tr>
        <td rowspan="3">Home Jersey</td>
        <td>Elliott Eagles</td>
        <td rowspan="3">$35.99</td>
</tr>
<tr>
        <td>Allentown Alligators</td>
</tr>
<tr>
        <td>Mt. Washington Presidents</td>
</tr>
<tr>
        <td rowspan="2">Hat</td>
        <td>Elliott Eagles</td>
        <td rowspan="2">$19.99</td>
</tr>
<tr>
        <td>Mt. Washington Presidents</td>
</tr>
</table>
```

Similar to rowspan, the colspan attribute allows a cell to occupy multiple columns. In effect, the column is now wider than a standard cell. The steps to colspan are similar to row spanning.

1. Count the number of columns to span.

2. Add the rowspan attribute to the first <td> cell.

3. Remove the additional <td>.

4. Optionally, have the first <td> on its own row.

Figure 6-4 and Code Block 6-8 show a table containing the schedule for a projector. Notice how Mr. Cottrell needs the projector from 8:00 to 10:00 on Tuesday, Wednesday, and Thursday. Each time period has one instructor using the projector for several days in a row. In the last block of time, Mrs. Czina needs the projector every day. A colspan would simplify this table and make the text more readable.

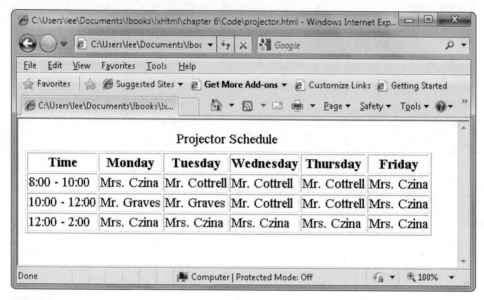

FIGURE 6-4 · A projector schedule before col spanning

CODE BLOCK 6-8

```
<table border="1">
    <caption>Projector Schedule</caption>
    <tr>
        <th>Time</th>
        <th>Monday</th>
        <th>Tuesday</th>
        <th>Wednesday</th>
        <th>Thursday</th>
        <th>Friday</th>
    </tr>
    <tr>
        <td>8:00 - 10:00</td>
        <td>Mrs. Czina</td>
        <td >Mr. Cottrell</td>
        <td>Mrs. Czina</td>
    </tr>
    <tr>
        <td>10:00 - 12:00</td>
        <td>Mr. Graves</td>
        <td>Mr. Graves</td>
        <td>Mr. Cottrell</td>
        <td>Mr. Cottrell</td>
        <td>Mrs. Czina</td>
    </tr>
```

```
        <tr>
                <td>12:00 - 2:00</td>
                <td>Mrs. Czina</td>
                <td>Mrs. Czina</td>
                <td>Mrs. Czina</td>
                <td>Mrs. Czina</td>
                <td>Mrs. Czina</td>
        </tr>
</table>
```

The following illustration shows the projector table after spanning columns. Notice that any instructors that use the projector on successive days are spanned. The code that generated the span is listed in Code Block 6-9.

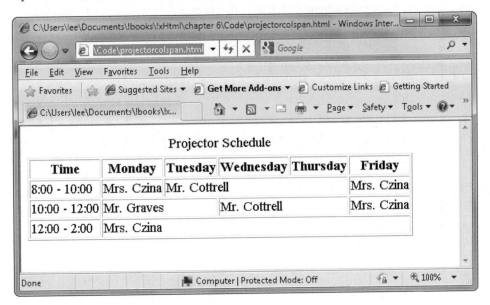

CODE BLOCK 6-9

```
<table border="1">
        <caption>Projector Schedule</caption>
        <tr>
                <th>Time</th>
                <th>Monday</th>
                <th>Tuesday</th>
                <th>Wednesday</th>
                <th>Thursday</th>
                <th>Friday</th>
        </tr>
```

```
        <tr>
            <td>8:00 - 10:00</td>
            <td>Mrs. Czina</td>
            <td colspan="3">Mr. Cottrell</td>
            <td>Mrs. Czina</td>
        </tr>
        <tr>
            <td>10:00 - 12:00</td>
            <td colspan="2">Mr. Graves</td>
            <td colspan="2">Mr. Cottrell</td>
            <td>Mrs. Czina</td>
        </tr>
        <tr>
            <td>12:00 - 2:00</td>
            <td colspan="5">Mrs. Czina</td>
        </tr>
</table>
```

Practice Row and Col Spanning

The dinner.html document created earlier in the chapter is a typical table. Row and col spanning will improve the document. You are going to span the rows for the employee bringing multiple meals and span the columns for the meal course.

1. Open the dinner.html document in your editor and browser.

2. Gina Czina is bringing three appetizers. You are going to span the rows for the appetizers. In the first <td> tag with Gina's name, enter the attribute rowspan="3".

   ```
   <td rowspan="3">Gina Czina</td>
   ```

3. Remove the next two <td> containing Gina Czina.

4. Save and refresh your page in the browser. It should look like the image shown here.

5. Find the entrée Spaghetti with Marinara provided by Les Graves. Start row spanning Les' contributions to the meal by adding the attribute **rowspan="2"** to the appropriate <td> holding Les' name.

6. Remove the next <td> holding Les' name under the <td> for Bacon wrapped filet mignon.

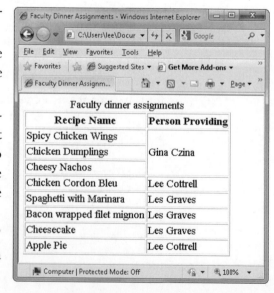

7. Your page after saving and refreshing should resemble this illustration:

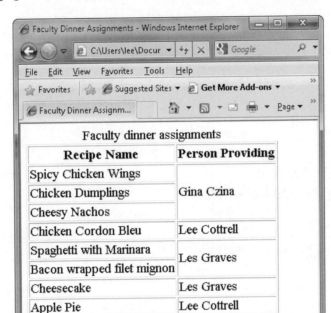

This table does a good job identifying who is bringing which dish. However, it does not identify the appetizers from the entrees or the desserts. Adding a new row identifying the course will make the table easier to read.

1. Click after the first </tr> for the header row. Add a new row.

```
<tr>
</tr>
```

2. Inside the new row, add a single <td> tag that row spans 2. Make the contents of this <td> tag say "Appetizers".

```
<td colspan="2">Appetizers</td>
```

3. Save and refresh your page. It will look like the following illustration:

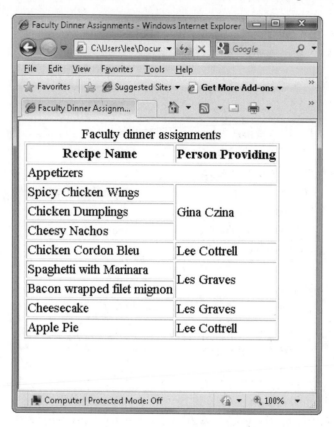

4. You will repeat for entrees and desserts. Find the </tr> after the entry for Cheesy Nachos. Add the following row and colspanned cell for Entrees after this </tr>.

```
<tr>
<td colspan="2">Entrees</td>
</tr>
```

5. Add the following colspanned cell for Desserts after the </tr> for Bacon wrapped filet mignon.

```
<tr>
        <td colspan="2">Desserts</td>
</tr>
```

6. Save and refresh your page in the browser. It will have three colspanned rows as shown in this image. The final code is shown in Code Block 6-10.

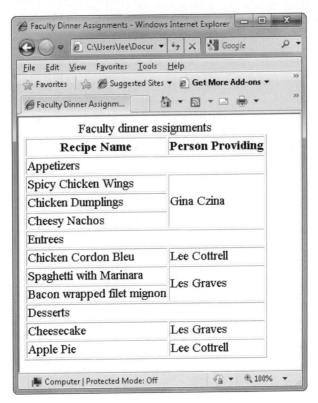

CODE BLOCK 6-10

```
<!DOCTYPE html PUBLIC "-//W3C//DTD XHTML 1.1//EN"
"http://www.w3.org/TR/xhtml11/DTD/xhtml11.dtd">
<html xmlns="http://www.w3.org/1999/xhtml" xml:lang="en">
    <head>
            <title>Faculty Dinner Assignments</title>
            <meta name="description"
             content="This month's faculty dinner assignments"/>
            <meta name="author" content="Lee M. Cottrell" />

    </head>
    <body>
    <table border="1">
    <caption>Faculty dinner assignments</caption>
    <tr>
            <th>Recipe Name</th>
            <th>Person Providing</th>
    </tr>
```

```
        <tr>
                <td colspan="2">Appetizers</td>
        </tr>
        <tr>
                <td>Spicy Chicken Wings</td>
                <td rowspan="3">Gina Czina</td>
        </tr>
        <tr>
                <td>Chicken Dumplings</td>
                </tr>
        <tr>
                <td>Cheesy Nachos</td>
        </tr>
        <tr>
                <td colspan="2">Entrees</td>
        </tr>
        <tr>
                <td>Chicken Cordon Bleu</td>
                <td>Lee Cottrell</td>
        </tr>
        <tr>
                <td>Spaghetti with Marinara</td>
                <td rowspan="2">Les Graves</td>
        </tr>
        <tr>
                <td>Bacon wrapped filet mignon</td>
        </tr>
        <tr>
                <td colspan="2">Desserts</td>
        </tr>
        <tr>
                <td>Cheesecake</td>
                <td>Les Graves</td>
        </tr>
        <tr>
                <td>Apple Pie</td>
                <td>Lee Cottrell</td>
        </tr>
        </table>
        </body>
    </html>
```

Formatting Tables

The tables produced in the chapter have been rather plain. Each had a simple border, and they were sized according to the needs of the table. Other than spanning, no time was spent on making the tables look better.

There are two methods of formatting tables. Several table attributes are available for formatting tables. Additionally, CSS provides advanced formatting options for tables.

Table Attributes

Table 6-1, shown at the start of this chapter, lists the attributes available for tables. The width attribute specifies how wide the table is. It accepts values in pixels, percents, inches, and several other measurements. Pixels and percents are the most useful.

Setting the width attribute to 100% will make the table as wide as the browser document. The table will be as high as it needs to be. Likewise, set the width attribute to 50% and the table will be half the width of the page. Percents result in a table that resizes itself based on the browser. There are times that a table needs a fixed size. Using a pixel value for the width attribute generates a fixed-sized table.

TIP *If your widths for the column or table are too small, browsers will ignore the width value and render the table as large as necessary.*

The width attribute can be applied to <tables>, <td>, and <th> tags. If used to adjust the width of a column, the attribute is only needed one time in any of the columns. Code Block 6-11 shows a table set to exactly 300 pixels, and a 200-pixel-wide first column and two 50-pixel columns. The output is shown in this image.

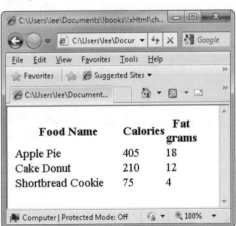

CODE BLOCK 6-11

```
<table width="300">
    <tr>
        <th width="200">Food Name</th>
        <th width="50">Calories</th>
        <th width="50">Fat grams</th>
    </tr>
    <tr>
        <td>Apple Pie</td>
        <td>405</td>
        <td>18</td>
    </tr>
```

```
        <tr>
                <td>Cake Donut</td>
                <td>210</td>
                <td>12</td>
        </tr>
        <tr>
                <td>Shortbread Cookie</td>
                <td>75</td>
                <td>4</td>
        </tr>
</table>
```

Tables are hard to read without borders and lines. The border attribute, as previously used, sets a border around the entire table and each cell. This is readable, although it can be unattractive. The rules and frame attributes, applied to the table tag, set the borders on the cells and tables respectively. Code Block 6-12 and the following illustration show the calories table with rules between the rows and a border below the table. Notice how Explorer 8 and Firefox 3 handle the borders differently.

CODE BLOCK 6-12

```
<table width="300" rules="rows" frame="below">
```

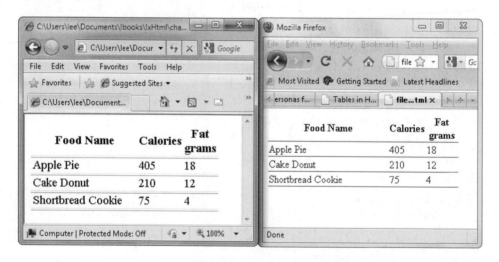

The cellspacing and cellpadding attributes control the amount of space around the contents of the <td> or <th>. The default setting for both values are one. Setting a value of zero will make the table seem smaller. Larger values will expand the table. Cellspacing controls the amount of space between the cells. Cellpadding controls the space between the contents of the cell and the cell border.

This space will be included in the width of the cell. The following illustration and Code Block 6-13 illustrate the use of cellspacing in our calorie table.

CAUTION *The cellspacing property acts differently in Internet Explorer and Firefox. Firefox seems to ignore the attribute, forcing it to stay at 0. Internet Explorer applies the attribute. Setting the attribute to 0 will cause Explorer to render the frame and rules similarly to Firefox.*

CODE BLOCK 6-13

```
<table width="300" rules="rows" frame="below" cellspacing="5">
```

Using CSS to Format Tables

Formatting a table using CSS provides more choices and a better-looking table. The border, rules, and frame attributes of tables can be set using CSS. Instead of a boring black line, you can choose colors, line thickness, and line-style. In addition to changing the line style, CSS makes it easy to change colors of the tables.

TIP *HTML includes three tags for formatting tables. They are thead, tbody, and tfooter. These are best combined with CSS to provide formatting for large tables. Unfortunately, browser support is quite spotty.*

Changing Borders with CSS

Consider Figure 6-2. The border attribute is set with the value of five. While this table looks reasonably good, CSS will make it look better. Figure 6-5 shows the border possibilities for tables with CSS. Code Block 6-14 shows the code that generated Figure 6-5.

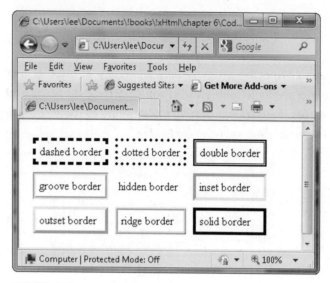

FIGURE 6-5 · CSS border examples

CODE BLOCK 6-14

```
<table cellpadding="5px" cellspacing="10px" style="border-
color:#000000;">
<tr>
      <td style="border-style:dashed;">dashed border</td>
      <td style="border-style:dotted;">dotted border</td>
      <td style="border-style:double;">double border</td>
</tr>
<tr>
      <td style="border-style:groove;">groove border</td>
      <td style="border-style:hidden;">hidden border</td>
      <td style="border-style:inset;">inset border</td>
</tr>
<tr>
      <td style="border-style:outset;">outset border</td>
      <td style="border-style:ridge;">ridge border</td>
      <td style="border-style:solid;">solid border</td>
</tr>
</tr>
</table>
```

TIP   *Only the dashed, dotted, and solid borders may accept a width.*

CSS border properties have more power than just style. You can set the color and width of several styles. Code Block 6-13 uses the border-color attribute to set the colors of each border to be black. Obviously, you can choose any color you wish. What may not be obvious is that you can set the color of each side. You could, if you wanted, have a black top border, a red right border, a green left border, and a blue bottom border. This example is extreme, but it shows the possibilities.

Table 6-2 lists the common border properties for CSS. Each accepts up to three values. The first value is the thickness. The second is one of the styles from Figure 6-5. The last is the color.

TIP *CSS borders are affected by the cellspacing. To achieve a continuous border, set the cellspacing to 0.*

Figure 6-2 only needs lines between the rows. To make this change, remove the border attribute from the table. Add the cellspacing="0" and cellpadding="2" attributes to the table. Finally, add the CSS shown in Code Block 6-15. The following illustration shows the newly formatted table.

CODE BLOCK 6-15

```
<style type="text/css">
    th{
        text-align:left;
        background-color:#000000;
        color:#ffffff;
    }
    td{
        border-bottom:2px solid #000000;
    }
</style>
<table cellspacing="0" cellpadding="2">
<!--rest of table omitted-->
</table>
```

TABLE 6-2 Common Border Properties for CSS

CSS Property	Description	Example
border	Sets the border for the entire table	border:double;
border–bottom	Sets the bottom border	border–bottom:1px solid #00ffff;
border–left	Sets the left border	border–left:1px solid #00ffff;
border–right	Sets the right border	border–right:1px solid #00ffff;
border–top	Sets the top border	border–top:1px solid #00ffff;

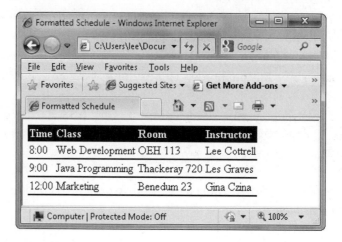

Practice Formatting Tables

The dinner menu needs to be formatted. To format the table, you will use the properties defined previously. To apply the formats, you will need to use a tag-level class.

A *tag-level* class is a named set of CSS rules. Apply the rules to the tag as often as necessary. It removes the problem of CSS entries applying where they are unwanted.

1. Open the dinner.html document in your browser and editor.

2. Remove the border="1" attribute from the <table>.

3. Add a style section to the head of the document.

```
<style type="text/css">

</style>
```

4. You are going to apply a line between courses brought by different instructors. Start by creating a td entry in the style section that sets a bottom-border of 1 pixel, uses the solid style, and is the #0000ff color.

```
td{
        border-bottom:1px solid #0000ff;
}
```

5. After saving and refreshing, your document should look like the image shown here:

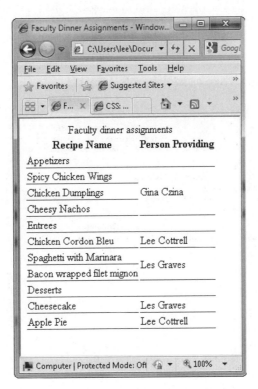

6. You only want the lines to separate the items brought by different teachers. For example, you want the line after Chicken Cordon Bleu and Cheesecake. Modify your td entry in the CSS section to read td.border. This creates a named tag-level class called border.

```
td.border{
     border-bottom:1px solid #0000ff;
     }
```

7. Save and refresh the page and the lines are all gone.

8. Find the row with Chicken Cordon Bleu. Inside of the attribute space for each td tag in this row, add the attribute class="border". This class applies the tag-level class you named border.

```
<tr>
     <td class="border">Chicken Cordon Bleu</td>
     <td class="border">Lee Cottrell</td>
</tr>
```

9. Repeat the class="border" to the two <td> in the row for Cheesecake.

```
<tr>
        <td class="border">Cheesecake</td>
        <td class="border">Les Graves</td>
</tr>
```

10. Save and refresh your page. It should have lines under Chicken Cordon Bleu and Cheesecake as shown in this image:

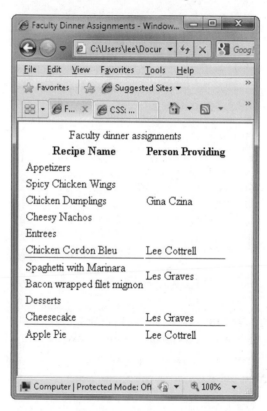

11. Look carefully at each line. There is a small break in the line. To remove the break, add the cellspacing="0" attribute to the table.

```
<table cellspacing="0">
```

12. Now you need to make the courses easier to identify. Again, we will use a tag-level class to format the desired <td>. Add a new td.course entry to your style section. Format with a background-color of #0000ff, a color of #ffffff, and font-size of 16pt.

13. Add the attribute class="course" to the <td> containing Appetizers, Entrees, and Desserts.

14. Save and refresh the page in the browser. It should have nicely formatted course names as shown here:

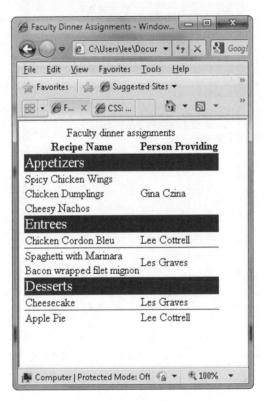

15. The header row now seems unnecessary. Remove the entire <tr> and </tr> containing the <th> tags.

16. Save and refresh your page. It should look like the following illustration. The final code is contained in Code Block 6-16.

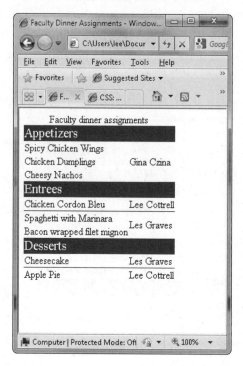

CODE BLOCK 6-16

```
<!DOCTYPE html PUBLIC "-//W3C//DTD XHTML 1.1//EN"
"http://www.w3.org/TR/xhtml11/DTD/xhtml11.dtd">
<html xmlns="http://www.w3.org/1999/xhtml" xml:lang="en">
      <head>
            <title>Faculty Dinner Assignments</title>
            <meta name="description" content=
            "This month's faculty dinner assignments"/>
            <meta name="author" content="Lee M. Cottrell" />
            <style type="text/css">
               td.border{
                   border-bottom:1px solid #0000ff;
               }
               td.course{
                   background-color:#0000ff; color:#ffffff;
                   font-size:16pt;
               }
</style>
      </head>
      <body>
      <table cellspacing="0">
      <caption>Faculty dinner assignments</caption>
```

```
       <tr>
          <td colspan="2" class="course">Appetizers</td>
       </tr>
       <tr>
          <td>Spicy Chicken Wings</td>
          <td rowspan="3">Gina Czina</td>
       </tr>
       <tr>
          <td>Chicken Dumplings</td>
       </tr>
       <tr>
          <td>Cheesy Nachos</td>
       </tr>
       <tr>
          <td colspan="2" class="course">Entrees</td>
       </tr>
       <tr>
          <td class="border">Chicken Cordon Bleu</td>
          <td class="border">Lee Cottrell</td>
       </tr>
       <tr>
          <td>Spaghetti with Marinara</td>
          <td rowspan="2">Les Graves</td>
       </tr>
       <tr>
          <td>Bacon wrapped filet mignon</td>
       </tr>
       <tr>
          <td colspan="2" class="course">Desserts</td>
       </tr>
       <tr>
          <td class="border">Cheesecake</td>
          <td class="border">Les Graves</td>
       </tr>
       <tr>
          <td>Apple Pie</td>
          <td>Lee Cottrell</td>
       </tr>
       </table>
       </body>
   </html>
```

Summary

This chapter covered HTML tables. You learned how to use a table and when tables are appropriate. You learned several methods of formatting a table. First, you learned the basic HTML formatting table attributes. Then you learned to span rows and columns. Finally, you formatted the table using CSS.

QUIZ

1. **This HTML tag creates structured data.**
    A. td
    B. th
    C. table
    D. h1

2. **This tag creates a row in a table.**
    A. tr
    B. td
    C. th
    D. caption

3. **The _____ attribute of a table controls where on the outside of the cell borders appear.**
    A. frame
    B. border
    C. rules
    D. width

4. **The _____ attribute of a table controls the distance from the cell contents to the cell border.**
    A. cellspacing
    B. cellpadding
    C. border
    D. width

5. **The _____ tag is centered and bold by default in all browsers.**
    A. td
    B. tr
    C. th
    D. caption

6. **The _____ produces a title for the table above the table.**
    A. td
    B. tr
    C. th
    D. caption

7. You want three cells in a row merged into one. Which of the following is the correct attribute and value?

   A. rowspan="3"
   B. rowspan="2"
   C. colspan="3"
   D. colspan="2"

8. The _____ tag creates a cell in the table.

   A. td
   B. tr
   C. th
   D. caption

9. The _____ attribute draws a line around the table and between all cells.

   A. frame
   B. border
   C. rules
   D. width

10. In the CSS code td.border, border is a _____.

   A. tag-level class
   B. td class
   C. generic class
   D. table class

chapter 7

Using Forms

This chapter will cover the HTML portion of forms. Not covered is the back end of forms: what to do with the data being sent. That is beyond the scope of this book.

CHAPTER OBJECTIVES

In this chapter, you will

- Describe the purpose of a form and create a form
- Use the input tag to place controls on a form
- Create drop-down lists
- Work with textareas
- Format a form

HTML is very good at delivering data to the user. This one-way delivery, similar to television's model, was very effective in the Web's early days. However, the Web has developed from a data delivery mechanism to a more collaborative, interactive experience.

Sites like MySpace, FaceBook, and YouTube depend on user submissions. HTML forms allow the user to send data to web sites. Forms allow users to order products, send messages, and even post videos.

Forms

Throughout your life, you have filled out forms. Standardized tests, applications for employment, and enrollment in social networking sites are all a type of form. Forms are a mechanism for collecting data. The mechanism asks questions in a set order and may limit responses to a question. For example, if the minimum age for working in your district is 16, then a job application form will reject any entries below 16.

You will use a form whenever you need to gather information from a user. You may gather any information you deem necessary. Rather than create a paper form, you will use HTML to generate the form.

HTML Forms

Creating a form is similar to creating tables. You start with a container tag, and then you place additional tags within the container.

The first tag to learn is the <form> tag. This tag begins the process of building a form. The form tag must have three attributes defined when the form is built. These attributes, defined in Table 7-1, control how the form works.

TABLE 7-1 The Three Required Form Attributes		
Form Attribute	**Description**	**Values**
action	Defines where the data will be sent.	A URL to a program that accepts the data
method	Describes the HTTP tool to send the data.	GET, POST
name	Names the form. Used by programmers to identify the form in code.	

Each of the attributes in Table 7-1 is important. The name attribute gives the form a unique identifier. This name is very important to the programmers who are working with the form. Unless you have specific instructions, you can name your form anything you want.

The method attribute describes how your web site will send the data. Two choices are available. A form may either POST data or GET data. There are several technical differences between POST and GET. Both deliver form data to the action URL. However, POST is more secure than GET. POST will hide the form contents from the user, while GET displays them. The following illustration shows the differences between a POST and a GET result from a login form. In the GET result, the data from the form is included in the URL. Notice that the password is clearly visible. The POST method hid the data. Unless I say otherwise, I recommend using POST for all form transactions.

Get example
http://leecottrell.com/phpclass/postback.php?username=lcottrell&password=password

Post example
http://leecottrell.com/phpclass/postback.php

The action attribute describes the program that will handle the data. This is typically a URL to a program written in PHP, ASP, or another programming language. The action will receive the data and respond to it in some fashion. While the subject is beyond the scope of the book, you do need to understand how this process works. The interaction between the form and the action script is known as Common Gateway Interface (CGI).

Code Block 7-1 illustrates a form that POSTs data to a PHP script on my web page. Pay attention to the attributes.

CODE BLOCK 7-1

```
<form name="example" method="POST"
 action="http://leecottrell.com/phpclass/postback.php">
</form>
```

Form Interaction

Forms gather data. However, the data is useless unless it has a purpose. Orders need to be processed, tweets need to be sent, and messages need to be written. This is the job of the program listed in the action attribute.

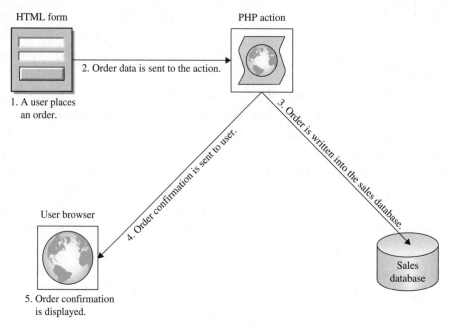

HTML form

2. Order data is sent to the action.

1. A user places an order.

PHP action

3. Order is written into the sales database.

4. Order confirmation is sent to user.

User browser

5. Order confirmation is displayed.

Sales database

FIGURE 7-1 • The process of placing an order through a web page

A form and an action interact in a standard manner. First, the user enters the data. The web site then sends it to the action. The action then takes the data and does something to it. Finally, the action returns an HTML page to the user displaying the results of the action. Figure 7-1 illustrates the process of placing an order through a web page.

 Still Struggling

The creation of the action is beyond the scope of this book. If you have programmed in the past, then you can learn how to create the action. Both PHP and ASP can be used to code an action. Purchase a book from McGraw-Hill such as *PHP: A Beginner's Guide* by Vikram Vaswani (2008) and start coding.

The Input Tag

To create a form, you start with the <form> tag. You add the required attributes defined in Table 7-1. Once this container tag is built, you need to start adding data collection items to the form. These items are better known as controls. Adding controls to a form requires more tags. The most used is the <input> tag.

The <input> tag takes many forms. Through its type attribute, the input tag can accept typed data, hidden password data, checkboxes, and radio buttons. In addition to gathering data, the input tag creates the buttons that send the data to the action. Table 7-2 lists the allowable values for the type attribute.

In addition to the type attribute, the <input> tag requires a name. Similar to the name attribute of the form, the name of the <input> tag allows the programmer to work with the data from the control.

The input tag technically does not require a closing tag for HTML, but XHTML does require it to be closed. The best solution is to self-close it as we have done for the <br /> and <img /> tags. All of my examples will self-close the <input> tag.

When rendered, browsers will display the <input> without a new line. If you want your controls on separate lines, either code a <br /> where desired or place your controls within a table. The table is preferred. Later in the chapter, you will add a table to a form.

TABLE 7-2   Allowable Values for the Type Attribute of the Input Tag

Value	Description
checkbox	Creates a series of controls that allow multiple selections. Users pick their choices by placing a check mark in the box.
file	Allows the user to browse to a file on their machine for submission to the web site.
hidden	Used to store data that the form needs but the user does not need to see.
image	Creates an image that sends the form data to the action.
password	Creates a box that allows users to type text. The text is hidden from the user.
radio	Creates a series of controls from which the user can select one choice.
reset	Creates a button that clears the form.
submit	Creates a button that sends the form data to the action.
text	Creates a box that allows users to type text.

TIP   *Unless you are working with a generic action or have written the action yourself, someone will tell you the valid names for your controls.*

Creating Text Controls

The most common usage of the input control is to create controls for text. Typically called text boxes or password boxes, these are the controls where users type their username, password, address, or any other form of data.

The most basic form of the text box is to code an input tag, use the type attribute, and provide a name. Code Block 7-2 shows two text boxes, and the illustration shows the form in Explorer.

CODE BLOCK 7-2

```
<input type="text" name="username"/><br />
<input type="password" name="password"/>
```

There are several things wrong with Code Block 7-2. First, the user does not know what to type in the boxes. Second, the user can type as much information as she wants in the box. This is a huge security breach in a web site. Placing too much data into a web form can crash the web server.

Solving these problems requires two additions. First, a simple text label before the <input> tag provides a prompt for the user. This prompt tells them what data to place in the box.

Fixing the second problem requires two additional attributes. The maxlength attribute restricts the number of characters typed into the text box. This property alone will protect your web site. The second attribute is for aesthetic purposes. The size property will adjust the number of characters visible in the text box. For values under 50, it is appropriate to make the maxlength and the size the same value. For maxlengths over 50, keep the size at 50. Code Block 7-3 and the following illustration show the corrected code.

CAUTION   *The maxlength protects your web site. Without this property, your site will accept any number of characters. If too many are sent to the web site, the server it is running on may crash.*

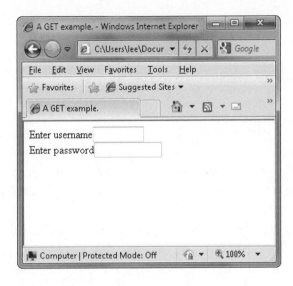

CODE BLOCK 7-3

```
Enter username <input type="text" name="username" maxlength="8"
size="8"/><br />
Enter password <input type="password" name="password"
maxlength="12" size="12" />
```

TIP *There are two possible ways to handle the size. I typically make the text box size match the maxlength. My designer friends make all the text boxes the same size. They claim it makes the form look better. We are both right.*

Creating Checkboxes

A checkbox allows the presentation of several choices to the user. The user is capable of selecting whichever of the choices he wants. Checkboxes render on the screen as a small box. When the box is selected, a mark will appear inside it.

To create the checkbox, again use the <input> tag. Set the type="checkbox" and set a name. Code Block 7-4 shows a group of checkboxes presenting choices for dinner at an all-you-can-eat restaurant. The illustration shows the output in Explorer with two choices selected.

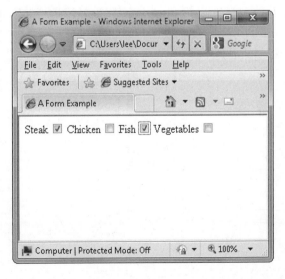

CODE BLOCK 7-4

```
Steak <input type="checkbox" name="steak"/>
Chicken <input type="checkbox" name="chicken"/>
Fish <input type="checkbox" name="fish"/>
Vegetables <input type="checkbox" name="vegetables"/>
```

Creating Radio Buttons

A radio button allows the presentation of several choices to the user. However, unlike when offered a checkbox, the user is capable of selecting only one of the choices. Radio buttons render on the screen as a small circle. When selected, it will include a smaller circle.

To create the radio button, again use the <input> tag. Set the type="radio" and set a name. To ensure the radio buttons work as expected, each must have the same name. In addition to the name, a value attribute must be set on each radio button. The value attribute holds the data that is sent to the server. Unless told otherwise, set the value equal to the prompt of the radio button. Code Block 7-5 shows a group of radio buttons presenting color choices, and the illustration shows the output in Explorer.

CODE BLOCK 7-5

```
Red <input type="radio" name="favoriteColor" value="red"/>
Green <input type="radio" name="favoriteColor" value="green"/>
Blue <input type="radio" name="favoriteColor" value="blue"/>
Purple <input type="radio" name="favoriteColor" value="purple"/>
```

Creating Buttons

HTML supports two form buttons: a submit button and a reset button. Once the form is created, the users need a way to send the data to the action. The submit type for the input tag does exactly this. Once clicked, the submit will send all of the form data to the action using the form's method. All forms must have a submit button. The reset button clears all form contents.

To build a submit button, start with the input tag, and set the type to submit. This will create a gray button on the web page. Without any other properties, the button will read Submit Query. While this is perfectly fine, you do have more control. The value property changes the text in the button. No name is typically required for a button.

Building a reset button is identical to the submit button. Simply replace submit with reset, and your button is finished. Code Block 7-6 and the following illustration show the input buttons.

CODE BLOCK 7-6

```
<input type="submit" value="Send Data" /><br />
<input type="reset" value="Clear Form" />
```

Creating Image Controls

The image type provides a graphical alternative to the submit button. Instead of a boring gray button, you can use a custom image. As with the img property, you need the src attribute to describe the image location. In addition, the height and width properties are used to provide enough room on the form. Alt and title tags are not necessary. The illustration and Code Block 7-7 show an image control.

TIP *The button was generated at flamingtext.com.*

CODE BLOCK 7-7

```
<input type="image" src="images/send.gif" height="43"
width="163"/>
```

Practice Creating a Form

You are going to create a simple form for a pizza shop. Your form will allow the ordering of one pizza. You can select the size and toppings. For practice, you are going to use my simple postback script. In reality, you will likely have a customized CGI script.

TIP *My postback script is available at http://leecottrell.com/phpclass/postback .php. It is a simple script that will simply return the information from your form. It does not track any usage data.*

1. Create a new file from your template named **pizza.html**. Save it in a chapter7 folder.

2. Create an appropriate title and meta information for the page.

3. Inside of the body, create a new form. Use the POST method and set the action to **http://www.leecottrell.com/phpclass/postback.php**.

```
<form name="example" method="POST"
action="http://www.leecottrell.com/phpclass/postback.php">

</form>
```

4. To make the form look nice, you will need a table within the form. The form will have two columns: The first column is for a label. The second column holds the actual form control. Add a table inside your form.

```
<table>

</table>
```

5. Create a row with two td tags.

```
<tr>
        <td>
        </td>
        <td>
        </td>
</tr>
```

6. Inside the first td tag, enter the text **Your name**.

7. Inside the second td tag, enter an input text control named customer. Set an appropriate maxlength and size. The complete row is shown here:

```
<tr>
        <td>
        Your name
        </td>
        <td>
        <input type="text" name="customer" maxlength="30"
         size="30" />
        </td>
</tr>
```

8. Create another row and input control for the address.

```
<tr>
        <td>
        Delivery address
        </td>
        <td>
        <input type="text" name="address" maxlength="100"
         size="50" />
        </td>
</tr>
```

9. Save and open the page in the browser. It should resemble the image shown here:

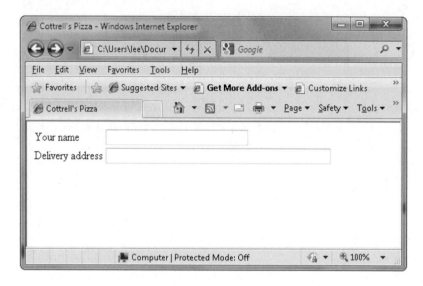

10. Create another row and input control for a phone number.

```
<tr>
     <td>
     Phone number
     </td>
     <td>
     <input type="text" name="phone" maxlength="15"
      size="15" />
     </td>
</tr>
```

11. You are now going to create controls for the pizza itself. Since you can only select one size for an individual pizza, you will use a radio button control. Create a radio button named size. Set the value and text after the control to say small.

```
<tr>
     <td>
     Size
     </td>
     <td>
     <input type="radio" name="size" value="small" />Small
     </td>
</tr>
```

12. Create two more radio buttons named size. Set their values and text to medium and large.

```
<input type="radio" name="size" value="medium" />Medium
<input type="radio" name="size" value="large" />Large
```

13. Save and refresh the page in the browser, it should resemble this image:

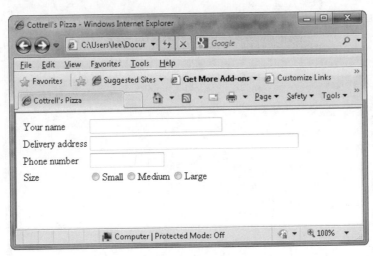

14. Now you need toppings. Multiple toppings are on a pizza. Create a new two-columned row with Toppings in the first td.

```
<tr>
     <td>
     Toppings
     </td>
     <td>

     </td>
</tr>
```

15. Inside the second td, create a checkbox control called pepperoni. Set the name, value, and text to pepperoni. Add a <br /> after the text pepperoni.

```
<input type="checkbox" name="pepperoni" value="pepperoni"
/>Pepperoni<br />
```

16. Create several additional toppings, similar to the pepperoni control.

```
<input type="checkbox" name="sausage" value="sausage" />
Sausage<br />
<input type="checkbox" name="mushrooms" value="mushrooms" />
Mushrooms<br />
<input type="checkbox" name="onion" value="onion" />Onion<br />
```

TIP   *The value and name of the checkbox will differ, depending on the code in the action script.*

17. Save and open the page in your browser. It will look like this image:

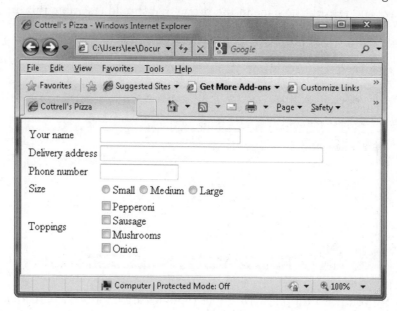

18. Now the form is complete. You need to test the action. Add a submit button and a reset button, after the table, but before the </form>.

```
<input type="submit" value="Order pizza" />
<input type="reset" value="Cancel pizza" />
```

19. Enter data in the fields and press the submit button. If everything is correct, then you should see what's shown in this illustration. This is the output from my postback script. If you get a 404 error, verify that the action URL is correct. The complete code is shown in Code Block 7-8.

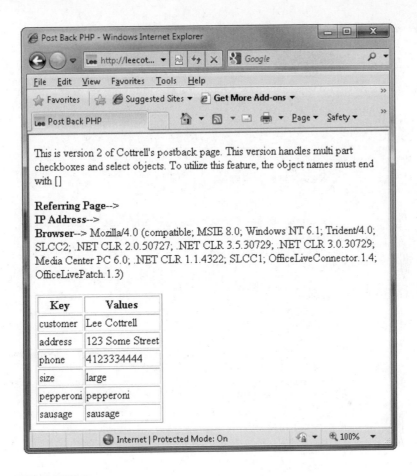

CODE BLOCK 7-8

```
<!DOCTYPE html PUBLIC "-//W3C//DTD XHTML 1.1//EN"
"http://www.w3.org/TR/xhtml11/DTD/xhtml11.dtd">
<html xmlns="http://www.w3.org/1999/xhtml" xml:lang="en">
    <head>
        <title>Cottrell's Pizza</title>
        <meta name="description" content="An order
         form for Cottrell's Pizza"/>
        <meta name="author" content="Lee M. Cottrell" />

    </head>
    <body>
    <form name="example" method="POST" action="http://
     leecottrell.com/phpclass/postback.php">
    <table>
    <tr>
```

```
            <td>
            Your name
            </td>
            <td>
            <input type="text" name="customer" maxlength="30"
             size="30" />
            </td>
      </tr>
      <tr>
            <td>
            Delivery address
            </td>
            <td>
            <input type="text" name="address" maxlength="100"
             size="50" />
            </td>
      </tr>
      <tr>
            <td>
            Phone number
            </td>
            <td>
            <input type="text" name="phone" maxlength="15"
             size="15" />
            </td>
      </tr>
      <tr>
            <td>
            Size
            </td>
            <td>
            <input type="radio" name="size"
             value="small" />Small
            <input type="radio" name="size"
             value="medium" />Medium
            <input type="radio" name="size"
             value="large" />Large
            </td>
      </tr>
      <tr>
            <td>
            Toppings
            </td>
            <td>
            <input type="checkbox" name="pepperoni"
             value="pepperoni" />Pepperoni<br />
            <input type="checkbox" name="sausage"
             value="sausage" />Sausage<br />
```

```
            <input type="checkbox" name="mushrooms"
             value="mushrooms" />Mushrooms<br />
            <input type="checkbox" name="onion"
             value="onion" />Onion<br />
            </td>
        </tr>
        </table>
        <input type="submit" value="Order pizza" />
        <input type="reset" value="Cancel pizza" />
        </form>
        </body>
    </html>
```

Drop-Down Lists

The input tag creates the majority of form controls. However, other controls work within a form. The <select> tag creates a drop-down list of choices for the user. Drop-down lists are a good method to deliver a large range of choices without taking a lot of screen space. A common use of drop-down lists is to create a list of states.

To create a drop-down list, start, name, and close a <select> tag. Within the <select> tag, add <option> tags. You will need one for each option in the list. The contents of the <option> tag are displayed in the list. Typically, the first choice provides a direction to the user. Alphabetize the remaining options to make it easier for your users to find. Code Block 7-9 shows a list box containing colors.

CODE BLOCK 7-9

```
<select name="favColors">
<option>Pick your favorite color</option>
<option>Black</option>
<option>Blue</option>
<option>Green</option>
<option>Orange</option>
<option>Red</option>
<option>Purple</option>
<option>White</option>
</select>
```

By default, HTML will send the contents of the selected <option> to the action script. Each <option> value may include a value attribute. Use the value attribute when the form is to send data other than what the list displays.

The developer of the action script will tell you what values to use in your lists. In Code Block 7-10, valid colors start at 0. The value –1 indicates that the user did not select a color. The following image shows the <select> tag:

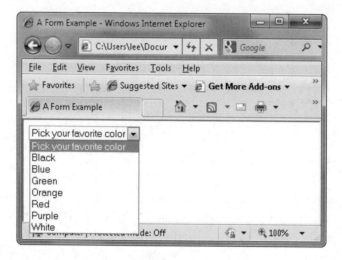

CODE BLOCK 7-10

```
<select name="favColors">
<option value="-1">Pick your favorite color</option>
<option value="0">Black</option>
<option value="1">Blue</option>
<option value="2">Green</option>
<option value="3">Orange</option>
<option value="4">Red</option>
<option value="5">Purple</option>
<option value="6">White</option>
</select>
```

TIP *You will use the value when the action script connects to a database. The value will hold the primary key of the displayed value.*

Textareas

The standard HTML input text box allows you to enter a line of text. If you want your form to accept paragraphs or multiple lines, the text box fails. The textarea fulfills this need.

The textarea control provides a large text box on the form. You can control the number of rows and columns that are visible. The rows equate to visible lines while the columns are approximate characters. Unlike when using the input text box, you cannot control the maximum number of characters entered in the textarea.

To create a textarea, open and name a <textarea> control. Close the tag immediately after the ending > for the control. Anything between the open and close <textarea> tags will be displayed in the box. This includes newlines, HTML code, and even spaces. Code Block 7-11 shows the code needed to generate a 5-row, 40-column textarea, shown in this image:

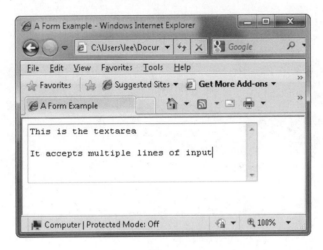

CODE BLOCK 7-11

```
<textarea name="comments" rows="5" cols="40"></textarea>
```

Practicing Use of Textareas and Drop-Down Lists

Your pizza form needs a little work. The owner of the shop wants to offer different sauce choices. The delivery drivers need a box for special directions to help them find the customer's house. You will add a drop-down list for the sauces and a textarea for the directions.

1. Open pizza.html in your browser and editor.
2. You are going to put a textarea between the address and phone inputs. In your editor, scroll down to immediately before the <tr> above the phone entry.
3. Follow the same table structure. Create a new row with two <td> tags.
4. Place the phrase **Delivery Instructions** in the first td.

5. In the second td, add a 2-row, 50-column textarea named directions.

```
<tr>
      <td>
      Delivery Instructions
      </td>
      <td>
      <textarea name="directions" rows="2"
       cols="50"></textarea>
      </td>
</tr>
```

6. Save and view the page in your browser. It should include the textarea as shown here:

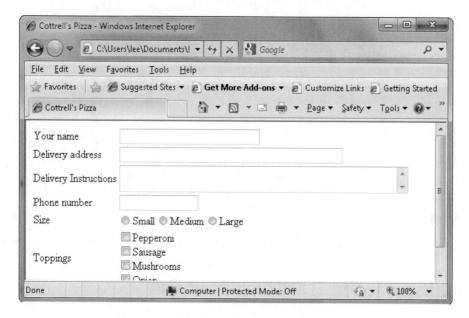

7. In the editor, scroll down to immediately before the <tr> for toppings.

8. Add another two-column row.

9. Place the phrase **Choose a sauce** in the first <td>.

10. Place a <select> option named sauce in the second <td>. Include at least three different sauce options. Remember to make the first <option> a direction to the user. There is no need to include the value attribute.

```
<tr>
      <td>
      Choose a sauce
      </td>
```

```
        <td>
        <select name="sauce">
        <option>Choose a sauce</option>
        <option>Buffalo</option>
        <option>Barbeque</option>
        <option>No sauce</option>
        <option>Red</option>
        <option>White</option>
        </select>
        </td>
    </tr>
```

11. Save and refresh your page in the browser. You should see a drop-down box similar to what's shown in the illustration. Code Block 7-12 contains the entire code for the form.

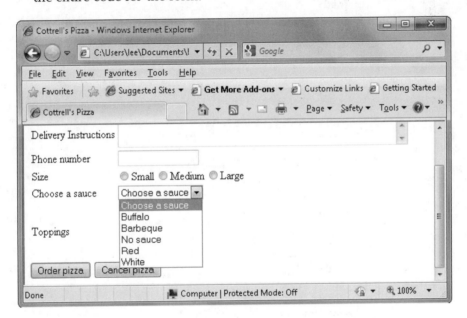

CODE BLOCK 7-12

```
<!DOCTYPE html PUBLIC "-//W3C//DTD XHTML 1.1//EN"
"http://www.w3.org/TR/xhtml11/DTD/xhtml11.dtd">
<html xmlns="http://www.w3.org/1999/xhtml" xml:lang="en">
    <head>
        <title>Cottrell's Pizza</title>
        <meta name="description" content="An order
         form for Cottrell's Pizza"/>
        <meta name="author" content="Lee M. Cottrell" />

    </head>
    <body>
```

```
<form name="example" method="POST" action="http://
leecottrell.com/phpclass/postback.php">
<table>
<tr>
      <td>
      Your name
      </td>
      <td>
      <input type="text" name="customer" maxlength="30"
       size="30" />
      </td>
</tr>
<tr>
      <td>
      Delivery address
      </td>
      <td>
      <input type="text" name="address" maxlength="100"
       size="50" />
      </td>
</tr>
<tr>
      <td>
      Delivery Instructions
      </td>
      <td>
      <textarea name="directions" rows="2"
       cols="50"></textarea>
      </td>
</tr>
<tr>
      <td>
      Phone number
      </td>
      <td>
      <input type="text" name="phone"
       maxlength="15" size="15" />
      </td>
</tr>
<tr>
      <td>
      Size
      </td>
      <td>
      <input type="radio" name="size"
       value="small" />Small
      <input type="radio" name="size"
       value="medium" />Medium
      <input type="radio" name="size"
       value="large" />Large
```

```
                  </td>
         </tr>
         <tr>
                  <td>
                  Choose a sauce
                  </td>
                  <td>
                  <select name="sauce">
                  <option>Choose a sauce</option>
                  <option>Buffalo</option>
                  <option>Barbeque</option>
                  <option>No sauce</option>
                  <option>Red</option>
                  <option>White</option>
                  </select>
                  </td>
         </tr>
         <tr>
                  <td>
                  Toppings
                  </td>
                  <td>
                  <input type="checkbox" name="pepperoni"
                   value="pepperoni" />Pepperoni<br />
                  <input type="checkbox" name="sausage"
                   value="sausage" />Sausage<br />
                  <input type="checkbox" name="mushrooms"
                   value="mushrooms" />Mushrooms<br />
                  <input type="checkbox" name="onion"
                   value="onion" />Onion<br />
                  </td>
         </tr>
         </table>
         <input type="submit" value="Order pizza" />
         <input type="reset" value="Cancel pizza" />
         </form>
         </body>
</html>
```

Formatting Forms

Tables for layout work well but are considered improper. Two new HTML tags, the label and fieldset when used with CSS, replace the table layout with a CSS layout. CSS provides the ability to jazz up the form. You can add borders, colors, and even have the object react when the user clicks into them.

To replace the tables in your forms will take a little work. First, you need to remove all table elements. The second step is to place the prompt and the input control into a paragraph tag. Finally, you need to identify the prompt as a label for the input control. The label tag includes the for attribute. The for attribute holds the name of the control that the label is associated with. The for attribute links the label to the control. Code Block 7-13 shows an example of two controls and associated labels.

CODE BLOCK 7-13

```
<p>
<label for="directions">Delivery Instructions</label>
<textarea name="directions" rows="2" cols="50"></textarea>
</p>
<p>
<label for="phone">Phone number</label>
<input type="text" name="phone" maxlength="15" size="15" />
</p>
```

Once each prompt has been labeled, CSS is used to format the labels. Spacing, color, and text alignment are possible. Code Block 7-14 shows a sample CSS layout for the layout element. For the width property, I used the em measurement instead of the px used in earlier chapters. The em rescales with changes in font size. Float left places the labels to the left of the input controls. Display block forces the elements to display as one big unit.

CODE BLOCK 7-14

```
label
{
        width: 8em;
        float: left;
        text-align: left;
        margin-right: 2em;
        display: block;
}
```

In addition to formatting the labels, each control can be formatted. The generic input style creates a style for all of the input tags in a form. You can also specify inputs for each individual type of input element. To specify the format for a text box only, you need to create a style header input[type="text"]. The word text specifies whether you are formatting a text box, a radio button, or some other input element. Code Block 7-15 creates a text box with a beige background, red border, and black text.

CODE BLOCK 7-15

```
input[type="text"]
{
border: 1pt solid #ff0000;
background-color:#F5F6CE;
color: #000000;
}
```

The final element that CSS controls on a table is the tag fieldset. The fieldset groups form controls. Visually, the form is surrounded with a light gray border. With the fieldset, you can create borders and colors around the entire form, or parts of the form. By default the fieldset will span to fit the entire page. Setting the CSS display property to inline will make the fieldset only as large as the largest form object.

The optional legend tag creates a visible title for the fieldset. Code Block 7-16 shows a formatted fieldset and a legend for a form.

CODE BLOCK 7-16

```
<form name="example" method="POST" action=" postback.php">
<fieldset>
<legend>Order form for Cottrell's Pizza</legend>
        <p>
        <label for="customer">Your name</label>
        <input type="text" name="customer" maxlength="30" size="30" />
        </p>
        <input type="submit" value="Order pizza" />
        <input type="reset" value="Cancel pizza" />
</fieldset>
</form>
```

The code blocks from this section modified the pizza.html file created earlier in the chapter to use the labels, fieldset, and legends. The following illustration shows the results of the work.

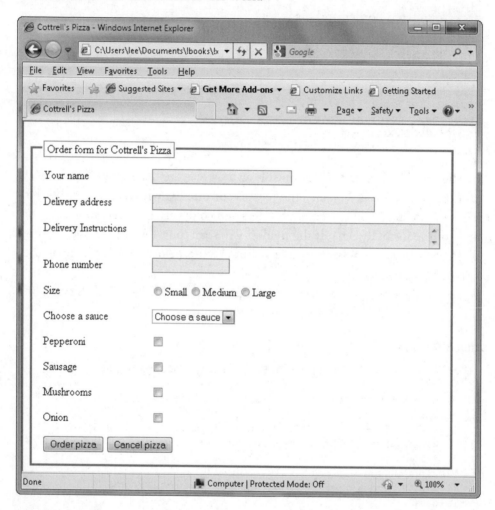

Form Pseudo-classes

Formatting a form allows more than changing the visuals. Forms can react to the user. Much of the reaction is scripted using JavaScript or some custom CGI. CSS allows the use of the hover and focus pseudo-classes.

The hover pseudo-class for form objects works similarly to the pseudo-class with the <a> tag. The CSS changes the format of the form control as the mouse hovers over the object. This pseudo-class helps users navigate the form by highlighting the mouse position.

In a form, focus means the currently selected object. The box you are typing in is the object with the focus. By formatting the focus object, the user can easily see the current object. Code Block 7-17 shows the code for the hover and focus pseudo-classes applied to the input and textareas. The hover formats the object with a red background color, while the focus sets the background color to yellow. The illustration shows the hover effect on the first text box and the focus on the second text box.

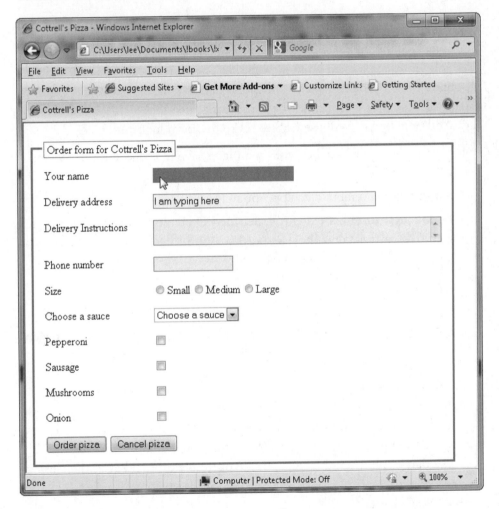

TIP   *The select object will not react to the hover or focus pseudo-class. JavaScript is needed to achieve the same effect.*

CODE BLOCK 7-17

```
input:hover, textarea:hover{
    background-color:#ff0000;
}

input:focus, textarea:focus, select:focus{
    background-color:#ffff00;
}
```

Practice Formatting Forms

The owners of the pizza shop have decided to create a frequent eaters club. The user will join using a form on their web site. They would like you to build the enrollment form. The form will gather the patron's name, street address, and e-mail address. You will format the form using the label, fieldset, and legend tags. Additionally, you will use CSS to make the form look very nice.

1. Create a new file based on your template. Save it as **enroll.html** into your chapter7 folder.

2. Set the title and meta data appropriately.

3. Build a new form named enroll. Set the POST method and the action to http://leecottrell.com/phpclass/postback.php.

   ```
   <form name="enroll" method="POST"
    action="http://leecottrell.com/phpclass/postback.php">
   </form>
   ```

4. Create a fieldset and legend entry. Set the legend text to read Frequent Eaters Enrollment Form. The code from Steps 4 through 9 will go between the form tags.

   ```
   <fieldset>
   <legend>Frequent Eaters Enrollment Form</legend>
   </fieldset>
   ```

5. You now need to start gathering the information. You will use input boxes and a submit button to gather the information. Each of the boxes will be in a paragraph tag and labeled. Inside of the fieldset and after the closing legend tag, create a new <p> tag asking for the customer's name.

   ```
   <p>Your Name</p>
   ```

6. Before the ending </p>, create a input text control called customer. Set the maxlength and size to 40.

   ```
   <input type="text" name="customer" maxlength="40" size="40" />
   ```

7. Now you will create the label. Open a label tag before the words Your Name. Close the label tag after Name and before the <input>. Set the for attribute of the label to customer. The following code shows the complete paragraph tag.

```
<p><label for="customer">Your Name</label> <input type="text"
name="customer" maxlength="40" size="40" /></p>
```

8. Repeat Steps 5 through 7 for the street address and e-mail address. Use appropriate names, maxlengths, and sizes.

```
<p><label for="streetAddress">Street Address</label>
<input type="text" name="streetAddress" maxlength="100"
size="50" /></p>
<p><label for="emailAddress">Email Address</label> <input
type="text" name="emailAddress" maxlength="50" size="50" /></p>
```

9. Add a submit button. Set the name to btnEnroll and the value to "Enroll in the club". The submit button does not need enclosed in a <p> tag.

```
<input type="submit" name="btnEnroll" value="Enroll in the
club" />.
```

10. Open the page in your browser. It should resemble this image:

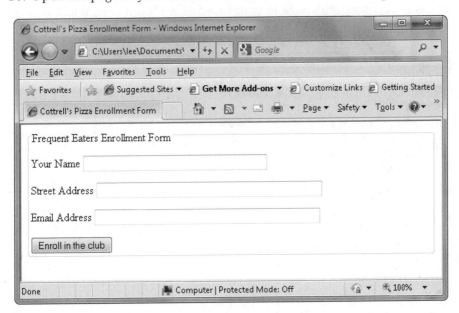

11. Create a css section in the header of the page. Alternatively, you could create a new CSS file and link it in the header.

12. We will first format the label. This will allow us to create a solid left margin for the text boxes. Create a label section in the CSS.

   a. Set the width property to a size that looks good. I used 7 em.

   b. Set the text-align property to right.

   c. The labels and the input boxes are a little cramped. Set a right margin to increase the space between the objects. I set it to 1em.

   d. Set the float property to left and the display property to block.

   e. Set the text-weight property to bold. If necessary, increase the width until your text fits on one line.

```
label
{
        width: 7em;
        float: left;
        text-align: right;
        margin-right: 1em;
        display: block;
text-weight:bold;
}
```

13. Save and refresh the page in your browser. It should resemble the image shown here:

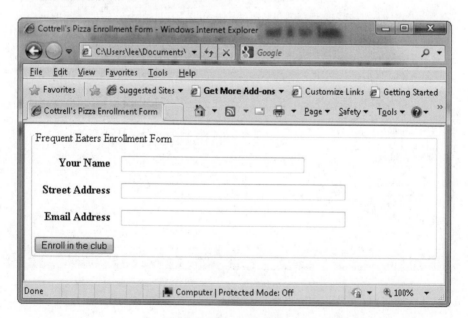

14. Now you want to color the form. Create a fieldset CSS entry.

    a. Set the background color to yellow, or another color of your choosing. Set the foreground color to blue, or another color.

    b. To eliminate the crowding, set a padding of 2px.

    c. Turn off the border.

```
fieldset
{
        background-color:#ffff00;
        color:#0000ff;
        display:Inline;
        padding:2px;
border:0pt;
}
```

15. Refresh the page in your browser. It will look like this:

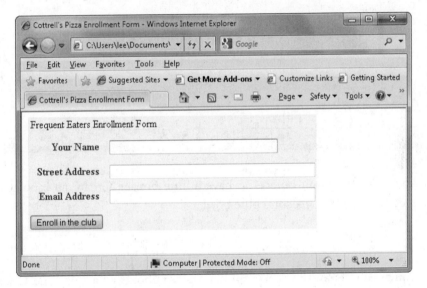

16. The legend needs to be formatted. Create a legend entry in the CSS section.

    a. Set the color to blue.

    b. Set the font-size to 14pt.

    c. Create a blue double border.

    d. Set left and right padding to 1 em.

```
legend
{
        color:#0000ff;
        border:double #0000ff;
```

```
            font-size:14pt;
            padding-left:1em;
            padding-right:1em;
    }
```

17. Save and refresh the page in your browser. It will look like the image shown here:

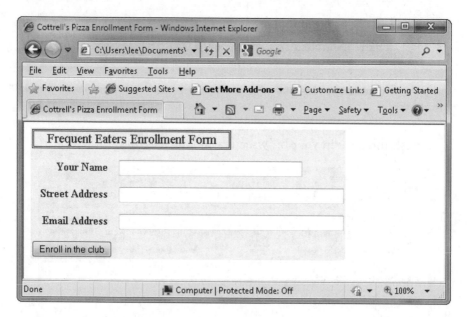

18. You want the input objects to have a blue border. Create an input CSS section and set a 1px solid blue border.

```
input{
        border:1pt solid #0000ff;
}
```

19. You need to color the background of the text boxes to a light blue. Create a CSS section for text boxes, and set the background color to light blue. I used #A0CFEC.

```
input[type="text"]
{
        background-color:#A0CFEC;
}
```

20. Save and refresh your browser to see what's shown in the following image:

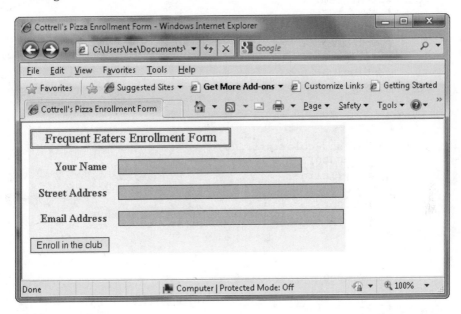

21. Finally, you want to change the format of the item with the focus. Create an input:focus CSS entry and set the background-color to a slightly darker blue. I used # 82CAFA.

```
input:focus
{
        background-color:#82CAFA;
}
```

22. Save and refresh the page in the browser. Click inside of a text box and the blue should change.

23. The final CSS and HTML are listed in Code Block 7-18.

CODE BLOCK 7-18

```
<!DOCTYPE html PUBLIC "-//W3C//DTD XHTML 1.1//EN"
"http://www.w3.org/TR/xhtml11/DTD/xhtml11.dtd">
<html xmlns="http://www.w3.org/1999/xhtml" xml:lang="en">
        <head>
                <title>Cottrell's Pizza Enrollment Form</title>
                <meta name="description" content="An enrollment
                 form for Cottrell's Pizza"/>
                <meta name="author" content="Lee M. Cottrell" />

<style type="text/css">
```

```
label
{
        width: 7em;
        float: left;
        text-align: right;
        margin-right: 1em;
        display: block;
        font-weight:bold;
}

fieldset
{
        background-color:#ffff00;
        color:#0000ff;
        display:Inline;
        padding:2px;
        border:0pt;
}

legend
{
        color:#0000ff;
        border:double #0000ff;
        font-size:14pt;
        padding-left:1em;
        padding-right:1em;
}

input{
        border:1pt solid #0000ff;
}

input[type="text"]
{
        background-color:#A0CFEC;
}

input:focus
{
        background-color:#82CAFA;
}
</style>
        </head>
        <body>
        <form name="enroll" method="POST" action="http://
        leecottrell.com/phpclass/postback.php">
        <fieldset>
        <legend>Frequent Eaters Enrollment Form</legend>
        <p><label for="customer">Your Name</label> <input
        type="text" name="customer" maxlength="40" size="40" />
        </p>
```

```
<p><label for="streetAddress">Street
Address</label> <input type="text"
name="streetAddress" maxlength="100" size="50" /></p>
<p><label for="emailAddress">Email Address</label>
<input type="text" name="emailAddress" maxlength="80"
size="50" /></p>
<input type="submit" name="btnEnroll" value="Enroll
in the club" />
</fieldset>
</form>
</body>
</html>
```

Summary

This chapter covered HTML forms. You learned how to create forms for data collection. Textboxes, radio buttons, checkboxes, drop-down lists, textareas, and buttons were presented. You learned how to format the form tables and the newer label tag.

QUIZ

1. This tag creates radio buttons, submit buttons, and text boxes.
   A. input
   B. control
   C. form
   D. data

2. The _____ attribute of a form describes how to send data to the CGI script.
   A. action
   B. name
   C. method
   D. encoding

3. The _____ attribute of input controls holds the data sent to the CGI script.
   A. name
   B. data
   C. value
   D. POST

4. The _____ attribute of a form describes the URL of the CGI script.
   A. action
   B. name
   C. method
   D. encoding

5. You wish to give your users a series of choices of which they can select only one. Which of the following controls is the best?
   A. checkbox
   B. submit button
   C. text box
   D. radio button

6. This tag surrounds a group of form controls.
   A. legend
   B. label
   C. fieldset
   D. div

7. This tag joins a prompt to its corresponding control.
   A. legend
   B. label
   C. fieldset
   D. div

8. **To make radio buttons work correctly, the _____ attribute must have the same data.**
   A. value
   B. name
   C. data
   D. class

9. **A _____ is used whenever the programmer needs to capture paragraphs of data.**
   A. radio button
   B. drop-down list
   C. textarea
   D. submit button

10. **To limit the number of characters sent to the script, the HTML form should use the _____ attribute for its input boxes.**
    A. size
    B. length
    C. maxlength
    D. value

chapter *8*

Page Layout with CSS

In this chapter you will use CSS to place page elements. You will master positioning, floating, and layering using the CSS Box Model.

In this chapter, you will

- Create classes
- Use the span and div tags
- Apply the CSS Box Model
- Build complex page layouts

I remember my first web page. It had a heading, several paragraphs, and a picture of my daughter. I made it as fancy as I could by placing the paragraphs and image in a table, which allowed me to move the picture beside the text. For the time, this was a cutting-edge use of a table.

Today, this layout is still valid, but generally avoided in the web design industry. CSS is used instead of tables. Through CSS I can replicate and improve my original page's layout. So far you have used CSS to format page elements. You have set font, colors, and pictures.

Classes

The easiest way to understand a class is to use an analogy. Consider automobiles. There are different classes of automobiles, each with their own distinct properties. Sports cars are small, sleek, and fast. SUVs are larger and tend to guzzle lots of gas. Family cars are roomy, safe, and relatively inexpensive. Simply stating a class of car produces an image of a car in most listeners' minds.

Imagine a car in the future. Instead of a fixed shape, it would be malleable. Before you got into the car, you would be able to pick the type of car you would drive that day. You could choose between sports, SUV, truck, or luxury sedan. Once selected, the appropriate properties would be applied to the vehicle.

CSS classes allow this functionality to HTML tags. By simply selecting a different class, you have elements receive different properties. The same type of element on the same page can have different formatting. Two types of classes exist in CSS: tag-level classes and generic classes.

Tag-Level Classes

A *tag-level* class is a class that works with a specific tag. You create the class and list the properties and their values. Once this is set, you then apply the class to the desired tags.

Cars have several classes that only work on certain types of cars. Consider the spoiler. Adding a spoiler to a sports car adds a set of properties to the car. It becomes a little faster with better traction. Adding the spoiler to a pickup truck just would not work.

The code to create a CSS tag-level class is very straightforward. Start by creating a new CSS entry with the tag. Create the class by adding a period and then a name for the class. Open and close the curly braces and set the properties and their values. Code Block 8-1 shows the creation of a tag-level class for the <h1> element.

TIP *Choose meaningful names for your classes. Make sure the names describe their function or appearance.*

CODE BLOCK 8-1

```
<style type="text/css" >
     h1.bookTitle{
           font-size:36pt;
           font-style:italic;
     }
</style>
```

Once the class is created, you need to apply where it is needed. To apply the class, you add the class attribute to the element. Set the value to the name of the class. Code Block 8-2 shows the application of a tag-level class to an <h1> element. The results of the code is shown in this image:

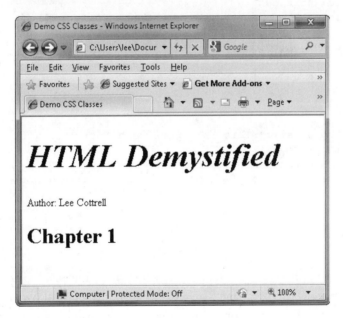

CODE BLOCK 8-2

```
<h1 class="bookTitle">HTML Demystified</h1>
<p>Author: Lee Cottrell</p>
<h1>Chapter 1</h1>
```

Generic Classes

Tag-level classes are designed to work with one class. There are times when you want the same format to apply to several different types of classes. Creating multiple tag-level classes would work but is inefficient. *Generic* class names allow you to build one format, and reuse it as many times as needed.

Tag-level classes are created in the CSS section. Class names are created using a period as the first letter of the name. They are applied in the same manner as tag-level classes, through the class attribute of the desired tag. Code Block 8-3 shows the creation and application of the generic class displayed in this illustration.

CODE BLOCK 8-3

```
<style type="text/css" >
.boldItalic
{
    font-weight:bold;
    font-style:italic;
}
</style>
</head>
<body>
<p class="boldItalic">This is a paragraph formatted with a
generic class.</p>
<p>This is a paragraph formatted with the defaults.</p>
<a href="http://www.google.com" class="boldItalic">Google.com</a>
</body>
```

Span and Div

Classes, when applied to a particular tag, affect only that tag. Quite often you want to format regions of a page. The <span> and <div> tags allow you to apply formats to multiple tags at one time. Through the use of these tags, named regions can be created on the page. Additionally, very complex formats can be achieved.

Span

The <span> tag is used to apply a format to a small amount of text. It is often used to create special formats or emphasis formatting within paragraphs or headings. A generic class will be applied to the class attribute of the <span> tag. The formatting rules in the class are set to the text enclosed within the <span>.

TIP *Using a span is similar to highlighting a region in Microsoft Word and applying a format.*

To use a <span> tag, you first have to create a generic class. Once this class is created, open the span tag before the text you wish to format. In the attribute space for the span, add a class attribute. Set its value to the name of the class. Close the span after the text.

Spans are an important tag for formatting. Code Block 8-4 shows a span applied within a <p> tag. The generic class of boldItalic from Code Block 8-3 is applied. The following illustration shows the result of the formatting.

CODE BLOCK 8-4

```
<p>Classes, when applied to a particular tag,
<span class="boldItalic">affect only that tag</span>. Quite often you
want to format regions of a page. The div and span tag allow you to apply
formats to <span class="boldItalic">multiple tags at one time</span>.
Through the use of these tags, named regions can be created on the page.
Additionally, very complex format can be achieved.</p>
```

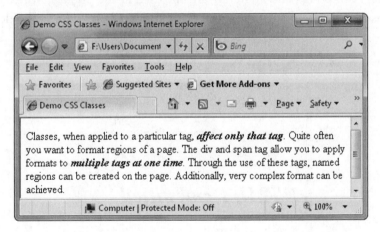

Division

The span tag is an inline tag that applies a generic class to a region of text. In contrast, the <div> tag, short for division, allows you to apply formats to large regions on the page. Many tags can be enclosed within the <div>.

Divisions of a page allow for the creation of very advanced layouts. Multiple columns of text are easily created. Elements can be stacked on top of each other. Independently scrolling regions are possible with divs. In short, most page layouts you wish to apply are created with a div tag.

TIP *Use a div tag to format large portions of a page. Typical formats include margins, font style, background colors, and borders. Individual styles can still be applied to objects within the div.*

Using a div tag is nearly identical to the use of a span tag. Div tags are not inline. This means that a new line will be created after the div. The second difference is the size of the div. Many tags can be included in the div. Code Block 8-5 shows the use of our .boldItalic class in a div tag.

CODE BLOCK 8-5

```
<div class="boldItalic">
<h1>HTML Demystified</h1>
<p>Author: Lee Cottrell</p>
<h2>Chapter 1</h2>
<p>HTML is cool!</p>
</div>
        <p>Out of the div tag. Default format is applied</p>
```

An h1 tag, two p tags, and an h2 tag are enclosed in the div tag. Notice that in this illustration, all of the text, except for the last paragraph, is bolded and italic.

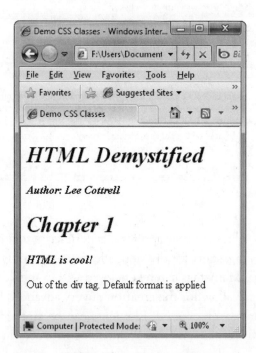

Standard Divisions on a Page

Modern web pages have three divisions: the header, the content section, and the footer. The header sits at the top of the web page. Headers typically contain an image for the web page. Additionally, a menu bar often sits in the header. By placing the header inside of a <div>, you can apply formatting differently than on the rest of the page.

The content section follows the header. The content section contains most of the body of the page. Content sections usually have a different font and margin than the header. Common formats in the content include centering the content on the page and creating multiple columns.

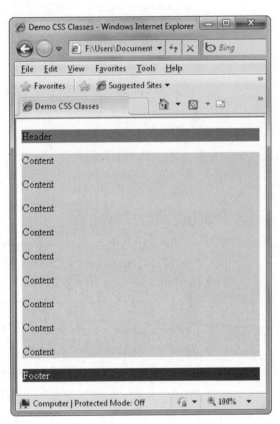

The last section is the footer. The footer contains many items related to the web page. The last update date of the page, copyright information, design credits, and e-mail contact information all exist in the footer.

Most modern web pages utilize some variant of the header, content, and footer layout. Throughout the remainder of this chapter, each page will be formatted using this configuration. Code Block 8-6 shows a header, content, and footer style sheet setting different colors in each section, and this illustration shows the output.

CODE BLOCK 8-6

```
<style type="text/css">
    .header{
        background-color:#ff0000;
    }
    .content{
        background-color:#00ff00;
    }
    .footer{
        background-color:#0000ff;
        color:#ffffff;
    }
```

```
          </style>
        </head>
        <body>
          <div class="header">
          <p>Header</p>
          </div>
          <div class="content">
          <p>Content</p>
          <p>Content</p>
          <p>Content</p>
          <p>Content</p>
          <p>Content</p>
          <p>Content</p>
          <p>Content</p>
          <p>Content</p>
          <p>Content</p>
          </div>
          <div class="footer">
          <p>Footer</p>
          </div>
        </body>
```

Practice Page Layout

You are going to build a page utilizing the standard page layout classes. You will build an HTML page and a CSS document with a header, a footer, and a content section. The content section will contain a picture and a paragraph describing the picture. Before you begin, acquire an image for the site.

1. Create a new page in your editor based on your template. Save it as **layout .html** in a folder called **chapter8**.

2. Create an appropriate title and meta tag information.

3. Create a new .css document titled **layout.css**. Save it in the chapter8 folder.

4. Create an **images** folder in your chapter8 folder.

5. Save your picture in the images folder.

6. Place the appropriate link tag in the head of boxImage.html.

   ```
   <link rel="stylesheet" href="layout.css"
     type="text/css"></link>
   ```

7. In the CSS document, create the generic classes for .header, .content, and .footer.

8. Add the text-align property to the header class to center the text.

```
.header{
     text-align:center;
}
```

9. For the footer, set the text-align property to center the text. Set the font size to 6pt.

```
.footer{
     text-align:center;
     font-size:6pt;
}
```

10. For the content class, set the font-size to 14pt. Set the margin property to 2em.

```
.content{
     font-size:14pt;
     margin:2em;
}
```

11. Save your document and switch to the boxImage.html document.

12. Create a div at the top of the body section that applies the header class.

```
<div class="header">

</div>
```

13. Inside of the div, create an <h1> titling the page.

14. Save and open your page in the browser. Your header should be centered in your window.

15. In your HTML code, after the </div> for the header, create a div class applying the content class.

```
<div class="content">

</div>
```

16. Use the <img> tag to show your picture. Be sure to set the alt, title, width, and height attributes.

```
<img src="images/firstday.jpg" alt="First day of school"
title="First day of school" width="634" height="401" />
```

17. Use the <p> tag to create a paragraph about your picture. Create at least three sentences about your picture.

```
<p>The first day of school is always an exciting time. My
children are excited to meet their teachers and see their
friends. The smiles on their faces say it all.</p>
```

18. Save and refresh the page in your browser. It should resemble the following illustration. You should see a distinct space between the left edge and the image and paragraph.

19. After the </div> for the content class, create a new div applying the footer class.

20. Add an <hr /> and create a paragraph citing the copyright year and your name.

```
<div class="footer">
<hr />
<p>Copyright 2010 Lee M. Cottrell</p>
</div>
```

21. Save and refresh the page in the browser. The footer text will resemble what's shown in the following illustration. The final CSS code is in Code Block 8-7. The final HTML code is in Code Block 8-8.

CODE BLOCK 8-7

```
/*Layout.css*/
.header{
     text-align:center;
}
.content{
     font-size:14pt;
     margin:2em;
}
.footer{
     text-align:center;
     font-size:6pt;
}
```

CODE BLOCK 8-8

```
<!DOCTYPE html PUBLIC "-//W3C//DTD XHTML 1.1//EN"
"http://www.w3.org/TR/xhtml11/DTD/xhtml11.dtd">
<html xmlns="http://www.w3.org/1999/xhtml" xml:lang="en">
<head>
<title>First day of school</title>
<meta name="description" content="First day of school"/>
<meta name="author" content="Lee M. Cottrell" />
<link rel="stylesheet" href="layout.css"
 type="text/css"></link>
</head>
<body>
<div class="header">
<h1>First day of school</h1>
</div>
<div class="content">
<img src="images/firstday.jpg" alt="First day of school"
title="First day of school" width="634" height="401" />
<p>The first day of school is always an exciting time. My
children are excited to meet their teachers and see their
friends. The smiles on their faces say it all.</p>
</div>
<div class="footer">
<hr />
<p>Copyright 2010 Lee M. Cottrell</p>
</div>
</body>
</html>
```

CSS Box Model

All HTML elements have a virtual box surrounding them. This box controls the screen space around the element. The box model allows you to control the size of the object, margins, border style, and padding around the object. Table 8-1 lists the CSS properties that modify the CSS box.

Understanding the box model is crucial to achieving good page layout. Understanding the relationship between the box components will allow you to tweak your page until it nears or reaches perfection. Good application of the model results in a beautiful page.

TABLE 8-1 CSS Box Model Properties

CSS Property	Description	Common Values
width	Controls the horizontal space taken up by the box.	Size—Measurement in px, em, in, or mm Percentage—Percentage of the screen
height	Controls the vertical space taken up by the box.	Size—Measurement in px, em, in, or mm Percentage—Percentage of the screen
visibility	Controls if the element can be seen by the user.	Visible—Object can be seen Hidden—Object cannot be seen but object still takes up space
margin	Controls the space between the border and other elements. Can control all four sides: margin-top, margin-bottom, margin-left, margin-right.	Size—Measurement in px, em, in, or mm margin: 2em;
border	Controls the border width, style, and color.	border: 2pt solid #ffff00; Border styles are dotted, dashed, solid, double, groove, ridge, inset, and outset.
padding	Controls the space between the element and the border. Can set padding-top, padding-bottom, padding-left, padding-right.	Size—Measurement in px, em, in, or mm padding: 2em;
float	Allows you to align elements side by side.	Left, right, none
clear	Ends the float element.	None, left, right, both
display	Controls how the box renders.	Block—Entire box is controlled by CSS formats None—Entire box is hidden without taking up space

Still Struggling

The CSS Box model is difficult to see on paper. It needs a good visual. The best place to see the box model in action is to visit www.csszengarden.com. This site is a showcase of CSS artists in action. The site has boilerplate text regarding CSS and several links to different CSS formats. Each CSS format utilizes the same classes, just in a unique manner.

Practice Using the Box Model

You are going to modify the layout.html page created earlier in the chapter. You will float the paragraph beside the image. Additionally, you will add borders and padding to the image.

1. Open the layout.html page in your browser and editor. Open the layout.css page in the editor.

2. Switch to the layout.css page. Create a tag-level class for the img called **img.border**.

   ```
   img.border{

   }
   ```

3. In img.border, set the CSS property border for 4pt solid black. Create 1em for padding. Finally, set the background color to a color that complements the picture. I choose dark green, #003300. These properties will create a "matte and frame" around the picture.

   ```
   img.border{
       border: 4pt solid #000000;
       padding:1em;
       background-color:#003300;
   }
   ```

4. Switch to layout.html. Apply the border class to your image.

   ```
   <img class="border" src="images/firstday.jpg" alt="First day
   of school" title="First day of school" width="634"
   height="401" />
   ```

5. Save and refresh your page in the browser. Your image should have a border similar to what's shown here:

6. Switch back to your css document.

7. You are going to float the image so that text appears to its right. Add the float:left property to the img.border class. Float:left means the image will appear on the left of following objects.

```
float:left;
```

TIP   *The float property is sticky. It continues to apply until it is turned off.*

8. Save and refresh the page in your browser. Your paragraph will be to the right of your image. Unfortunately, your footer is also to the right of the image and the paragraph is too close to the image. The following illustration highlights these errors:

9. To fix the crowding, add a margin-right:1em to the img.border class.

10. Placing the footer under the image and paragraph requires using the clear property of the box model. Add clear:left to the footer class. Save and refresh the page in the browser. The footer is where it belongs. Code Block 8-9 displays the final CSS code. Code Block 8-10 shows the final HTML code.

CODE BLOCK 8-9

```
.header{
    text-align:center;
}

.content{
    font-size:14pt;
    margin:2em;
}
```

```
.footer{
     text-align:center;
     font-size:6pt;
     clear:left;
}

img.border{
     border: 4pt solid #000000;
     padding:1em;
     margin-right:1em;
     background-color:#003300;
     float:left;
 }
```

CODE BLOCK 8-10

```
<!DOCTYPE html PUBLIC "-//W3C//DTD XHTML 1.1//EN"
"http://www.w3.org/TR/xhtml11/DTD/xhtml11.dtd">
<html xmlns="http://www.w3.org/1999/xhtml" xml:lang="en">
<head>
<title>First day of school</title>
<meta name="description" content="First day of school"/>
<meta name="author" content="Lee M. Cottrell" />
<link rel="stylesheet" href="layout.css"
 type="text/css"></link>
</head>
<body>
<div class="header">
<h1>First day of school</h1>
</div>

<div class="content">
<img class="border" src="images/firstday.jpg" alt="First day
of school" title="First day of school" width="634"
height="401" />
<p>The first day of school is always an exciting time. My
children are excited to meet their teachers and see their
friends. The smiles on their faces say it all.</p>
</div>
<div class="footer">
<hr />
<p>Copyright 2010 Lee M. Cottrell</p>
</div>
</body>
</html>
```

Complex Page Layouts

The header, content, and footer layouts are not any better designed than a standard web page. The div and classes allow formatting of each area, but no fancy formatting. Using additional classes and div tags, very complex formatting can be achieved.

For the remainder of this chapter, you are going to use the same page formatted several different ways. The next practice section will create this page using the Latin dummy text of lorem ipsum. You should concentrate on the div tags and the classes and not the content of the page.

Creating a Practice Page

In this practice, you will build an HTML page that will be used for the next two examples. After completing this practice, your page will include div tags for header, content and footer, but will have no formatting applied.

1. Create a new page called **complex.html**. Save it in your chapter8 folder.

2. Create a new CSS page titled **complex.css**. Save it in the same folder.

3. In your CSS page, create the standard page layout classes of .header, .content, and .footer.

   ```
   .header{
   }
   .content{
   }
   .footer{
   }
   ```

4. Switch to your HTML page. In the body, create three div tags applying the classes of header, content, and footer.

   ```
   <div class="header">
   </div>
   <div class="content">
   </div>
   <div class="footer">
   </div>
   ```

5. Create an <h1> tag in the header div saying Complex Page Layout.

   ```
   <div class="header">
   <h1>Complex Page Layout</h1>
   </div>
   ```

6. In the footer div, create a <p> tag holding copyright date and your name.

   ```
   <div class="footer">
   <p>Copyright 2010 Lee M. Cottrell</p>
   </div>
   ```

7. Visit www.lipsum.com/. In the second column, near the bottom is a form. Enter **40** and select the radio button for words. Click the button Generate Lorem Ipsum.

8. Copy the results on the page.

9. In the content section, create a <p> tag. Paste the generated text into the <p> tag.

```
<p>Lorem ipsum dolor sit amet, consectetur adipiscing elit.
Mauris metus lectus, congue vel posuere eget, euismod in
tellus. Nullam luctus libero et nulla sollicitudin non
aliquet diam congue. Sed lectus justo, sollicitudin ac
pretium quis, ullamcorper vel enim. Sed nec.</p>
```

10. In your browser, click the back button and repeat Steps 7 through 9 three more times. Your content div will have four paragraphs.

11. In the head section of your HTML page, add a <link> tag for the complex .css stylesheet.

```
<link rel="stylesheet" href="complex.css" type="text/css"></
link>
```

12. Save and view the page in your browser. It should look like the image shown here:

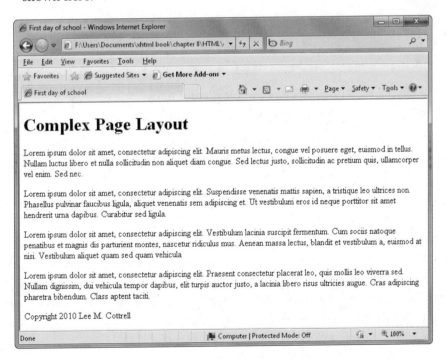

Multiple Columns

One of the more common layouts is using multiple columns. The content section of the page is broken into two or more columns. Each column contains content for the page. Examples of multiple-column web pages include youtube.com and msn.com.

There are as many different uses for the columns as there are pages using the columns. Some pages treat the columns like a newspaper, with each column holding content. Others have one main column of content and a sidebar of related links. Still others use columns to lay out categories of links.

Practice Using Multiple Column Pages

You are going to split complex.html into two columns of equal width. Each column will have two paragraphs. The columns will be controlled by generic classes named .left and .right.

1. Open complex.html in your editor and browser. Save complex.html as **complex2column.html**. Open complex.css in your editor.

2. Add two generic classes to your CSS document titled .left and .right.

   ```
   .left
   {
   }
   .right
   {
   }
   ```

3. Save the CSS document as **complex2column.css**.

4. Switch to complex.html. Edit the <link> href property to point to complex2column.css instead of complex.css.

   ```
   <link rel="stylesheet" href="complex2column.css"
     type="text/css"></link>
   ```

5. Find the first <p> tag in your document. Open a <div> tag that applies the .left class.

   ```
   <div class="left">
   ```

6. Close this <div> after the end of the second paragraph and before the beginning of the third paragraph. Your div will enclose two paragraphs. The following code shows the relationship between the <div> and the <p> tags. I abbreviated the paragraphs for clarity.

   ```
   <div class="left">
   <p>Lorem ipsum dolor sit amet, </p>
   ```

```
<p>Lorem ipsum dolor sit amet, </p>
</div>
```

7. Before the beginning of the third paragraph, and immediately after the </div> tag, open a <div> tag that applies the .right class.

```
<div class="right">
```

8. Close this </div> before the beginning of the <div> class for the footer. Again, your <div> will enclose two paragraphs. There will be two </div>s, one ending the content div, the other ending the right div.

```
<div class="right">
<p>Lorem ipsum dolor sit amet, </p>
<p>Lorem ipsum dolor sit amet, </p>
</div>
```

9. Save your .html document. There will be no change if viewed in the browser.

10. Switch to the .css document. In the .left class, set the float property to left and the width to 45%.

```
.left{
width:45%;
float:left;
}
```

11. In the .right class set the float property to right and the width to 45%.

12. Save and view the page in your browser. It will resemble the image shown here. Notice that the footer is between the columns.

13. Recall from earlier in the chapter that the float property stays on until it is turned off. You need to turn off the float in the footer. Set the clear attribute to both to turn off the float.

14. Save and refresh the page. The footer is now where it should be.

15. For a bit of fanciness, you can add borders to the columns. You will add a 2px border between the columns. To the .left class, add a border-right property setting a solid 2 point blue border. Also set the padding to 5%.

```
padding-right:5%;
border-right:2px solid #0000ff;
```

16. Save and refresh the page. Your two-column layout is complete and will look like this illustration. The final CSS code listing is in Code Block 8-11. The final HTML code listing is in Code Block 8-12.

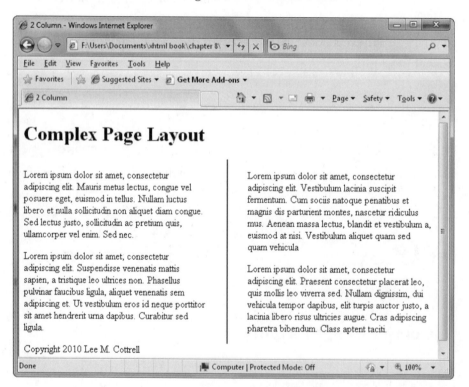

CODE BLOCK 8-11

```
.header{
}
.content{
}
```

```
.footer{
     clear:both;
}
.left{
width:45%;
float:left;
padding-right:5%;
border-right:2px solid #0000ff;
}
.right{
float:right;
width:45%;
}
```

CODE BLOCK 8-12

```
<!DOCTYPE html PUBLIC "-//W3C//DTD XHTML 1.1//EN"
"http://www.w3.org/TR/xhtml11/DTD/xhtml11.dtd">
<html xmlns="http://www.w3.org/1999/xhtml" xml:lang="en">
    <head>
        <title>2 Column</title>
        <meta name="description"
         content="First day of school"/>
        <meta name="author" content="Lee M. Cottrell" />
        <link rel="stylesheet" href="complex2column.css"
         type="text/css"></link>
    </head>
    <body>
      <div class="header">
      <h1>Complex Page Layout</h1>
      </div>

        <div class="content">
        <div class="left">
        <p>Lorem ipsum dolor sit amet</p>
        <p>Lorem ipsum dolor sit amet</p>
        </div>
        <div class="right">
        <p>Lorem ipsum dolor sit amet</p>
        <p>Lorem ipsum dolor sit amet</p>
        </div>
        </div>
        <div class="footer">
        <p>Copyright 2010 Lee M. Cottrell</p>
        </div>
    </body>
</html>
```

Floating Layouts

Another complex layout is the *floating* layout. In this layout, a background image is used. This image is often one that cannot easily be used with text. The web content is placed in a block that is centered on the page. This block typically has a solid background that complements the background image. I call it a floating image because the block seems to float above the background.

Still Struggling

Centering items in CSS is not as difficult as it seems. For tips on centering many different elements and tips on many other CSS tricks, visit www.w3.org/Style/Examples/007/.

More needs to be said about the centering. The center tag is deprecated. To center, a CSS trick is needed. The trick is to set the width of the block to a value that is less than 100%. Then you will set the margin-left and margin-right properties to auto. Setting both to auto will instruct the browser to create equal margins on both sides of the block, thus centering the image. The text within the block is not centered.

Practice Creating a Floating Layout

You are going to modify the complex.html file to use the floating layout. I will place the content and footer in a new div. This new div will block the content and footer sections. The block will be centered within the browser. The box will be centered in every browser. An alternative layout would include the header in the div as well.

TIP *The code in this section creates a block using a percentage. Other pages use a fixed width and height instead of a percentage.*

1. Open the complex.html and complex.css documents in your editor.
2. Save the complex.html document as **complexfloat.html**. Save the complex.css document as **complexfloat.css**.

3. Change the href property of link tag in the head of the .html document to point to complexfloat.css.

```
<link rel="stylesheet" href="complexfloat.css" type="text/
css"></link>
```

4. Switch to the CSS document.

5. Add a body element. Set the background-image property to read the background image you downloaded. I used the wall.gif file. Also set a background color that matches the predominate color in your image. I used a dark gray, #434a3a.

```
body{
background-image:url("images/wall.gif");
background-color:#434a3a;
}
```

6. Save and preview your page in the browser. Verify that your background image is loading.

7. Your header text needs a little formatting. In the header class in the CSS, format the font so that it looks good with the background. I chose white.

```
color:#ffffff;
```

8. In your CSS document, create a new generic class called .floatBox.

```
.floatBox{
}
```

9. Set the width property for floatBox to 80%.

```
width:80%;
```

10. Set the margin-left and margin-right for floatBox to auto.

```
margin-left:auto;
margin-right:auto;
```

11. Set the background-color and color for floatBox to colors that coordinate with your background. I used a lighter gray for the background and dark green for the color.

```
background-color:#c0c0c0;
color:#009933;
```

12. Create a 2pt solid border for floatBox using a color that coordinates with your page. I used the same dark green for the border color.

```
border:2pt solid #009933;
```

13. Add a 1em padding to floatBox.

```
padding:1em;
```

14. Save your .css document.

15. Switch to the .html document.

16. Create a new div applying the floatBox class above the div for the content. Close the div after the </div> closing the footer, immediately above the </body>. The following illustration shows the placement in my copy of Programmer's Notepad.

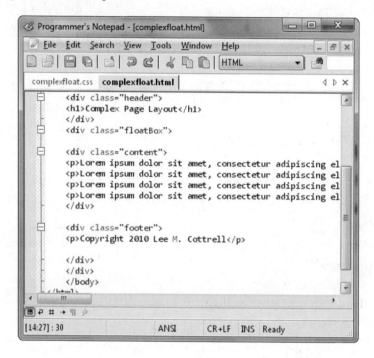

17. Save and refresh your page in the browser. Your content and footer should be enclosed within a box that is centered on the page. The next image shows how mine looks.

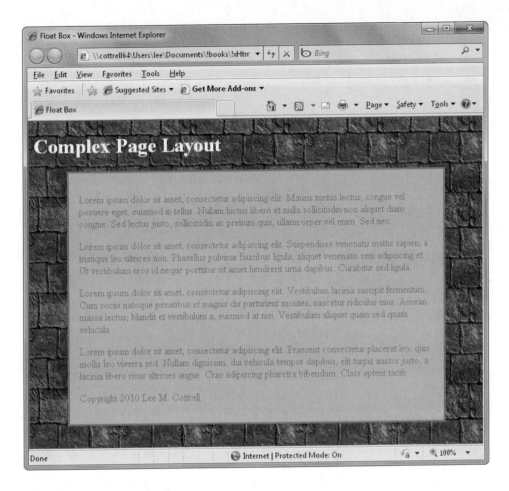

Creating Your Own Layouts

The layouts presented here are just two common layouts. You are limited only by your imagination and desire to code CSS. Typically any CSS trick that you see will work in your page. For example, the following illustration shows the float layout with two columns enabled. There are more CSS layouts than I can fit within this chapter.

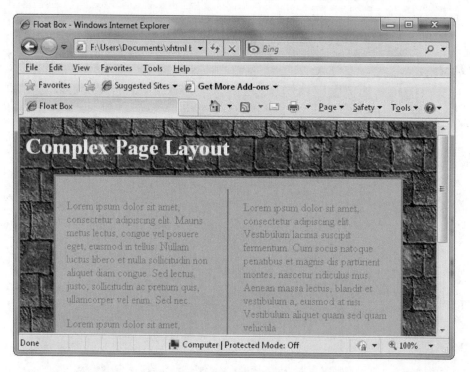

For more help with layouts, search the Web for pages that you like. View the source code and read the CSS. Find the CSS code that powers the feature you like and implement it on your own site. It is considered polite to cite your influences for your page design in a comment in your code.

Still Struggling

If you do not want to create your own custom layouts, there are several sites on the Web that can help. My personal favorite is freecsstemplates.com.

Summary

You learned that CSS is the best way to achieve a page layout. Through the creation of generic and tag-level classes, you can create many different layouts. The new div and span classes allow you to apply the formatting in any part of the web page. Two-column and floating layouts proved that a complex layout is possible with CSS.

QUIZ

1. **Which of the following is a correctly named generic class in CSS?**
   A. header
   B. .header
   C. body.header
   D. class="header"

2. **To center a block, set the margin-left and margin-right properties to _____.**
   A. center
   B. dynamic
   C. auto
   D. fixed

3. **This HTML tag applies formats to large sections of your page.**
   A. div
   B. span
   C. body
   D. class

4. **The CSS property of _____ provides space between the text and the border.**
   A. space
   B. z-index
   C. margin
   D. padding

5. **This HTML tag applies formats to small amounts of text on your page.**
   A. div
   B. span
   C. body
   D. class

6. **We divided a normal HTML page into _____ distinct regions.**
   A. 2
   B. 3
   C. 4
   D. 5

7. **The float property is sticky. To turn it off, use the CSS property _____.**
   A. float
   B. clear
   C. padding
   D. reset

8. **To hide an element without taking up any space, the _____ property is needed.**
   A. display
   B. hidden
   C. visibility
   D. show

9. **The CSS _____ controls how screen objects are formatted.**
   A. layout
   B. formatting
   C. rendering
   D. box

10. **The following line of CSS code shows an example of a(n) _____.**

```
p.layout{
}
```

   A. layout
   B. tag-level class
   C. generic class
   D. error

chapter 9

JavaScript

This chapter will show you how to use JavaScript. It is not intended as a primer on programming. This chapter will not teach you how to program. It will show you how to include JavaScript in your pages.

CHAPTER OBJECTIVES

In this chapter, you will

- Define JavaScript
- Create JavaScript statements
- Use existing script libraries

HTML is an excellent choice for delivering information to the user. It is capable of formatting data, displaying pictures, and capturing input. By itself, however, it is not capable of reacting to the user. HTML depends on additional languages for this functionality.

JavaScript is the most popular of the languages that can be used to script HTML pages. JavaScript allows you to create objects that the user can interact with. JavaScript allows you to change colors, change pictures when the mouse rolls over, and verify that form data is correct.

JavaScript

JavaScript is a lightweight scripting language. It is lightweight because it is limited on what it can do. For security reasons, JavaScript can only affect the web page. It is intended to allow you to add interactivity to your web page.

JavaScript is a client-side scripting language. This means that the program will run in the user's browser on the user's web page. By running on the client's computer, your web site will load faster.

JavaScript can be used for many things on your web page. One item JavaScript can handle is reacting to an event. An event is an action performed by the user. Clicking a button, loading a page, or hovering over a picture are all events that JavaScript can react to. Event-driven programming is part of the basis of modern programming.

In addition to handling events, JavaScript can read and create cookies. A cookie is a file created by a web page. The cookie holds information about the user's session with the web page. Items ordered, date last visited, or even page preferences can be held in the cookie file.

Finally, JavaScript can modify the HTML on your page. Through creative uses of JavaScript, HTML, and CSS, you can create very unique web pages. This combination is referred to as Dynamic HTML (DHTML). DHTML is the subject of the next chapter.

JavaScript Objects

Objects have many meanings. In the physical world, an object is something that you can touch and use, and that has properties. A car radio is an object. It can be turned on, the station changed, and the volume adjusted. The radio has several functions that you interact with. You can change the volume, set the station, and adjust the sound features. The properties of the radio include the number of watts it generates and the current station. Notice that you are capable of changing one of the properties.

Computer objects are similar in function to a car radio. The primary difference is that you cannot touch a computer object. Consider the icons on your computer desktop. Double-clicking the icon will run the associated program. The icon has properties that affect how it works.

In JavaScript, you will work with several objects. In each case, you will work with them as if they were a radio. You will utilize the object's functions and modify its properties. To use an object in code, you will type its name. Following the name is a period and the function or property you wish to use. Table 9-1 lists the common JavaScript objects.

TIP   *For more information about JavaScript objects, visit devguru.com.*

The Document Object Model

The Document Object Model (DOM) is a standardized platform designed to unify JavaScripting across all browsers. Browsers will read the HTML into a format that the DOM can manipulate. Every JavaScript script uses the DOM in some way.

It is important that you know that the DOM exists and provides JavaScripting functionality. It is important that you know how to code JavaScript to utilize the DOM. Unless you are a hard-core web programmer, it is not important that you understand everything about the DOM.

TABLE 9-1 Common JavaScript Objects

Object	Description
Date	Handles date and time.
Document	Access and control the current page in memory.
Form	Provides access to the form and form data.
History	Keeps a list of every page visited by the browser session.
Image	Allows the programmer to adjust the image.
Navigator	Provides information about the user's browser.
String	Strings are words and paragraphs.
Window	Use to modify the browser window.

Still Struggling

Most HTML books spend pages on the DOM. Relax. Unless you are a computer programmer, you will spend very little time using the DOM. Most likely, you will either be given working JavaScript code from a seasoned programmer, or you will borrow JavaScript from an online repository and use it in your code.

Creating Scripts

Scripts run inside of your web page. You need to learn where to place the scripts. You have two choices of script placement. Your first choice is *inline* scripts. Inline scripts are written within the HTML code. Sometimes you want your scripts to run after clicking a button. These types of scripts are called *event* scripts.

The actual JavaScript code for your scripts may exist in one of three places. For simple scripts, the code is placed where it is run. For example, an inline script will be written completely inside of the body. The second place your scripts will exist is in a JavaScript section in the heading of your page. When using the heading section, you will create named blocks of JavaScripts called functions. The functions can be called either inline or through events.

TIP *Functions are very hard for the beginning programmer to understand. A function is merely a name that runs a large block of code. As an example, in your word processing program, there is a button that runs the spell checker. The spell checker is a named block of code.*

The last place your scripts may be held is in a script library. Script libraries are text files with a .js extension. They hold functions that your HTML page can run. Many free script libraries exist on the Internet. One of the most popular is the JQuery library. You will encounter more on this later in the chapter.

Creating Inline Scripts

Creating inline scripts requires the <script> tag. This tag encloses the JavaScript. The <script> requires the type attribute. Type holds the name of the scripting language. For JavaScript, you set the attribute to text/JavaScript.

```
<script type="text/JavaScript">
```

Code Block 9-1 shows the placement of two inline scripts. Both display HTML content onto the page. The Document object is used to write the output to a screen. Write is a method of the Document object. Write places the text in the () onto the browser screen.

TIP *Write is a method of the Document object. Methods provide functionality for the document.*

CODE BLOCK 9-1

```
<body>
<h1>A sample JavaScript</h1>
<script type="text/JavaScript">
document.write("<p>Welcome to JavaScripting!</p>");
</script>
<h2>More scripts below</h2>
<script type="text/JavaScript">
document.write("<p>Document.write places output on the screen.</p>");
</script>
</body>
```

Code Block 9-1 is not very exciting. There is nothing in this script that you could not do with pure HTML. The purpose of the block was to show how to write an inline script. Our next example will be more exciting. It will identify the browser.

TIP *If you write this script and save it on your computer, Internet Explorer will throw a security warning your way. Allow the scripts to run.*

Correcting Errors

Typing JavaScript is very hard. Your JavaScript code has to be perfect. The smallest error from missing a semicolon to forgetting a double quote will cause your program to crash, and show an error as the following illustration shows. To see the dialog box, you will need to double-click the yellow exclamation mark in the lower-right corner of the Explorer window. Once the dialog box appears, click on Show Details.

TIP *With the exception of function statements, all JavaScript lines end with a semicolon.*

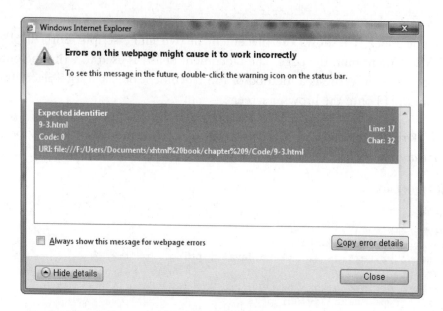

Firefox error messages are more detailed than Internet Explorer's. The next illustration shows how Firefox attempts to point out where the error is located. In the example, I used a period (.) instead of a plus (+) sign. The steps to see Firefox's errors are a little different. Start by clicking the Tools menu and then Error Console.

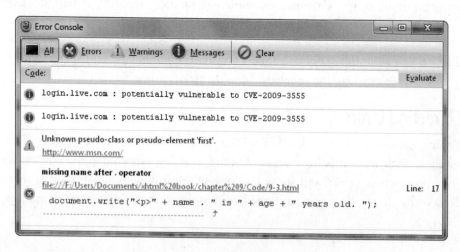

Still Struggling

I strongly recommend using Firefox to write JavaScript. The error console is much more robust than Internet Explorer's. Also, Firefox more closely adheres to the Document Object Model.

Remember that you are not learning how to program JavaScript, you are learning how to use it in HTML. You should feel very comfortable finding JavaScript from a web site and using it in your code.

When you get an error, relax. They happen to all programmers. The trick is to know how to fix them. For code blocks in this book, be sure that *every character, space, and symbol* in your code matches my code. When copying and pasting code from the Internet, be sure to follow any directions included with the JavaScript.

Making Decisions in JavaScript

The Navigator object defined in Table 9-1 provides the user with information regarding the browser. The name and version of the browser are identifiable using the Navigator object. Navigator.appName will return a shortened name for the browser. Navigator.userAgent will return nearly everything about the user's web environment. A common usage is to check the browser compatibility with a web site. For example, YouTube.com checks your browser to see if it can display the videos on its site.

Decisions in JavaScript are made using the if statement. An if statement checks a condition and reacts according to whether the condition is true or false. We use if statements every day in our life. If it is raining, we open an umbrella; otherwise, we close the umbrella. Your if statements will be similar. If the browser is Internet Explorer, do one chunk of code; otherwise, do something else. Code Block 9-2 displays a message to the user based on which browser she is using. If the browser is Internet Explorer, a message to the Internet Explorer user is displayed. Otherwise, a message is displayed to the non–Internet Explorer user. The following illustrations display the output in Internet Explorer (left) and in Firefox (right).

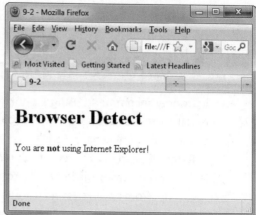

CODE BLOCK 9-2

```
<body>
<h1>Browser Detect</h1>
<script type="text/JavaScript">
if(navigator.appName == "Microsoft Internet Explorer"){
    document.write("You are using Internet Explorer!");
}
else
{
    document.write("You are <b>not</b> using Internet Explorer!");
}
</script>
</body>
```

Variables

Quite often programmers need to hold data in their programs. Data is held in a variable. A variable, similar to algebra class, can hold many things. JavaScript variables can hold anything from your name, to your age, to a text box from a form. JavaScript programs use variables to save and store data for future use. By using a variable, you can reduce the amount of code you have to type.

Creating a variable in JavaScript is much easier than in other programming languages. JavaScript does not care what type of data is stored in its variables. All that you have to do is create the variable by using the var keyword, followed by a word that identifies the variable.

TIP *Variable names should reflect what you intend for them to hold. Additionally, they cannot contain spaces, nor start with a number.*

Many different examples of a variable exist. Code Block 9-3 shows the JavaScripting creating three variables holding my name, my age, and my age in dogYears. DogYears is calculated by multiplying my current age by 7. I display the name, age, and dogYears variables in document.write lines.

CODE BLOCK 9-3

```
<script type="text/JavaScript">
var name="Lee Cottrell";
var age = 40;
var dogAge = age * 7;
document.write("<p>" + name +" is " + age + " years old. ");
document.write("If he were a dog, he would be " + dogAge +
" years old!</p>");
</script>
```

To display the content of the variable, I created a <p> tag. Inside I put the words I wanted displayed inside of a set of double quotes. The variables are held outside of the quotes, surrounded by plus (+) signs. The plus signs add the value of the variable to the words in the paragraph. Notice that the value of the variable is displayed. The output is shown in this illustration.

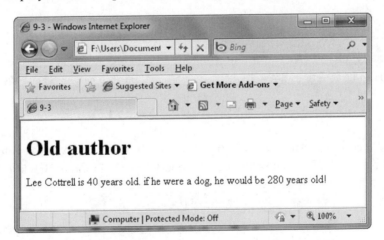

Practice Creating Inline Scripts

In this section you will create a greeting script. A variable called today will be created holding the current date and time. The variable today will be created using the Date object. The Date object will generate the current time and place it within the today variable. Finally, the getHours method will return the military time. If the time is before 12, a good morning message will be returned.

Times between 12 and 17 hours will return a good afternoon message. Times after 17 will return a good evening message.

1. Create a new folder titled chapter9. Create a new HTML document titled **greet.html**. Save it in the chapter9 folder.

2. Inside of the body section, create a <script> tag. Include the type attribute equal to text/JavaScript.

3. Create a variable called today and set it equal to new Date().

```
var today = new Date();
```

4. Create an if statement that compares today.getHours() >=0 and < 12. Make the code block display good morning.

```
if((today.getHours() >= 0) && (today.getHours() <12))
{
        document.write("Good morning from Lee Cottrell! ");
}
```

5. Add the else if statement that compares today.getHours() >=12 and < 17. Make the code block display good afternoon.

```
else if((today.getHours() >= 12) && (today.getHours() <17))
{
        document.write("Good afternoon from Lee Cottrell! ");
}
```

6. Finally add an else statement. Make the code block display good evening.

```
else if((today.getHours() >= 17) && (today.getHours() <=23))
{
        document.write("Good evening from Lee Cottrell! ");
}
```

7. Save and view the page in your browser. It will resemble the following illustration. The final version of the code appears in Code Block 9-4.

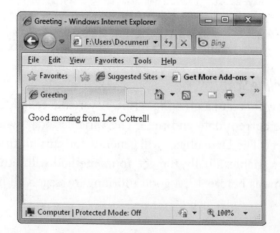

CODE BLOCK 9-4

```
<!DOCTYPE html PUBLIC "-//W3C//DTD XHTML 1.1//EN"
"http://www.w3.org/TR/xhtml11/DTD/xhtml11.dtd">
<html xmlns="http://www.w3.org/1999/xhtml" xml:lang="en">
<head>
<title>Greeting</title>
<meta name="description" content="Template"/>
<meta name="author" content="Lee M. Cottrell" />
</head>
<body>
<script type="text/javascript">
      var today = new Date();
      if((today.getHours() >= 0) && (today.getHours() <12))
      {
            document.write("Good morning from Lee Cottrell! ");
      }
      else if((today.getHours() >= 12) && (today.getHours() <17))
      {
            document.write("Good afternoon from Lee Cottrell! ");
      }
      else if      ((today.getHours() >= 17) &&
      (today.getHours() <=23))
      {
            document.write("Good evening from Lee Cottrell! ");
      }

      </script>
   </body>
</html>
```

Using Scripts in the Head

The greeting script presented in Code Block 9-4 is a good script. It produces a customized greeting based on the time of day. However, as an inline script, it makes the HTML hard to read. Most programmers will not place scripts this long inline; instead, they will move them to the head section of the document, create them as a named function, and call the function where they want it.

Wow! There was a lot in that last sentence. We need to break that sentence apart and describe its component parts. I will use Code Block 9-3 for our example. Starting in order, creating a script section in the head is straightforward. In the head section, create a <script> tag, identical to the one you created in the <body>. Be sure to close the </script> tag!

```
<script type="text/JavaScript">
</script>
```

Once the script section is created, you need to define a function. A function is a named chunk of JavaScript code. You create a JavaScript function with the function keyword, followed by a name. The name is followed by a set of parentheses that can either be empty or have values in them. Ours will have nothing in them.

```
function oldAuthor()
```

The function has a name but no body, or substance. After the close parenthesis, open a curly brace ({). Press ENTER a few times then close the curly brace (}). Like CSS classes, JavaScript functions are stored inside of blocks. The code that is currently in your body will need to be moved into the function. Drag the code from the body to between the open and close curly braces.

TIP *Dragging code is a quicker way to cut and paste. It works in nearly every editor and word processor.*

```
function oldAuthor()
{
var name="Lee Cottrell";
var age = 40;
var dogAge = age * 7;
document.write("<p>" + name + " is " + age + " years old. ");
document.write("if he were a dog, he would be " + dogAge +
" years old!</p>")
}
```

Now you need to call the function. Calling a function is similar to calling a dog. Unless you call your dog's name, he will not come to you. Calling a function in JavaScript means typing the name of the function where you want the code to appear. In our case, we will call the function inline inside of the body, where the code originally appeared.

```
<h1>Old author</h1>
<script type="text/JavaScript">
oldAuthor();
</script>
```

In addition to making the body section of your page more readable, functions make your code reusable. You may call your function as many times as you like, and it will always run. Code Block 9-5 shows the final version with the function oldAuthor called five times. The following illustration shows the output of all five calls.

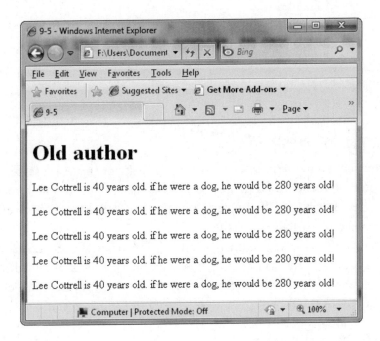

CODE BLOCK 9-5

```
<!DOCTYPE html PUBLIC "-//W3C//DTD XHTML 1.1//EN"
"http://www.w3.org/TR/xhtml11/DTD/xhtml11.dtd">
<html xmlns="http://www.w3.org/1999/xhtml" xml:lang="en">
    <head>
    <title>9-5</title>
    <meta name="description" content="Template"/>
    <meta name="author" content="Lee M. Cottrell" />
    <script type="text/JavaScript">
    function oldAuthor()
    {
    var name="Lee Cottrell";
    var age = 40;
    var dogAge = age * 7;

    document.write("<p>" + name + " is " + age + " years old. ");
    document.write("if he were a dog, he would be " + dogAge +
    " years old!</p>");
    }
    </script>
    </head>
```

```
<body>
  <h1>Old author</h1>
        <script type="text/JavaScript">
        oldAuthor();
        oldAuthor();
        oldAuthor();
        oldAuthor();
        oldAuthor();
        </script>
  </body>
</html>
```

Creating Script Files

The script section in the head of a page creates a script that is reusable for that page. However, this does not help if you want the script reusable for a site or even a series of web sites. To create scripts that are reusable across several web sites, you need to create a script file.

The script file is a text document with a .js extension. Just as CSS files only hold CSS code, a JS file will hold only JavaScript. This file is accessed through a script section in the head. A new attribute of the <script> tag is needed. The src attribute tells the browser where the JavaScript file is stored.

Practice Creating a Script File

In this section you are going to create a script file holding one new function called pageDate. PageDate will display the date the page was last modified. This script is very important on your web site. It allows your viewers to know when your content was last updated.

This script will use the Document object. The Document object's property lastModified retrieves the date and time the page was saved. This property is a Date object. So as in the greet script, Date methods will generate the desired output.

The output depends on a programming idea called *concatenation*. Concatenation simply means joining lines of text together. These lines, called strings, can form a longer string through concatenation. The JavaScript symbol for concatenation is the plus (+) sign.

1. Open the greet.html document created earlier in the chapter in your editor and browser.

2. Create a new document in your editor. Save it in the chapter9 folder as **script.js**.

3. Create a function in script.js titled pageDate().

```
function pageDate()
{
}
```

4. Inside of the function, create a variable named lastMod of type Date.

```
var lastMod = new Date();
```

5. You need to make lastMod hold the date the page was last modified. Place document.lastModified inside of the () after date. By placing the object inside of the (), you will cause lastModified to be converted to a Date object, allowing you to use the Date methods.

```
var lastMod = new Date(document.lastModified);
```

6. You now need to print out the date the page was last modified. Start by using the document.write method to start a paragraph holding "Document Last Modified".

```
document.write("<p>Document last modified ");
```

7. You will print the date in American style. Start by displaying the date's month using the getMonth method inside of a document.write.

```
document.write(lastMod.getMonth());
```

8. After the () and before the closing) add a + and then "-" to concatenate the dash onto the date. After the "-", add another + and lastMod .getDate().

```
document.write(lastMod.getMonth() + "-" + lastMod.getDate());
```

9. Finish the date with another + "-" + and lastMod.getFullYear().

```
document.write(lastMod.getMonth() + "-" + lastMod.getDate() +
"-" + lastMod.getFullYear();
```

10. Finish the paragraph by adding another document.write holding "</p>".

```
document.write("</p>");
```

11. You still need to call the function. Switch to your HTML file.

12. In the head section, before your existing script entry, create a <script> section using the src attribute that holds script.js.

```
<script type="text/javascript" src="script.js"></script>
```

13. Now scroll to the end of your body section. As the last line of the body, create a script section calling the pageDate() function.

14. Save and view the page in your browser. Notice that the date is displayed in your browser. Also notice that it is off by one month. This is shown in the next illustration. This is because programming languages start counting at 0. Thus January is month 0, while December is month 11. The simple fix is to add one 1 the month returned.

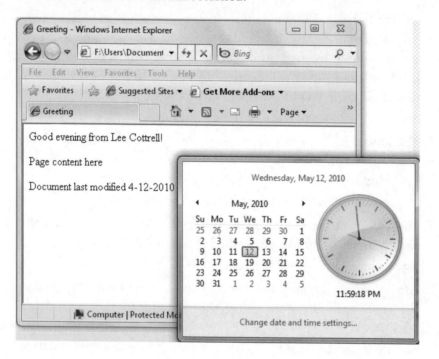

15. Switch back to your .js file.

16. Surround the existing lastMod.getMonth() with a set of parentheses.

```
(lastMod.getMonth() )
```

17. After getMonth() add the mathematical operation + 1. The parentheses allow this to be a math operation, not a string concatenation. The full line of code is shown here:

```
document.write((lastMod.getMonth() +1) + "-" +
lastMod.getDate() + "-" + lastMod.getFullYear());
```

18. The correct output is shown in the following illustration. Final code listing is in Code Block 9-6.

CODE BLOCK 9-6

```
/*script.js*/
function pageDate()
{
        var lastMod = new Date(document.lastModified);

        document.write("<p>Document last modified ");
        document.write((lastMod.getMonth() +1) + "-" +
        lastMod.getDate() + "-" + lastMod.getFullYear());
        document.write("</p>");


}
<!--Final html code-->
<!DOCTYPE html PUBLIC "-//W3C//DTD XHTML 1.1//EN"
"http://www.w3.org/TR/xhtml11/DTD/xhtml11.dtd">
<html xmlns="http://www.w3.org/1999/xhtml" xml:lang="en">
    <head>
        <title>Greeting</title>
        <meta name="description" content="Template"/>
        <meta name="author" content="Lee M. Cottrell" />
      <script type="text/javascript" src="script.js"></script>
      <script type="text/javascript">
      /*code hidden for clarity */
      </script>
    </head>
    <body>
```

```
<script type="text/javascript">
greet();
</script>
<p>Page content here</p>
<script type="text/javascript">
pageDate();</script>
</body>
</html>
```

Using Existing Scripts

As stated several times earlier, this chapter is about using JavaScript; it is not about learning JavaScript. My goal was to show you how to include JavaScript in your pages. I assumed that you would leave the actual coding of JavaScript to others.

There are thousands of competent JavaScript programmers in the world. Many write scripts and post them to repositories all over the Internet. One excellent source for quality JavaScripts is javascript.internet.com. As of this writing, this site boasted 1420 scripts freely available for download. The site provides the JavaScript. You need to copy and paste the script into your code. If adjustments are needed, the site clearly explains the adjustments.

JQuery

Another outstanding source of online JavaScripts is the JQuery repository. Housed at JQuery.com, they call their repository the "Write Less, Do More, JavaScript Library." The library has thousands of ready-made scripts that accomplish phenomenal tasks. My Graphic Designer friends swear by this site whenever they need JavaScript.

TIP *JQuery accepts scripts from many sources. Their code is generated by the Internet community at large. Given this, you will find many different categories of JQuery scripts.*

JQuery offers several tutorials for the budding JavaScripter. At your stage, I recommend the tutorials "How JQuery Works," "Getting Started with JQuery," and "JQuery for Designers." All three show you how to use the library to your best advantage. Other tutorials show you how to build new plug-ins for addition to the JQuery library.

Using JQuery

JQuery takes a little getting used to. Reading their tutorials is very important. Their beginning tutorials focus on the ready function. The ready function allows you to call an event when the DOM is ready. This solves a problem with events running before they should.

Since JQuery is a library, you need to have a copy of jquery.js. They recommend that you download their library for speed purposes. The production, or minified, version is recommended. If you depend on JQuery, I recommend updating your download at least once a week.

To get JQuery, use Internet Explorer to visit JQuery.com. Click the Download Now button and save your file as jquery.js. If you use Firefox, the link will open in a window. From there, save the file as jquery.js.

Using the JQuery plugins is a little strange. You will first include a link to the jquery.js file at the end of the *head section* of your document. From there, you will create another script section. This section will create the JQuery call. The normal syntax is (html object).plugin(parameters). Code Block 9-7 uses JQuery's ready function to make an image grow.

CODE BLOCK 9-7

```
<script type="text/javascript" src="jquery.js"></script>
<script type="text/javascript">
    $(document).ready(function(){
      $("img").click(function(event){
      $('img').animate({left:0,width:"50%",top:0,
      height: "50%"},"slow");
      });
    });
</script>
```

This script will resize a picture on clicking. The $(document).ready(function() line lets the page fully load. $("img").click(function(event){ creates the event code for when a user clicks on the image. $('') can hold any HTML object. The next line calls the JQuery plugin animate. Animate causes the image to change size. The width and height of the object are set to 50% of the page. The slow attribute tells animate to grow slowly. The complete code appears in Code Block 9-8. The before and after images appear in the following illustration.

CODE BLOCK 9-8

```
<!DOCTYPE html PUBLIC "-//W3C//DTD XHTML 1.1//EN"
"http://www.w3.org/TR/xhtml11/DTD/xhtml11.dtd">
<html xmlns="http://www.w3.org/1999/xhtml" xml:lang="en">
<head>
<title>Image Resize</title>
<meta name="description" content="JQuery Example"/>
<meta name="author" content="Lee M. Cottrell" />
<script type="text/javascript" src="jquery.js"></script>
<script type="text/javascript">
$(document).ready(function(){
$("img").click(function(event){
$('img').animate({left:0,width:"50%",top:0,height: "50%"},"slow");
});
});

    </script>
 </head>
 <body>
  <img src="images/firstday.jpg" height="10"></img>
    </body>
</html>
```

Still Struggling

JQuery has outstanding documentation. It has an even better community of users. Every time I need an effect, I Google "JQuery effect". In nearly every case, I find a working example on the first link, usually through JQuery's forums. My hat is off to that community for saving me uncountable amounts of time.

Summary

This chapter showed how to use JavaScript. It demonstrated how to create inline scripts, header scripts, and JavaScript files. A little time was devoted to discussing the art of programming. You should understand how to include JavaScript in your pages. You should also look to the Web for working JavaScript. Two repositories were discussed: JavaScript.internet.com and JQuery were presented as valid alternatives to writing your own code.

QUIZ

1. JavaScript is said to be a _____ scripting language because it runs in the user's browser.
   A. server-side
   B. interpreted
   C. client-side
   D. automated

2. JavaScript depends on the _____ to create a unified programming experience across browsers.
   A. object
   B. DOM
   C. JQuery
   D. JS file

3. Most JavaScript lines end with a _____ .
   A. period (.)
   B. dash (-)
   C. exclamation mark (!)
   D. semicolon (;)

4. JavaScript files have a ._____ extension.
   A. js
   B. jp
   C. css
   D. java

5. _____ is the "Write Less, Do More" library.
   A. JavaScript.Internet.com
   B. JQuery.com
   C. DevGuru.com
   D. Google.com

6. A _____ is a named chunk of JavaScript code.
   A. variable
   B. function
   C. element
   D. object

7. **To display text on the page using JavaScript, the _____ method of the document class is used.**

    A. display
    B. page
    C. load
    D. write

8. **For our greet and pageDate script to run, you created a variable of type _____.**

    A. Time
    B. Calendar
    C. Date
    D. Clock

9. **Making a decision in JavaScript requires the use of a(n) _____ statement.**

    A. if
    B. decision
    C. then
    D. function

10. **Programmers use _____ to store data for a program.**

    A. objects
    B. classes
    C. variables
    D. functions

chapter 10

Dynamic HTML

This chapter will act as a cookbook, presenting simple DHTML techniques. As with the preceding chapter, this is not a complete reference. Instead, you should get a feel for some of the things DHTML can do for your web site. You are encouraged to learn more about this technology.

CHAPTER OBJECTIVES

In this chapter, you will

- Create functions in JavaScript
- Pass parameters to a JavaScript function
- Use the DOM to adjust page formatting
- Use the DOM to adjust page content
- Create a rollover

The computer world loves to merge technologies. DHTML is a combination of HTML, CSS, and JavaScript, or other programming languages. DHTML allows the designer to create interactive web pages. Through DHTML, the user can customize fonts, colors, and even layout of the page. Web developers can use DHTML to change page content based on user choices, and create simple animation.

The term DHTML may be a little dated. Some books refer to DHTML as DOM scripting. The concepts are the same; just the name has changed. Regardless of what you call it, the techniques are applicable to all modern browsers.

Using Functions in JavaScript

DHTML will combine the three skills you have learned in this book. The HTML and the CSS are relatively easy. The JavaScript is the hard part. You have to not only know what you want done, you need to learn how to do it. Most of the DHTML presented in tutorials will utilize the power of JavaScript functions.

Chapter 9 presented a basic JavaScript function. Here I will add the concept of a parameter. A parameter is data passed to a function. This data allows the function to be completely reusable. Code Block 10-1 shows a JavaScript function with two parameters.

CODE BLOCK 10-1

```
<!DOCTYPE html PUBLIC "-//W3C//DTD XHTML 1.1//EN"
"http://www.w3.org/TR/xhtml11/DTD/xhtml11.dtd">
<html xmlns="http://www.w3.org/1999/xhtml" xml:lang="en">
    <head>
        <title>Function Example</title>
        <meta name="description" content="Function Example"/>
        <meta name="author" content="Lee M. Cottrell" />
        <script type="text/JavaScript">
        function addEm(num1, num2)
        {
        var sum;
        sum = num1 + num2;
        document.write("<p>" + num1);
        document.write(" + " + num2);
        document.write(" = " + sum);
        document.write("</p>");
        }
        </script>
```

```
        </head>
        <body>
        <script type="text/javascript">
               addEm(7, 3);
               addEm(20, 30);
        </script>
        </body>
</html>
```

Function addEm has two parameters, called num1 and num2. The function takes the two values and adds them together. It then displays the two numbers and their sum in a paragraph. The function is called two times with two different sets of values. In the first call, num1 receives the value of 7 and num2 receives 3. The second call sends 20 to num1 and 30 to num2. By using parameters, you can reuse the parameters as many times as needed. The following illustration shows the two lines of output.

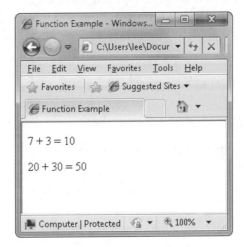

TIP   *You could have produced that output without JavaScript. Function addEm is merely designed to show the function and parameter syntax.*

DHTML Visual Examples

Most developers' first exposure to DHTML is through changing colors on the page. This script will demonstrate the basics of adjusting the style of the document through the DOM. The DOM includes an object called the body. This object represents the body of the HTML document.

The body object includes a property called style. Unfortunately, style is not the CSS style you learned earlier. It is a special style property with dozens of subproperties. Two of these properties are background and color. Background does as its name indicates. It changes the background color of the page. The color property changes the foreground color. The code to set the property is

```
document.body.style.background='red';
```

TIP *For a complete listing of the style subproperties, visit www.w3schools.com/ jsref/dom_obj_style.asp.*

Practice Changing Page Styles

In this practice, you will create an HTML form that selects colors and fonts on the page. Rather than post to a server, each form object will use the onclick event. This event runs whenever a user clicks the object, and will change a property on the page. Chapter 9 introduced events. This chapter will use them to great advantage.

1. Create a new folder called **chapter10**.

2. Create a new document called **colorChange.html** and save it in the chapter10 folder.

3. Inside of the body element, create a new form called control. Set the action to null and the method to post.

   ```
   <form id="control" method="post" action="">
   </form>
   ```

4. Inside of the form, create a paragraph tag. Inside of the <p>, type the word **Red** and create a radio button named optColor.

   ```
   <p>Red <input type="radio" name="optColor" /></p>
   ```

5. Repeat for at least two more colors.

   ```
   <p>Yellow<input type="radio" name="optColor" /></p>
   <p>White<input type="radio" name="optColor" /></p>
   ```

6. Create three more radio controls named optFont. Set the prompts for Arial, Times, and Verdana.

   ```
   <p>Arial <input type="radio" name="optFont" /></p>
   <p>Times <input type="radio" name="optFont" /></p>
   <p>Verdana <input type="radio" name="optFont" /></p>
   ```

7. After the form, create a paragraph tag with a few sentences. The content does not matter; I used the lipsum content again.

```
<p>Lorem ipsum dolor sit amet, consectetur adipiscing elit.
Integer viverra leo quis lectus faucibus et iaculis quam
blandit. Mauris quam elit, vestibulum quis auctor non,
viverra at libero. Sed blandit dictum libero id mattis. Cras
mauris sapien, consequat non hendrerit a,mattis a purus.
Aenean elit eros, posuere vel volutpat in, scelerisque sit
amet nunc.Etiam quis turpis sed enim volutpat aliquet. </p>
```

8. Save and view the page in the browser. It should resemble the following image:

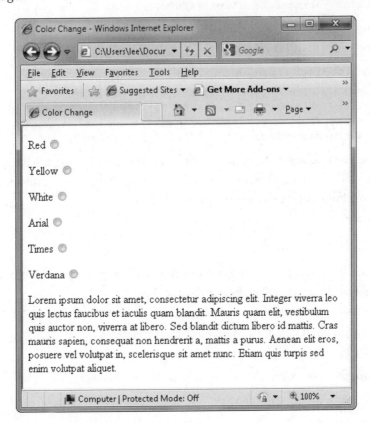

9. Create a Script section in the head of your document. Set the type to text/javascript.

10. Create a new function called changeBackcolor that accepts one parameter called bgColor.

```
function changeBackcolor(bgColor)
{
}
```

11. Add the functionality to the function. Code a line that sets the document .body.style.background property to the parameter passed in.

```
document.body.style.background=bgColor;
```

12. Now you have to call the function. Create an onclick event in the first radio button.

```
<input type="radio" name="optColor" onclick=""/>
```

13. Onclick will call the changeBackcolor function. It will pass the color of the first radio button.

```
<input type="radio" name="optColor"
onclick="changeBackcolor('#ff0000');"/>
```

14. Save and refresh the page in the browser. Click in the red radio button. Your page should turn red.

15. Repeat the onclick call for the other two colors.

```
<p>Yellow <input type="radio" name="optColor"
onclick="changeBackcolor('#ffff00');"/></p>
<p>White <input type="radio" name="optColor"
onclick="changeBackcolor('#ffffff');"/></p>
```

16. Now you will adjust the font on the page. Instead of using the background, you will set the fontFamily to a font name. Add a new function titled changeFont with a parameter titled fontName.

```
function changeFont(fontName)
{
}
```

17. Add a line of code to the function that will set the document.body.style .fontFamily property to the fontName parameter.

```
document.body.style.fontFamily=fontName;
```

18. Now you need to call the function. Find the radio button for Arial. Create an onclick event for this object.

```
<input type="radio" name="optFont" onclick=""/>
```

19. Onclick will call the changeFont function. Make it pass in the string Arial.

```
<input type="radio" name="optFont"
onclick="changeFont('Arial');"/>
```

20. Save and preview the page in the browser. Click the Arial radio button. Your font should change.

21. Repeat the onclick call for the other two fonts. Use the strings Times and Verdana.

```
<p>Times <input type="radio" name="optFont"
onclick="changeFont('Times');"/></p>
<p>Verdana <input type="radio" name="optFont"
onclick="changeFont('Verdana');"/></p>
```

22. Save and preview your page in the browser. Your font radio buttons should change the font.

23. The final code is listed in Code Block 10-2. An example of the running program is shown in this illustration:

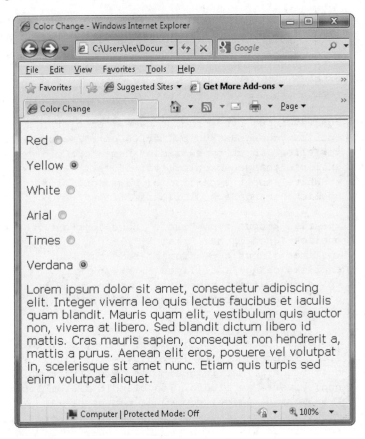

CODE BLOCK 10-2

```
<!DOCTYPE html PUBLIC "-//W3C//DTD XHTML 1.1//EN"
"http://www.w3.org/TR/xhtml11/DTD/xhtml11.dtd">
<html xmlns="http://www.w3.org/1999/xhtml" xml:lang="en">
    <head>
        <title>Color Change</title>
        <meta name="description" content="Color Change"/>
        <meta name="author" content="Lee M. Cottrell" />
        <script type="text/javascript">
        function changeBackcolor(bgColor)
        {

                document.body.style.background=bgColor;

        }

        function changeFont(fontName)
        {
                document.body.style.fontFamily=fontName;
        }
        </script>
    </head>
    <body>
    <form id="control" method="post" action="">
    <p>Red <input type="radio" name="optColor"
    onclick="changeBackcolor('#ff0000');"/></p>
    <p>Yellow <input type="radio" name="optColor"
    onclick="changeBackcolor('#ffff00');"/></p>
    <p>White <input type="radio" name="optColor"
    onclick="changeBackcolor('#ffffff');"/></p>

    <p>Arial <input type="radio" name="optFont"
    onclick="changeFont('Arial');"/></p>
    <p>Times <input type="radio" name="optFont"
    onclick="changeFont('Times');"/></p>
    <p>Verdana <input type="radio" name="optFont"
    onclick="changeFont('Verdana');"/></p>
    </form>

    <p>Lorem ipsum dolor sit amet, consectetur adipiscing
    elit. Integer viverra leo quis lectus faucibus et iaculis
    quam blandit. Mauris quam elit, vestibulum quis auctor
    non, viverra at libero. Sed blandit dictum libero id mattis.
    Cras mauris sapien, consequat non hendrerit a, mattis a
    purus. Aenean elit eros, posuere vel volutpat in,
    scelerisque sit amet nunc. Etiam quis turpis sed enim
    olutpat aliquet. </p>
    </body>
</html>
```

Rollovers

Rollovers are a common sight on the Web. A *rollover* is typically a button on the web page that reacts whenever the mouse hovers over it. The reaction is usually a visual effect, changing colors or font face. The effect is similar to the a:hover code from earlier in the text.

In this practice, you will create several buttons in two different colors, red and blue, for example. You will display the red image when the page loads. Whenever the user hovers over the red button, it will turn blue. Whenever the mouse leaves the button, it will revert to red. The images will be used to create a menu system for a web site. Instead of creating multiple pages, your <a href> will point to #. This will make the links think that they are working.

A JavaScript function called changePic will handle the rollover. ChangePic will accept two parameters. The first is the id of the <img> you wish to change. The second parameter is the path to the new image. The JavaScript will change the src property of the <img>.

TIP *The images I used for my code are available for download from www .mhprofessional.com/computingdownload.*

1. Create an **images** folder in your chapter10 folder.

2. Visit www.flamingtext.com and click the buttons link. Select a button style that you like.

3. Create three buttons using blue text. The text for each will be Home, Softball, and Baseball. Save each in the images folder as homeblue.gif, softballblue.gif, and baseballblue.gif.

4. Create three more buttons using red text. As in the previous step, the text for each will be Home, Softball, and Baseball. Save each in the images folder as homered.gif, softballred.gif, and baseballred.gif.

5. Create a new page called **rollover.html**. Save it in your chapter10 folder.

6. At the top of the body section, create a div called **header**.

7. Inside of the div tag, create three <a> tags pointing to #. Set the title attributes to say "Link to home", "Link to baseball", and "Link to softball" respectively. Place nothing between the tags.

```
<a href="#" title="Link to home"></a>
<a href="#" title="Link to baseball"></a>
<a href="#" title="Link to softball"></a>
```

8. Inside of the <a> tag for home, use the img tag to display the homeblue .gif image. Set the width, height, and alt appropriately for your image.

```
<a href="#" title="Link to home"><img
src="images/homeblue.gif" width="128" height="25"
alt="home image"/></a>
```

9. Repeat for the baseball and softball images.

```
<a href="#" title="Link to baseball"><img
src="images/baseballblue.gif" width="128" height="25"
alt="baseball image"/></a>
<a href="#" title="Link to softball"><img
src="images/softballblue.gif" width="128" height="25"
alt="softball image"/></a>
```

10. Save and preview in your browser. Your screen should resemble the following image:

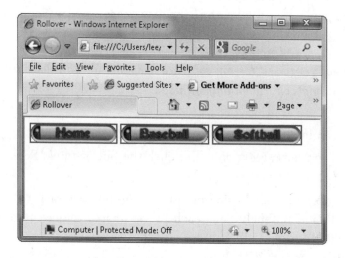

11. The blue border around the images is unnecessary and ugly. Create a style section in the head of your page.

```
<style type="text/css">
</style>
```

12. Inside of the style section, add an img element that sets the CSS border property to 0.

```
img{
      border:0;
}
```

13. Save and refresh your page in the browser. The lines will disappear.

14. To simplify the rollover code, you will name each of your images with the id attribute of the img. Inside of the attribute space of the homeblue.gif image, add id="home".

```
<img id="home" src="images/homeblue.gif" width="128"
height="25" alt="home image" />
```

15. Set id attributes for the baseball and softball images.

```
<img id="baseball" src="images/baseballblue.gif" width="128"
height="25" alt="baseball image"/>
<img id="softball" src="images/softballblue.gif" width="128"
height="25" alt="softball image"/>
```

16. Create a script tag for javascript in the head of your page, after the </style>.

```
<script type="text/javascript">
</script>
```

17. Inside of the script section, create a new function called changePic. Set changePic to accept two parameters, called imgObject and newPic.

```
function changePic(imgObject, newPic)
{
}
```

18. Inside of the {} add a line of JavaScript code that sets the src attribute to the newPic parameter.

```
imgObject.src=newPic;
```

19. Now you need to call the function in the onmouseover and onmouseout events for the homeblue.gif image. Onmouseover will pass in parameters for home and images/homered.gif. Onmouseout will pass in parameters for home and images/homeblue.gif. In the attribute space of the first image, add the following two events.

```
onmouseover="changePic(home, 'images/homered.gif');"
onmouseout="changePic(home, 'images/homeblue.gif');"
```

TIP *The second parameter is surrounded by single quotes. These are needed because the entire event code is surrounded by double quotes.*

20. Save and preview your page in the browser. Your home image should react when the mouse goes over and leaves the image. The following illustration shows my first image reacting.

21. Set the events for the baseball images. Use images/baseballred.gif and images/baseballblue.gif.

```
onmouseover="changePic(baseball, 'images/baseballred.gif');"
onmouseout="changePic(baseball, 'images/baseballblue.gif');"
```

22. Finally, set the events for the softball images. Use images/softballred.gif and images/softballblue.gif.

```
onmouseover="changePic(softball, 'images/softballred.gif');"
onmouseout="changePic(softball, 'images/softballblue.gif');"
```

23. The final code listing appears in Code Block 10-3.

CODE BLOCK 10-3

```
<!DOCTYPE html PUBLIC "-//W3C//DTD XHTML 1.1//EN"
"http://www.w3.org/TR/xhtml11/DTD/xhtml11.dtd">
<html xmlns="http://www.w3.org/1999/xhtml" xml:lang="en">
    <head>
    <title>Rollover</title>
    <meta name="description" content="Rollover"/>
    <meta name="author" content="Lee M. Cottrell" />
    <style type="text/css">
    img{
        border:0;
    }
    </style>
```

```
<script type="text/javascript">
function changePic(imgObject, newPic)
{
        imgObject.src=newPic;
}
</script>
</head>
<body>
<div id="header">
<img id="home"
onmouseover="changePic(home, 'images/homered.gif');"
onmouseout="changePic(home, 'images/homeblue.gif');"
src="images/homeblue.gif" width="128" height="25"
alt="home image"/>
<img id="baseball"
onmouseover="changePic(baseball, 'images/baseballred.gif');"
onmouseout="changePic(baseball, 'images/baseballblue.gif');"
src="images/baseballblue.gif" width="128" height="25"
alt="baseball image"/>
<img id="softball"
onmouseover="changePic(softball, 'images/softballred.gif');"
onmouseout="changePic(softball, 'images/softballblue.gif');"
src="images/softballblue.gif" width="128" height="25"
alt="softball image"/>
</div>

        </body>
</html>
```

DHTML Content Examples

The rollover and colorChange examples demonstrated how DHTML can be used to change how the page looks. While this is important, it is not DHTML's only use. DHTML can also change the content on the page.

By utilizing JavaScript events and the HTML id attributes, headers and paragraphs can be changed as desired. Through cookies, the user's preferences are saved for future visits. While not a topic in this book, DHTML can interact with PHP to read from a database. In summary, you can do anything with DHTML that you wish.

Change Paragraph Content

In this practice, you will change a page's content by clicking an object. You will change a heading and a paragraph's contents. To do this with JavaScript will take a lot of difficult code. Rather than struggling with this code, we will use a function from the JQuery library.

The JQuery script will utilize the html property of an object. The html property sets the text of an object. We will modify the rollover.html page created in this chapter. To make this JQuery function work, you will need to create an <h1> element and a <p> element, both with appropriate id tags. You will also need to remove each of your <a> tags.

1. Open the rollover.html document in your editor.

2. Save it into the chapter10 folder as **contentChange.html**.

3. Download the newest copy of the JQuery repository from jquery.com. Save it as **jquery.js** in the chapter10 folder.

4. Since this page will not actually link to another page, remove each of the <a> and </a> tags. Be sure to leave the <img> tags intact.

5. Inside of your body, after the </div>, create a new div called **content**.

6. Inside of this div, create an <h1> for home and a short paragraph describing your home page. My document is about a sports organization.

```
<div id="content">
<h1>Home Page</h1>
<p>The Community Youth Sports League supports the development
of young minds and bodies. Through our programs we teach
leadership, team work, and the value of fun.</p>
</div>
```

7. Save and preview your page in your browser. It should look like this image:

8. For the JQuery to work, you need to give the heading and paragraph an id. Set the id for the <h1> tag to be heading and the id for the <p> tag to be paragraph.

```
<div id="content">
<h1 id="heading">Home Page</h1>
<p id="paragraph">The Community Youth Sports League supports
the development of young minds and bodies. Through our
programs we teach leadership, team work, and the value of
fun.</p>
</div>
```

9. Now that the HTML is finished, you need to work on the JavaScript. Before the currently existing <script> tag in your header, add a <script> tag with a src pointing to jquery.js.

```
<script type="text/javascript" src="jquery.js"></script>
```

10. After the } for the existing function, create an entry for the $(document) .ready(function(){ });. Recall from Chapter 9 that the ready function drives when the page is ready to run DOM events.

```
$(document).ready(function() {
});
```

11. You are going to code the baseball link first. Recall that you set the id attribute of the image to "baseball".

12. Inside of the { } for the ready function create a new JQuery click event for the baseball image. $("#baseball") is how JQuery refers to the baseball image.

```
$("#baseball").click(function() {
});
```

13. Inside of the {} for the click function, create the JQuery code to change the HTML for the heading entry.

```
$("#heading").html("Baseball");
```

14. After the heading code, create the JQuery code to change the HTML for the paragraph entry.

```
$("#paragraph").html("Baseball is America's game. We offer
leagues for players from 4 to 18.");
```

15. Save and preview in your browser. Click the baseball image, your page should change as shown here:

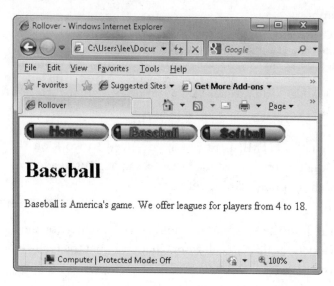

16. Now you will create the click event for softball. Placement is crucial. You currently have two sets of punctuation marks like these });. These mark the end of functions. You will begin the click event for softball between the two sets. Click your cursor between the two sets of });.

17. Using the $(#softball) object, create a click event to change the header and the paragraph.

```
$("#softball").click(function() {
$("#heading").html("Softball");
$("#paragraph").html("Softball is anything but soft. We offer
leagues for players from 4 to 18.");
});
```

18. Finally, you need to code the home button. Use the $(#home) object and create a click event to change the header and the paragraph.

```
$("#home").click(function() {
$("#heading").html("Home Page");
$("#paragraph").html("The Community Youth Sports League
supports the development of young minds and bodies. Through
our programs we teach leadership, team work, and the value of
fun.");
});
```

19. Save and refresh your page in a browser. Each button should react when clicked.

20. The final code is shown in Code Block 10-4.

CODE BLOCK 10-4

```
<!DOCTYPE html PUBLIC "-//W3C//DTD XHTML 1.1//EN"
"http://www.w3.org/TR/xhtml11/DTD/xhtml11.dtd">
<html xmlns="http://www.w3.org/1999/xhtml" xml:lang="en">
    <head>
    <title>Rollover</title>
    <meta name="description" content="Rollover"/>
    <meta name="author" content="Lee M. Cottrell" />
    <style type="text/css">
    img{
        border:0;
    }
    </style>
    <script type="text/javascript" src="jquery.js"></script>
    <script type="text/javascript">
    function changePic(imgObject, newPic)
    {
        imgObject.src=newPic;
    }
    $(document).ready(function() {
        $("#baseball").click(function() {
        $("#heading").html("Baseball");
        $("#paragraph").html("Baseball is America's game.
        We offer leagues for players from 4 to 18.");
        });

        $("#softball").click(function() {
        $("#heading").html("Softball");
        $("#paragraph").html("Softball is anything but
        soft. We offer leagues for players from 4
        to 18.");
        });

        $("#home").click(function() {
        $("#heading").html("Home Page");
        $("#paragraph").html("The Community Youth Sports
        League supports the development of young minds
        and bodies. Through our programs we teach
        leadership, team work, and the value of fun.");

    });
    });


    </script>

    </head>
```

```
<body>
<div id="header">
<img id="home"
onmouseover="changePic(home, 'images/homered.gif');"
onmouseout="changePic(home, 'images/homeblue.gif');"
src="images/homeblue.gif" width="128" height="25"/>
<img id="baseball"
onmouseover="changePic(baseball, 'images/baseballred.gif');"
onmouseout="changePic(baseball, 'images/baseballblue.gif');"
src="images/baseballblue.gif" width="128" height="25"/>
<img id="softball"
onmouseover="changePic(softball, 'images/softballred.gif');"
onmouseout="changePic(softball, 'images/softballblue.gif');"
src="images/softballblue.gif" width="128" height="25"/>
</div>
<div id="content">
<h1 id="heading">Home Page</h1>
<p id="paragraph">The Community Youth Sports League supports
the development of young minds and bodies. Through our
programs we teach leadership, team work, and the value of
fun.</p>
</div>
        </body>
</html>
```

Cookies

Cookies! Yum!! Wait, wrong type of cookies. A cookie for a web page is a small file that holds information for a web page. Contrary to popular belief, most cookies are harmless. They do not slow your computer down, and they cannot steal all of your information.

Web sites set cookies, or persistent cookies, to track data. Your local computer is used to hold the data. The cookie will hold information about the domain creating the cookie, how long the cookie lasts, and any information you desire. Once a cookie is set, the web site generating the cookie can read and use the cookie data.

Most web sites utilize cookies in some fashion. Amazon remembers the items you looked at in your last visit. Shopping carts at several online retailers depend on cookies to store your selections.

TIP *Browsers allow you to clear your cookies. In Internet Explorer 8 clear your cookies by selecting the Tools menu | Internet Options and then clicking Delete under Browsing History. For Firefox, select Tools | Clear Recent History.*

You are going to write a cookie for the colorChange.html page. Our code will write two cookies. In general, you need to set one cookie per data value you want to set. The first cookie will hold the color, and the second cookie will hold the font choice. The document.cookie property will hold the content and an expiration date. The syntax for the cookie is variable=data;expirationDate. You will write a JavaScript function called setCookie to write the cookie.

Once the cookie is set, the information is readable by the browser. Your computer will send the cookie along with the request for the web page. A JavaScript function called readCookie will parse through the contents of the cookie.

ReadCookie will call a third function called getCookieData that will strip the variables set by setCookie. GetCookie accepts a parameter holding the name of the data you wish to read. GetCookie will send it back to the ReadCookie function. ReadCookie will then set the value to the page.

Practice Writing Cookies

In this practice, you will create a cookie for a DHTML web page. The cookie will remember your color choice from the last time you visited the page.

1. Open the colorChange.html file in your editor.

2. Save the file as **colorCookie.html**.

3. Inside of the JavaScript section, create a new function called setCookie ().

```
function setCookie()
{
}
```

Still Struggling

This is the most complex code in the book. I present this code for completeness. If you feel intimidated by the code, do not feel upset. You are not alone! Cookies are very strange.

If you get confused during the step-by-step, refer to the code listing at the end of the section.

Rather than struggling with the step-by-step typing, you can download the complete code from www.mhprofessional.com/computingdownload.

4. SetCookie needs to get the current date for the expiration value of the cookie. Create a variable called expire that holds the current date and time.

```
var expire=new Date();
```

5. Your cookie will expire in one year. Modify the expire variable for one year from now.

```
expire.setDate(expire.getDate()+365);
```

6. Create two more variables called colorChoice and fontChoice that are set to the appropriate document.body.style property.

```
var colorChoice = document.body.style.background;
var fontChoice = document.body.style.fontFamily;
```

7. Set the document.cookie value for the colorChoice. Set the variable to backColor.

```
document.cookie="backColor=" +escape(colorChoice) +
";expires="+expire.toUTCString();
```

8. Set the document.cookie value for the fontChoice. Set the variable to optColor.

```
document.cookie="optFont=" +escape(fontChoice) +
";expires="+expire.toUTCString();
```

9. Call the setCookie function by adding the line **setCookie( );** as the second statement in the existing functions changeBackColor and changeFont.

10. Now you have to read the cookie contents. Create a new function called getCookieData that accepts a parameter named cookVar.

```
function getCookieData(cookVar){
}
```

11. The function getCookieData will read the cookie and find the value. It finds the value by stripping the data from after the = and before the ; in the cookie. Start by verifying that the cookie contains data. If the cookie is empty, then stop the function. Place this code inside of the curly braces for getCookieData.

```
if (document.cookie.length>0)
{
}
return "";
```

12. Find the = sign in the cookie. Set the location of the = to the cookStart variable. Add the following inside of the {} for the if statement.

```
cookStart=document.cookie.indexOf(cookVar + "=");
```

13. Check to see that cookStart actually found the = sign. If the value is not equal to –1, then the = was found. Place the following code after the cookStart line:

```
if (cookStart!=-1)
{
}
```

14. Inside of the curly braces for the if statement you just added, add the length of the cookie variable's name to the location of the cookStart. This finds the exact location of the beginning of the value.

```
cookStart=cookStart + cookVar.length+1;
```

15. After the cookStart line, determine if a ; follows the value. Then adjust the end of the value.

```
cookEnd=document.cookie.indexOf(";",cookStart);
if (cookEnd==-1)
{
        cookEnd=document.cookie.length;
}
```

16. Send the value of the cookie back to the browser. Place this code after the ending } from the if statement you just added.

```
return unescape(document.cookie.
substring(cookStart,cookEnd));
```

17. For clarity, the complete code listing for getCookieData appears here:

```
function getCookieData(cookVar)
{
        if (document.cookie.length>0)
        {
        cookStart=document.cookie.indexOf(cookVar + "=");
        if (cookStart!=-1)
        {
                cookStart=cookStart + cookVar.length+1;
                cookEnd=
                document.cookie.indexOf(";",cookStart);
                        if (cookEnd==-1)
                        {
                                cookEnd=document.cookie.length;
                        }
                        return
                        unescape(document.cookie.
                        substring(cookStart,cookEnd));
                }
        }
        return "";
}
```

18. Now you will assign the values read from the cookie to the page. Create a new function called readCookie(). Be sure it is outside of any curly braces.

```
function readCookie()
{
}
```

19. Inside of the { }, create a variable called bgColor. Set its value to a call to getCookieData for backColor.

```
var bgColor = getCookieData('backColor');
```

20. Create another variable called fontName. Set its value to a call to getCookieData for optFont.

```
var fontName = getCookieData('optFont');
```

21. Set the document.body.style background and fontFamily properties to bgColor and fontName.

```
document.body.style.background=bgColor;
document.body.style.fontFamily=fontName;
```

22. Finally, you need to call readCookie(). Create an onload event for the body tag. Call readCookie() there. The onload event fires when the page is loaded in memory or refreshed.

```
<body onload="readCookie();">
```

23. Save and refresh your page in the browser. Select a color and a font. Refresh the page, the color should change.

24. The complete JavaScript section is shown in Code Block 10-5.

CODE BLOCK 10-5

```
<script type="text/javascript">
function changeBackcolor(bgColor)
{
        document.body.style.background=bgColor;
        setCookie();
}
function changeFont(fontName)
{
        document.body.style.fontFamily=fontName;
        setCookie();
}
function readCookie()
{
        var bgColor = getCookieData('backColor');
        var fontName = getCookieData('optFont');
```

```
        document.body.style.background=bgColor;
        document.body.style.fontFamily=fontName;
}
function setCookie()
{
        var expire=new Date();
        expire.setDate(expire.getDate()+365);
        var colorChoice = document.body.style.background;
        var fontChoice = document.body.style.fontFamily;
        document.cookie="backColor=" +escape(colorChoice) +
        ";expires="+expire.toUTCString();
        document.cookie="optFont=" +escape(fontChoice) +
        ";expires="+expire.toUTCString();
}
function getCookieData(cookVar)
{
        if (document.cookie.length>0)
        {
                cookStart=document.cookie.indexOf(cookVar + "=");
                if (cookStart!=-1)
                {
                        cookStart=cookStart + cookVar.length+1;
                        cookEnd=document.cookie.indexOf
                        (";",cookStart);
                        if (cookEnd==-1)
                        {
                                cookEnd=document.cookie.length;
                        }
                        return
                        unescape(document.cookie.substring
                        (cookStart,cookEnd));

                }
        }
        return "";
}
</script>
```

Summary

In this chapter, you wrote several functions. Each function accessed the Document Object Model (DOM) and modified the page. You learned how to allow the user to change the color and font on the site. You then created a page with rollovers. This rollover page was modified to change page contents using the .html property of JQuery objects. Finally, you set and read cookies to create persistent user settings.

QUIZ

1. DOM stands for _____ .
   A. Document Object Model
   B. Document Orientation Mode
   C. Document Object Maintenance
   D. Document Object Mode

2. To change a format in the web page, you access the style property of the _____ object.
   A. body
   B. document
   C. document.body
   D. page

3. The _____ event fires when the page comes into the browser.
   A. onload
   B. onpageload
   C. onbrowserload
   D. onloadpage

4. The _____ event fires when the mouse is over an object.
   A. onhover
   B. onmouseover
   C. onmouse
   D. onmousemove

5. The _____ property of JQuery allows you to change the contents of a tag.
   A. text
   B. src
   C. contents
   D. html

6. The _____ event fires when you click an object.
   A. onclick
   B. onmouse
   C. onmousepress
   D. onmousebutton

7. A _____ is data passed to a function.
   A. variable
   B. parameter
   C. constant
   D. value

8. To make the <a href> point to the current page, use the _____ symbol.
    A. $
    B. #
    C. @
    D. %

9. Cookies contain two pieces of data. Which is the correct syntax for the cookie?
    A. expirationData;variable=data
    B. variable=data;expirationDate
    C. data;variable;exiprationDate
    D. variable;data; exiprationDate

10. Use the _____ attribute to name HTML objects for use in JavaScript.
    A. name
    B. title
    C. id
    D. alt

chapter 11

Effectively Using Multimedia

In this chapter, you will learn how to embed common multimedia elements onto your pages. You will start with sound. From sound, you will move to flash animations and finally movies. In each section, I place emphasis on the proper usage of the technology.

CHAPTER OBJECTIVES

In this chapter, you will

- Play sounds on a web page
- Embed Flash videos
- Play movies on a web page

Multimedia is a term from an older era. The term was coined when computers were first being able to play authentic sounds and display quality graphics simultaneously. While the term is dated, the concepts are still valid. A multimedia web site is one that plays sounds, images, and even videos at the same time.

When multimedia first hit the scene, few people knew how to use the technologies. Many developers thought that the more multimedia, the better. They threw sounds, pictures, animations, and movies on every page. Thankfully, the technology has matured into a powerful tool.

Sound

Computers can play the most realistic sounds. Nearly every computer has a high-quality sound card built in. Most are capable of playing full surround sound over at least five separate channels. Computers store sounds in a special type of file.

There are dozens of different types of sound files. The three most common are waveform (WAV) files, Musical Instrument Digital Interface (MIDI), and MP3 files. Each file type has an appropriate usage.

TIP   *Be very careful using sounds on a web site. The vast majority of sounds available are copyrighted to another person. Before using any sound, make sure that you either own the sound or have total legal rights to the sound. As for MP3 files, never use them unless you happen to be a part of the band that owns the copyright to the song.*

Typically, WAV sounds play short sounds. Recordings of sounds, people speaking and some computer-animated sounds are stored as WAV files. On a Windows computer, all of the sounds played by Windows are WAV files.

MIDI files hold computer-generated versions of sounds. The MIDI file contains actual recordings of actual instruments. Thus, the MIDI file can sound exceptional when crafted by a professional musician. A good source online for MIDI files is www.mididb.com/.

Lastly, there is the MP3 file. The MP3 file holds a recording of a song. MP3s are created by sampling the song at a certain interval. This sampling degrades the quality of the sound but makes it small enough for storage on your computer. There is no reason to play a MP3 file directly on your page.

TIP *MP3 and WAV files can both store songs on your computer. The difference is quality and file size. The WAV file will sound true to life, while taking up about 1MB per second of song. MP3 files are of lower quality but take up about 1MB per minute of song, or 60 times less space. In practical terms, a 1GB MP3 player will hold about 5 three-minute WAV songs, or about 300 three-minute MP3 songs.*

Embedding Sounds

An embedded sound is one that plays whenever the page is loaded. If done poorly, it can really irritate the viewer. Only use an embedded sound if it truly adds to the page. A good example would be a spooky web site. Spooky music when the page loads might add to the experience. However, the music might interfere with other sounds the user is playing.

Embedded sounds will play through a helper object. Depending on your system setup, the helper could be Windows Media Player, Winamp, QuickTime, or some other media player. While each has its own fans, each does what is needed to play your sounds.

TIP *Picking a background sound is like picking a background image. It should not interfere with the page. Extremely loud or annoying sounds will cause your user to leave your page.*

There are two methods of embedding sounds in a web site. The current recommended method is the <object> tag. The object tag allows the inclusion of nearly any type of file. However, it is rather difficult to code. Code Block 11-1 shows an example of the embed code to play a MIDI file called rhapsody.mid.

CODE BLOCK 11-1

```
<body>
<object classid="clsid: 22D6F312-B0F6-11D0-94AB-0080C74C7E95">
<param name="FileName" value="rhapsody.mid" />
</object>
</body>
</html>
```

Wow, look at all of the random numbers. Those numbers are not random; they are the identifying number for a version of Microsoft Windows Media Player. Different objects have a different number. Inside of the <object> tag is the param tag. This tag passes information to the <object> tag; similar to how a parameter passes information to a JavaScript function. The file I am playing is a MIDI file called rhapsody.mid.

The following illustration shows the visual output of Code Block 11-1. Notice that a media player bar appears, allowing the user to stop the music. If you choose to embed music, you should include a way to stop the music.

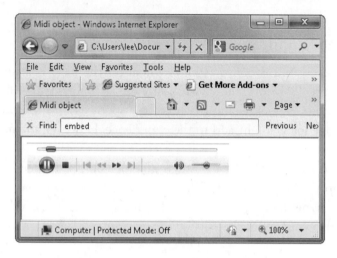

The object tag is the correct and verifiable way to embed music in your page. However, it does not work on all browsers. The tag that does work is the <embed> tag.

The <embed> tag has been around the HTML community for several years. Every major browser supports it. However, it is not included in the current HTML recommendation. This means that using <embed> will result in a page that cannot be validated.

TIP   *Recall that the W3C stands for the World Wide Web Consortium. W3C creates and maintains HTML specifications.*

You might be thinking, why use a tag that is not recognized by the W3C? The reason is that W3C has included the <embed> tag in the upcoming HTML 5 standard. HTML 5 has streamlined the use of all multimedia objects, including sound, flash animations, and movies. Embed is an officially recognized tag. Modern browsers support the HTML 5 version. Unless your company insists on strict validation, use the embed tag instead of the <object> tag.

Code Block 11-2 shows the same MIDI file using the embed tag. It is much cleaner than the object tag. No random letters and a simple one-line tag. This image shows the embed tag in Internet Explorer:

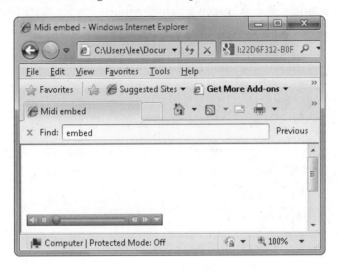

CODE BLOCK 11-2

```
<body>
<embed src="rhapsody.mid"/>
</body>
```

TIP *Install the QuickTime plug-in for Firefox to allow Code Block 11-2 to run.*

Embed has three additional properties that are useful. The height and width properties set the size of the object on screen. Setting both to 0 will effectively hide the object from the user, but the sound will still play. I have found that a height of 10 will make the bar small enough to tuck into the corner of a header or footer section of the page, yet still be large enough to control the file. The loop property, when set to true, will continuously play the sound.

Playing Sounds on Demand

This is the preferred method of playing sounds. Let the user click a link and the sound will play. Sites that sell music like itunes.com and amazon.com include this on every song. Click a button and a portion of the song plays.

The simplest method of playing a sound on demand is to use a hyperlink. Create an <a> tag pointing to the sound. When the link is clicked, the browser will offer to play or save the sound file. The following image shows Internet Explorer's choice of saving the sound or opening it. Opening the file will create a new window for the helper objects. Firefox will play the WAV or MIDI sound in a Firefox window. It will launch a helper application for MP3 files.

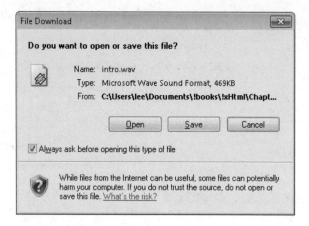

Practice Playing Sounds on Demand

Before starting, gather three sounds, a WAV file, a MP3 file, and a MIDI file. I used intro.wav, rhapsody.mid, and dollars.mp3. There are many web sites specializing in sound files.

1. Create a folder titled **chapter11**.

2. Under chapter11, create a folder titled **sounds**.

3. Place your three sound files into the chapter11\sounds folder.

4. Create a new document titled **ondemand.html**. Save in the chapter11 folder.

5. Create an appropriate title and meta tag information.

6. Create a \<h1\> tag holding Sounds On Demand.

   ```
   <h1>Sounds On Demand</h1>
   ```

7. Under the \<h1\>, create a link to the first sound. Be sure to set the title attribute of the link appropriately.

   ```
   <a href="sounds/intro.wav" title="link that plays intro.wav">
   intro.wav</a>
   ```

8. Save and view the page in your browser. Click the link. Select Open to play the file.

9. Repeat for your other files. Verify that each works on click. The next illustration shows Firefox playing rhapsody.mid in a window using my default helper application QuickTime.

10. The final code listing appears in Code Block 11-3.

CODE BLOCK 11-3

```
<!DOCTYPE html PUBLIC "-//W3C//DTD XHTML 1.1//EN"
"http://www.w3.org/TR/xhtml11/DTD/xhtml11.dtd">
<html xmlns="http://www.w3.org/1999/xhtml" xml:lang="en">
     <head>
          <title>OnDemand Sounds</title>
          <meta name="description"
          content="OnDemand Sounds"/>
          <meta name="author" content="Lee M. Cottrell" />
     </head>
     <body>
     <h1>Sounds On Demand</h1>
     <a href="sounds/intro.wav"
     title="link that plays intro.wav">intro.wav</a>
     <a href="sounds/dollars.mp3"
     title="link that plays dollars.mp3">dollars.mp3</a>
     <a href="sounds/rhapsody.mid"
     title="link that plays rhapsody.mid">rhapsody.mid</a>
     </body>
</html>
```

Flash

One of the most popular types of multimedia application found on the Web is the Flash file. Flash is a trademark of Adobe. Flash files are typically created using Adobe Flash Professional.

Flash can create many types of animations. I have seen menus, movies, games, and even entire pages built with Flash. In the hands of a trained designer, Flash can create wondrous things. Flash files are stored with a .swf extension.

TIP *SWF has many meanings. Small Web Format is the proper meaning. However in practice, it stands for ShockWave Flash.*

To create Flash, you need Adobe Flash Professional. Flash Professional by itself retails for nearly $700. Alternatively, Flash is part of the Adobe Creative Suite, which retails for nearly $1800. Before plunking this amount of money for a product, try it out. Adobe offers trials of nearly all of its products. These are available from www.adobe.com/downloads/. To use Flash on your web site, you need the free Flash Player installed on your system. The Flash plug-in is available from www.adobe.com/products/flashplayer/.

Creating Flash animations is beyond the scope of this book. It is an excellent second class in web design, though. If you want to get your feet wet using Flash, w3schools has a good basic tutorial at www.w3schools.com/flash/flash_howto.asp.

TIP *My demystified.swf file is available for download from www.mhprofessional .com/computingdownload.*

Embedding Flash

Normally, Flash videos are embedded in a page, playing automatically after the page loads. The video will appear in a player box sized per your code. Code Block 11-4 lists the bare minimum code needed to embed a Flash video. To run this code, substitute moviename.swf for the name of your movie. Set the width and height accordingly.

CODE BLOCK 11-4

```
<object width="300" height="400">
<param name="movie" value="movieName.swf">
<embed src="movieName.swf" width="300" height="400">
</embed>
</object>
```

FIGURE 11-1 · Demystified playing in Internet Explorer

This is rather complicated. Two different tags for embedding appear. The object tag works in Internet Explorer while the embed tag works everywhere else. The width and height attributes set the size of the Flash window. The src or value properties set the name of the SWF file to play. Figure 11-1 shows my simple Flash video playing in Explorer.

Code Block 11-4 is the minimum code to play Flash. You can use other parameters. The clsid parameter for the first object tag completely identifies the object as a Flash file. Additionally, the clsid will direct Internet Explorer to download the player if it is not installed. The second object directs Firefox to play the flash file. Code Block 11-5 shows a simple yet complete embedding of a SWF file. As in the preceding example, replace movieName.swf with the name of your SWF file.

CODE BLOCK 11-5

```
<div><object classid="clsid:d27cdb6e-ae6d-11cf-96b8-444553540000"
width="300" height="400">
<param name="movie" value="movieName.swf">
```

```
<param name="play" value="true" />
<object type="application/x-shockwave-flash" data="movieName.swf"
width="300" height="400"></object>
</object>
</div>
```

This is a lot of code. However, you may not need to remember it all. Flash Professional generates the complete code for your movie. When you publish your movie in Flash Professional, it will create the .SWF file and an HTML file. The HTML holds correct values for the width, height, clsid, and plugsinpage attributes. Additional parameters such as color depth, quality, and loop may also be set. Copy and paste the code from the HTML to your page.

TIP *Flash Professional's code will not validate. To fix this problem, remove the align property from the first object.*

Practice Embedding a Flash Animation

You are going to embed a SWF file into a web page. You will set the preferred size, set the high quality, and cause it to play at load. You will ensure that the file plays in all browsers. If you have not downloaded my demystified.swf file, you can do so at www.mhprofessional.com/computingdownload.

1. Create a new page based on your template called **flash.html**. Save it in your chapter11 folder.

2. Set an appropriate title and meta tag information.

3. Create a div tag. Objects should be included within another tag. The div is only for validation.

4. In the div tag, create the object tag for Internet Explorer. Use the clsid to D27CDB6E-AE6D-11cf-96B8-444553540000. Set the width to 600 and the height to 300.

   ```
   <object classid="clsid:d27cdb6e-ae6d-11cf-96b8-444553540000"
   width="600" height="300">
   </object>
   ```

5. Inside of the object, create a param tag. Set the name attribute to movie and the value attribute to demystified.swf.

   ```
   <param name="movie" value="demystified.swf" />
   ```

6. Create another param tag. Set the name attribute to play and the value to true.

```
<param name="play" value="true" />
```

7. Finally, set the param for high quality.

```
<param name="quality" value="high" />
```

8. Save and view your page in Internet Explorer. It should look like Figure 11-1.

9. This file will not load in Firefox or Chrome. You need to use another object. Right before the current </object> tag, create another object tag. Set the type to application/x-shockwave-flash. If you placed the object correctly, you will have back-to-back close object tags.

```
<object type="application/x-shockwave-flash">
</object>
```

10. The Shockwave object accepts more parameters than the IE one. Inside of the attribute space for your new object, create a data attribute with the value of demystified.swf.

```
<object type="application/x-shockwave-flash"
data="demystified.swf" >
</object>
```

11. Add attributes of height and width to your object. The final object is here:

```
<object type="application/x-shockwave-flash"
data="demystified.swf"
width="600" height="300">
</object>
```

12. Inside of your Shockwave object, set the parameter for high quality as you did in Step 7.

```
<param name="quality" value="high" />
```

13. Save and open your file in Firefox. It will resemble the illustration shown next. The final code is in Code Block 11-6.

CODE BLOCK 11-6

```
<!DOCTYPE html PUBLIC "-//W3C//DTD XHTML 1.1//EN"
"http://www.w3.org/TR/xhtml11/DTD/xhtml11.dtd">
<html xmlns="http://www.w3.org/1999/xhtml" xml:lang="en">
    <head>
        <title>Flash</title>
        <meta name="description" content="Flash"/>
        <meta name="author" content="Lee M. Cottrell" />
    </head>
    <body>
    <div>
    <object classid="clsid:d27cdb6e-ae6d-11cf-96b8-
    444553540000" width="600" height="300">
            <param name="movie" value="demystified
            .swf" />
            <param name="play" value="true" />
            <param name="quality" value="high" />
            <object type="application/x-shockwave-
            flash" data="demystified.swf"
            width="600" height="300">
```

```
                    <param name="quality" value="high" />
                    </object>
        </object>
        </div>
        </body>
    </html>
```

Movies

Just a few years ago, movies on the Web were very rare. Then YouTube.com launched and millions of people (including myself) found a way to display their movies. With the launch of YouTube, videos started appearing on many web sites.

You have many decisions to make when creating videos for the Internet. Your first choice is where to host the video. You can host your videos on your own site or at a third-party hosting site like YouTube. Hosting the movie on your own site has a few advantages. The first is speed. Sites on your own server are likely to launch faster than from a different server. Second, you have complete control over the video. Some third-party sites add advertisements to the videos. The downside of self-hosting is server space and bandwidth issues. Movies take up a lot of space on a server. Having many movies would require a large amount of disk space. Bandwidth issues are a little fuzzy. Many web-hosting plans include a bandwidth cap. This cap controls the amount of data sent from your server. Exceeding the cap will cost extra money.

Off-site, or third-party, hosting is very popular. However, the benefits and drawbacks are reversed for self-hosted videos. Load time can be slower, and you may have ads forced upon your page. However, space and bandwidth issues are nonexistent.

For a professional-level page, you should host the video on your server. By hosting the file on your server, you enable your viewers to enjoy the movie at the highest speed. For other sites, self-hosting video files is not necessary. Off-

Still Struggling

Bandwidth caps are very similar to minute limits on a cell phone plan. Exceed your minutes and you pay dearly.

site hosting through YouTube or another online video hosting service is appropriate.

The second choice you need to make is the type of video. The most commonly used video types are Windows Media, RealVideo and QuickTime videos. Unfortunately, each needs a different object type with different parameters. I recommend deciding on a consistent video type and generating a template page for videos. This way, you only need to learn one form of video object code.

Playing Movies on a Click

The simplest way to use videos on your site is to link to them. You provide a link to the movie to play. Once clicked, the movie plays in a helper object on the user's machine. This helper object is either Windows Media Player, Winamp, QuickTime, VLC, or another video player. Once clicked, the user can choose to download or play the video. The illustration here shows the demystified .wmv file playing in Winamp. Code Block 11-7 shows the <a> tag necessary to play a movie.

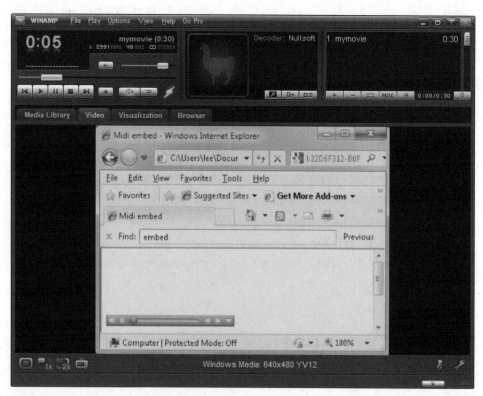

CODE BLOCK 11-7

```
<a href="mymovie.wmv" title="Link to a movie">Play Movie</a>
```

There are many downsides to linking to the movie. The first is the assumption that the user has the appropriate player and codec. A *codec* is a small program that tells your video player how to access and use the video. The second is users may not trust a linked video. There are many instances of Trojan horses embedded inside of videos. Finally, when your video opens in another window, your customer leaves your page.

Embedding Movies

Actually embedding a movie into your site takes more work. As with the Flash videos from earlier, you need to create objects to run the movies. As with Flash, Internet Explorer uses different helpers than Firefox. This requires you to code two separate objects.

Recall the choices from earlier. If you hosted your movie on YouTube.com, then they have done all of the work for you. The page showing the desired video includes a link to the correct HTML code to embed the video into your site.

Practice Embedding YouTube Videos

In this practice, you will embed a YouTube video directly onto your web page. The steps will link to a movie I created for this book. However, you can substitute my movie for something that you enjoy.

1. Create a new file based on your template called **youTubeEmbed.html**. Save it in the chapter11 folder.

2. Set an appropriate title and meta tag information.

3. Create a div tag inside of the body.

   ```
   <div>
   </div>
   ```

4. Browse to YouTube.com. Search for "mrcottrellbradford demystified".

5. Click the video to start playing it.

6. As shown in this illustration, click the Embed button, which is below and to the right of the image.

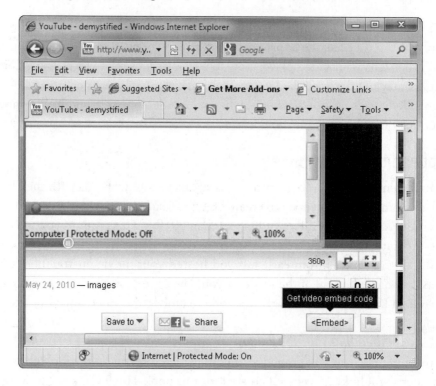

7. Copy the object code from the text box.

8. Paste the code inside of the div.

9. Save and view in your browser. Figure 11-2 shows the video before playing. Notice the YouTube logo in the lower-right corner. The final code is in Code Block 11-8.

CODE BLOCK 11-8

```
<!DOCTYPE html PUBLIC "-//W3C//DTD XHTML 1.1//EN"
"http://www.w3.org/TR/xhtml11/DTD/xhtml11.dtd">
<html xmlns="http://www.w3.org/1999/xhtml" xml:lang="en">
    <head>
        <title>YouTube embed</title>
        <meta name="description" content="YouTube embed"/>
        <meta name="author" content="Lee M. Cottrell" />
    </head>
    <body>
    <div>
    <object width="480" height="385"><param name="movie"
```

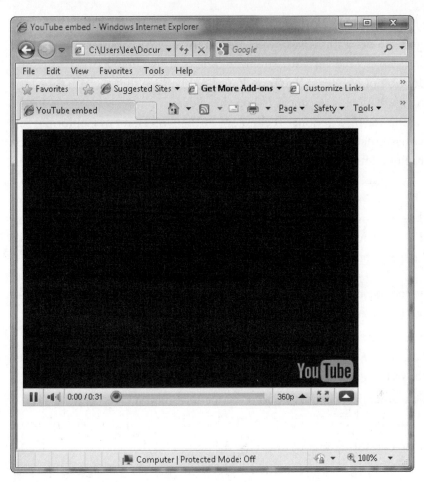

FIGURE 11-2 • Demystified starting to play from YouTube.com

```
value="http://www.youtube.com/v/eBDP68Gbonw&hl=en_
US&fs=1&rel=0">
</param><param name="allowFullScreen" value="true"></param>
<param name="allowscriptaccess" value="always"></param>
<embed src="http://www.youtube.com/v/eBDP68Gbonw&hl=en_
US&fs=1&rel=0" type="application/x-shockwave-flash"
allowscriptaccess="always" allowfullscreen="true" width="480"
height="385"></embed></object>
        </div>
        </body>
</html>
```

Practice Playing Movies Hosted on Your Site

You are going to use a third-party web site to generate the complex code needed to play a video hosted on your site. My code will use demystified.wmv, the same video you played from YouTube. You should notice that the YouTube logo visible in Figure 11-2 is not included on this video.

The Center for Instructional Technology at the University of California, San Francisco has created an Embedded Media HTML Generator. Hosted at cit .ucsf.edu/embedmedia/step1.php, this site will ask a few questions and then generate the code to play your movie.

Before beginning this practice, download the demystified.wmv file from www.mhprofessional.com/computingdownload. Save the movie file in the chapter11 folder. You may use any video of your choice, but you will have to adjust the directions.

TIP *The code generated in the following example will play on both Explorer and Firefox. The players will look a little different between the two browsers.*

1. Create a new file based on your template. Save it in the chapter11 folder as **movieEmbed.html**.

2. Create an appropriate title and meta tag information.

3. Use your browser to navigate to cit.ucsf.edu/embedmedia/step1.php.

4. For the demystified.wmv file, select Windows Media.

5. The second page requires some input. Do not place anything in the server field. Put demystified.wmv in the file path field. The optimal size of the video is 640 × 480, although a smaller size would work. Set the last properties as you desire, although I checked off start automatically. Click the Submit button when you are ready. The next illustration shows my completed form.

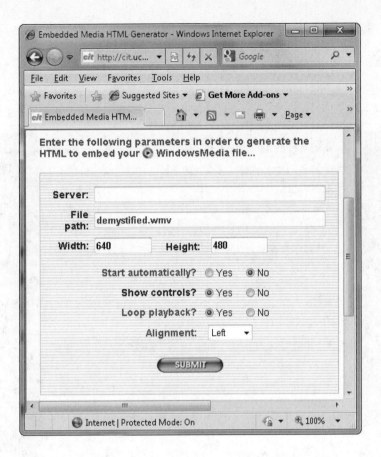

6. The third page shows the completed code. The test buttons will not work because your video is on your hard drive rather than a web site. Copy the created code, starting after the first line with <?>.

7. Paste the code into your HTML file between the body tags.

8. Save and preview in a browser. Click the Play button. Your movie should be playing as in shown in the following image.

9. The final code is in Code Block 11-9.

CODE BLOCK 11-9

```
<!DOCTYPE html PUBLIC "-//W3C//DTD XHTML 1.1//EN"
"http://www.w3.org/TR/xhtml11/DTD/xhtml11.dtd">
<html xmlns="http://www.w3.org/1999/xhtml" xml:lang="en">
    <head>
        <title>Movie embed</title>
        <meta name="description" content="Movie embed"/>
        <meta name="author" content="Lee M. Cottrell" />
    </head>
    <body>
    <!-- begin embedded WindowsMedia file... -->
    <table border='0' cellpadding='0' align="left">
```

```
    <tr><td>
    <OBJECT id='mediaPlayer' width="640" height="525"
    classid='CLSID:22d6f312-b0f6-11d0-94ab-0080c74c7e95'
    codebase='http://activex.microsoft.com/activex/
    controls/mplayer/en/nsmp2inf.cab#Version=5,1,52,701'
    standby='Loading Microsoft Windows Media Player
    components...' type='application/x-oleobject'>
    <param name='fileName' value="demystified.wmv">
    <param name='animationatStart' value='true'>
    <param name='transparentatStart' value='true'>
    <param name='autoStart' value="false">
    <param name='showControls' value="true">
    <param name='loop' value="true">
    <EMBED type='application/x-mplayer2'
      pluginspage=
      'http://microsoft.com/windows/mediaplayer/en/download/'
      id='mediaPlayer' name='mediaPlayer' displaysize='4'
      autosize='-1'
      bgcolor='darkblue' showcontrols="true" showtracker='-1'
      showdisplay='0' showstatusbar='-1' videoborder3d='-1'
      width="640" height="525"
      src="demystified.wmv" autostart="false"
      designtimesp='5311' loop="true">
    </EMBED>
    </OBJECT>
    </td></tr>
    <!-- ...end embedded WindowsMedia file -->
  <!-- begin link to launch external media player... -->
    <tr><td align='center'>
    <a href="demystified.wmv"
    style='font-size: 85%;' target='_blank'>
    Launch in external player</a>
    <!-- ...end link to launch external media player... -->
    </td></tr>
    </table>
    </body>
  </html>
```

HTML 5 Preview

As evidenced by the complex code in this book, HTML 4.01 does a lousy job of handling videos. Needing to use different players in the most popular browsers is very inefficient.

HTML 5, while not yet official as of this printing, will simplify video playing. Rather than depend on separate players controlled through the object tag,

HTML 5 introduces the video tag. The complex code generated in Code Block 11-9 is reduced to

```
<video src="demystified.wmv" controls="controls" width="640"
 height="480" />
```

Do not try this code. It is currently only supported in Internet Explorer 9, Firefox 3.5, all versions of Safari, Chrome, and Opera. I use the word supported very loosely here. The standard, while nearly complete, is still changing. Additionally, HTML 5 videos will need to utilize a new technology called WebM Transcodes. Without this technology, video playing will be as complex as it is currently.

Summary

Multimedia additions to your web site, if handled correctly, will have a positive impact on your user's experience. The sound file is the first type of multimedia file you learned how to include. You learned to play the sound on a click and embed the song as a background sound. From sounds, you moved on to the most prevalent form of animation on the Web, the Flash video. Like sounds, you learned how to play a video on demand. Finally, you learned to embed movies from YouTube and those hosted on your own site.

QUIZ

1. **This is the most common type of animation.**
   A. Flash
   B. MP4
   C. WMV
   D. Ogg

2. **The _____ tag is the easy way to create a background sound.**
   A. object
   B. wav
   C. winamp
   D. embed

3. **To play a video in Internet Explorer, you need the correct _____, set to a seemingly random series of letters and numbers.**
   A. object
   B. clsid
   C. src
   D. name

4. **Passing a value into the object tag is the job of the _____ tag.**
   A. value
   B. param
   C. data
   D. send

5. **Flash files are stored with a(n) _____ extension.**
   A. fla
   B. swf
   C. wmv
   D. fsh

6. **To play a sound on a click, you should use a _____ tag.**
   A. sound
   B. embed
   C. a
   D. link

7. **In HTML 5, the _____ tag will be used to play movies.**
   A. embed
   B. video
   C. flash
   D. movie

8. **The recommended tag for playing flash, sounds, or movies in Internet Explorer is the _____ tag.**

    A. object

    B. embed

    C. video

    D. link

9. **Creating a Flash file requires _____ .**

    A. Adobe Creative Suite

    B. Adobe Illustrator

    C. Adobe Flash Professional

    D. Adobe Dreamweaver

10. **Storing your movies on _____ requires a lot of space and high bandwidth.**

    A. YouTube

    B. Hulu

    C. your web site

    D. Google

chapter **12**

Using Frames

In this chapter, you will create a web site that uses frames. Frames provide an excellent, if dated, way to arrange your pages.

CHAPTER OBJECTIVES

In this chapter, you will

- Define frames
- Create frames
- Navigate through frames
- Format frames
- Use iFrames

Up to now, you have had one HTML page per browser window. A frame allows you to display multiple pages in one window. Frames, when used correctly, create an efficient navigation structure for a web page.

Frames are rarely used in modern HTML. The reasons are many. First, navigating framed pages is difficult for the visually impaired. Second, a framed page loads slower than a single page. Finally, CSS layout techniques have replaced the framed layout.

Briefly, a frame is an excellent, simple way to organize your web site. Despite this, the web design community has turned their backs on frames in favor of CSS. After reading through the chapter, you can make up your own mind.

Defining Frames

Frames break your browser window into several panes. Each pane holds a separate HTML document. The most common usage for frames was creating page navigation. One pane, typically a left pane or the top pane, had links. These links changed the page loaded in a content pane. The panes themselves required a frameset document defining the positioning and sizes of the panes.

Designing layouts with frames is easier than using CSS. The CSS layouts we presented earlier in the book required a thorough understanding of the CSS box model. The developer is required to code several CSS properties to make divisions float. Frames simplify layout by reducing the layout to rows and columns. This simplicity does have its drawbacks. A framed document only contains rectangular panes. CSS documents are capable of creating sections of varying sizes and shapes.

Creating Frames

Creating frames in HTML is much different than creating a standard page. The first difference is the number of pages that need to be created. For a page with two frames, you need to create three documents. You create two HTML documents for the contents of the frames, and one frameset document that describes the frame.

This frameset document provides the second big difference from creating a standard web page. The frameset page has no body. In the place of the body tag, you create <frameset> tags. The <frameset> tags describe the number and sizes of rows and columns in the window. The frameset tag will hold one attribute:

either rows or cols. Regardless of the attribute selected, the value will be a list of the sizes of the panes. The number of values indicates the number of panes. Code Block 12-1 shows the frameset tag for a three-column frameset. The first and last column each represents 25 percent of the page, while the middle column is the remaining 50 percent.

TIP *The sizes for rows or cols can be represented in pixels.*

CODE BLOCK 12-1

```
<frameset cols="25%, 50%, 25%">
</frameset>
```

TIP *If you use an asterisk (*) in the list for the size value, the browser will use the remaining space for the corresponding row or column.*

Contained within the frameset tag will be the <frame> tag. The frame tag contains several attributes, the most important of which are listed in Table 12-1. As a bare minimum, the frame tag should contain the src attribute. Like the <img> tag, the src provides the URL for the HTML page to be displayed in the frame.

Viewing Code Block 12-1 will result in a blank page in your browser. The frameset tag needs three frame tags nested within it, one for each column. Each frame tag will point to a unique HTML document. This document will provide the content for the pane. Code Block 12-2 shows the three frame tags. Pay special attention to the src attributes of each frame tag. Notice that each has a unique file name.

TABLE 12-1 Attributes of the Frame Tag

Attribute	Description	Values
frameborder	Toggle turning the border on or off.	1 = border on 0 = border off
marginheight	Width of margin between frame border and text.	Pixels
marginwidth	Width of margin between frame border and text.	Pixels
name	The name of the pane. Be sure that your names are very descriptive.	
noresize	Toggle describing if the frame can be resized.	
src	URL to the contents of the page.	

CODE BLOCK 12-2

```
<frameset cols="25%, 50%, 25%">
    <frame src="leftFrame.html" name="leftFrame"></frame>
    <frame src="middleFrame.html" name="middleFrame"></frame>
    <frame src="rightFrame.html" name="rightFrame"></frame>
</frameset>
```

TIP *The frame tags should be listed in the order that you wish the frames to appear.*

Not all browsers display frames. Your code needs to reflect this. After the last frame tag, you need to include a noframe tag. This tag will contain a valid HTML body. The body will contain a message describing the frame layout, and contain links to the pages contained within the frames. Code Block 12-3 shows the completed frameset page. This illustration shows the frames in Internet Explorer.

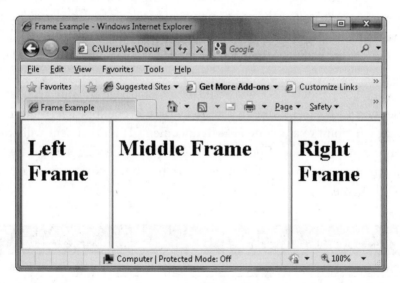

CODE BLOCK 12-3

```
<!DOCTYPE html PUBLIC "-//W3C//DTD XHTML 1.0 Frameset//EN"
"http://www.w3.org/TR/xhtml1/DTD/xhtml1-frameset.dtd">
<html xmlns="http://www.w3.org/1999/xhtml" xml:lang="en">
```

```
<head>
        <title>Frame Example</title>
        <meta name="description" content="Code Block 12-1"/>
        <meta name="author" content="Lee M. Cottrell" />
</head>
<frameset cols="25%, 50%, 25%">
        <frame src="leftFrame.html" name="leftFrame"></frame>
        <frame src="middleFrame.html" name="middleFrame"></frame>
        <frame src="rightFrame.html" name="rightFrame"></frame>
        <noframes>
        <body>
        <p>This page contains frames. Your browser is not
        displaying them. The page contents follow.</p>
        <ul>
        <li><a href="leftFrame.html" title="Link to left frame">
        </a></li>
        <li><a href="middleFrame.html" title="Link to middle frame">
        </a></li>
        <li><a href="rightFrame.html" title="Link to right frame">
        </a></li>
        </ul>
        </body>
        </noframes>
    </frameset>
</html>
```

Code Block 12-3 shows the final difference between normal web pages and frameset documents. The doctype in the first line is different than the ones presented throughout this book. Up until this point, we have been using the strict doctype. The strict doctype does not support frames. While the page would work, it would not validate. For your frameset documents, be sure to use the doctype shown here:

```
<!DOCTYPE html PUBLIC "-//W3C//DTD XHTML 1.0 Frameset//EN"
"http://www.w3.org/TR/xhtml1/DTD/xhtml1-frameset.dtd">
```

Nested Framesets

Code Block 12-3 presented a three-column frameset. By changing the cols attribute in the frameset to rows, your page will be displayed in rows as shown in the next illustration. I left the original frame src entries to prove that changing layout was very easy.

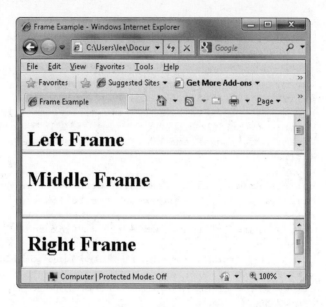

You need to nest framesets if you want both rows and columns. Nesting means to place a frameset tag within a frameset tag. You will place the frameset tag precisely where you want the additional frameset. The code in Code Block 12-4 produces the three-column, two-row frameset displayed in this illustration. I wanted to modify the middle column, so I placed the nested frameset tag immediately after the first column. This nested frameset generates two rows within the second column. Inside of the inner frameset, I included two frame tags creating the horizontal frame elements.

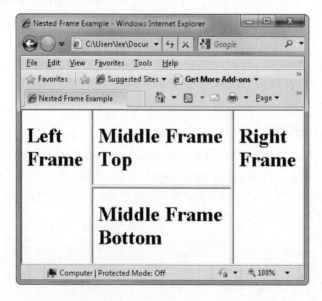

CODE BLOCK 12-4

```
<!DOCTYPE html PUBLIC "-//W3C//DTD XHTML 1.0 Frameset//EN"
"http://www.w3.org/TR/xhtml1/DTD/xhtml1-frameset.dtd">
<html xmlns="http://www.w3.org/1999/xhtml" xml:lang="en">
     <head>
          <title>Nested Frame Example</title>
          <meta name="description" content="Code Block 12-4"/>
          <meta name="author" content="Lee M. Cottrell" />
     </head>
     <frameset cols="25%, 50%, 25%">
          <frame src="leftFrame.html" name="leftFrame"></frame>
          <frameset rows="50%, *">
              <frame src="middleFrameTop.html" name="midTop">
                  </frame>
              <frame src="middleFrameBottom.html" name="midBottom">
                  </frame>
          </frameset>
          <frame src="rightFrame.html" name="rightFrame"></frame>
          <noframes>
          <body>
          <p>This page contains frames. Your browser is not displaying
              them. The page contents follow.</p>
          <ul>
          <li><a href="leftFrame.html" title="Link to left frame">
              </a></li>
          <li><a href="middleFrameTop.html"
              title="Link to middle top frame"></a></li>
          <li><a href="middleFrameBottom.html"
              title="Link to middle Bottom frame"></a></li>
          <li><a href="rightFrame.html"
              title="Link to right frame"></a></li>
          </ul>
          </body>
          </noframes>
     </frameset>
</html>
```

Practice Creating Nested Framesets

In this practice, you are going to create a frameset about music with three panes. You will have two rows. The top row will contain a banner. The second row is split into two panes. The left pane will handle navigation for the page.

The right pane will display the content for the page. This practice will only configure the frames. Later in the chapter, you will actually create the functionality.

1. Create a new folder called **chapter12**.

2. Create four new files based on your template. Save them as **frameset.html**, **banner.html**, **navigation.html**, and **content.html**. Save them in the chapter12 folder.

3. Switch to the banner.html file. Create a <h1> holding Music Types.

   ```
   <h1>Music Types</h1>
   ```

4. Switch to the navigation.html file. For now just put a <h3> holding Links.

   ```
   <h3>Links</h3>
   ```

5. Switch to the content.html file. For now just put a <h1> holding Content.

   ```
   <h1>Content</h1>
   ```

6. Switch to the frameset.html document.

7. Change the doctype at the top of the document to the frameset doctype.

   ```
   <!DOCTYPE html PUBLIC "-//W3C//DTD XHTML 1.0 Frameset//EN"
   "http://www.w3.org/TR/xhtml1/DTD/xhtml1-frameset.dtd">
   ```

8. Change the title to Music Types. Set the meta tag appropriately.

9. Delete the open and close body tags.

10. Create a frameset tag defining two rows. The first row is 100 pixels high. The second row is the remaining portion of the page.

    ```
    <frameset rows="100,* ">
    </frameset>
    ```

11. Create a frame tag inside of the frameset. Set the src to banner.html and the name as banner.

    ```
    <frame src="banner.html" name="banner"></frame>
    ```

12. After the ending frame tag, create a nested frameset defining two columns. Set the first column to 10%. Use the remaining space for the second column.

    ```
    <frameset cols="10%, *">
    </frameset>
    ```

13. Create two frame tags inside of the nested frameset. Set the src of the first to navigation.html and name it navigation. Set the src of the second to content.html and the name to content.

```
<frame src="navigation.html" name="navigation"></frame>
<frame src="content.html" name="content"></frame>
```

14. After the end of the nested frameset tag, create the noframes tag.

```
<noframes>
</noframes>
```

15. Inside of the noframes tag, create a body tag.

```
<body>
</body>
```

16. Inside of the body tag, create a paragraph describing the framed document. We will add the links later in the chapter.

```
<p>This page requires frames</p>
```

17. Save and view frameset.html in your browser. It should look like the following illustration. The final code listing for frameset.html is in Code Block 12-5.

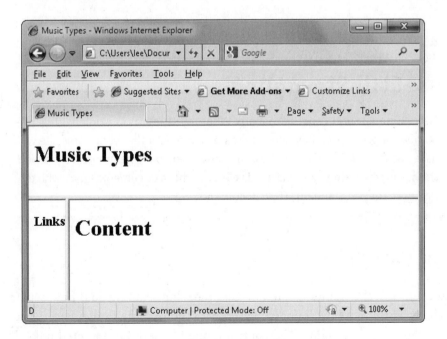

CODE BLOCK 12-5

```
<!DOCTYPE html PUBLIC "-//W3C//DTD XHTML 1.0 Frameset//EN"
"http://www.w3.org/TR/xhtml1/DTD/xhtml1-frameset.dtd">
<html xmlns="http://www.w3.org/1999/xhtml" xml:lang="en">
    <head>
        <title>Music Types</title>
        <meta name="description"
        content="Music types frameset"/>
        <meta name="author" content="Lee M. Cottrell" />
    </head>
    <frameset rows="100,* ">
    <frame src="banner.html" name="banner"></frame>
    <frameset cols="10%, *">
    <frame src="navigation.html" name="navigation"></frame>
    <frame src="content.html" name="content"></frame>
    </frameset>
    <noframes>
    <body>
    <p>This page requires frames</p>
    </body>
    </noframes>
    </frameset>
</html>
```

 Still Struggling

Frames are a tough concept to learn. What my students struggle with is the number of pages that they need to create. Remember that your frame site will have one page defining the frames, and at least one page per frame. So in a web site having five frames, you will need at least six .html documents—one with the frameset, the rest standard HTML documents.

Navigating Through Frames

Theoretically, the frames created in the preceding section could hold separate content. This is not how frames are used. Most commonly, frames have a *control* frame and a *content* frame. The control frame is a series of targeted links. The target is the name of the content frame. Consider the two-column frame in Code Block 12-6:

CODE BLOCK 12-6

```
<frameset cols="175, *">
<frame src="links.html" name="links"></frame>
<frame src="home.html" name="content"></frame>
</frameset>
```

Each frame has a unique name. By naming the right pane, a link can place HTML content into the pane. Code Block 12-7 shows the links that can control the content pane. Pay close attention to the target of each link. The target is the name of the content pane. The illustration shows the output after clicking the page 2 link.

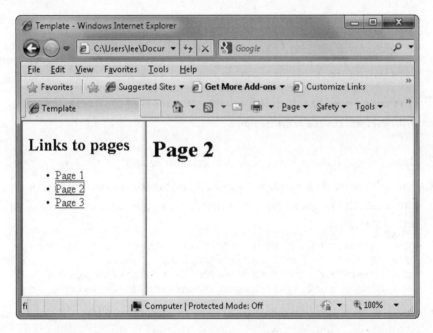

TIP   *Like intra-page anchors covered in Chapter 4, the names of your frames are case sensitive. Be sure to select easy-to-spell yet meaningful names.*

CODE BLOCK 12-7

```
<h2>Links to pages</h2>
<ul>
<li><a href="page1.html" target="content">Page 1</a></li>
<li><a href="page2.html" target="content">Page 2</a></li>
<li><a href="page3.html" target="content">Page 3</a></li>
</ul>
```

Practice Navigating Through Frames

In this section, you will modify the framed music page you created earlier. You will create four web pages about four different types of music. You will then modify the navigation page to view the pages in the content pane.

1. Create four pages based on your template named rock.html, rap.html, pop .html, and country.html. Save them in the chapter12 folder.

2. Edit each file to have a <h1> tag displaying the type of music the page represents. Type a short paragraph describing the music. I provide an example of my rock.html page here:

```
<h1>Rock and Roll</h1>
<p> The original music of rebellion, rock has defined the
modern music scene for over 60 years. Artists ranging from
Chuck Berry to Pink Floyd to Daughtry have defined their own
version of rock. Most modern music has a rock influence.p>
```

TIP *There is no need to set a title for the content pages of the frame. The title of the frameset will cover the entire page.*

3. Open the navigation.html page you created earlier.

4. You will create four links. Set the href to the appropriate music page. Be sure to set the target's value to content. Add your links after the h3 tag in your document.

```
<p><a href="country.html" target="content">Country</a></p>
<p><a href="pop.html" target="content">Pop</a></p>
<p><a href="rap.html" target="content">Rap</a></p>
<p><a href="rock.html" target="content">Rock</a></p>
```

5. Save and view your frameset.html page in a browser. After clicking on the rock link, you will see a page similar to the image shown next.

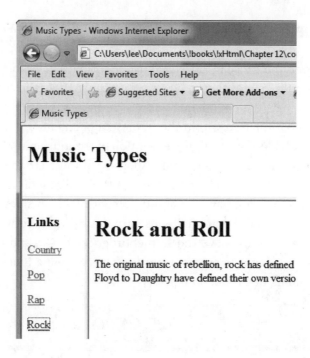

6. The complete code listing for the navigation page is in Code Block 12-8.

CODE LISTING 12-8

```
<!DOCTYPE html PUBLIC "-//W3C//DTD XHTML 1.0 Frameset//EN"
"http://www.w3.org/TR/xhtml1/DTD/xhtml1-frameset.dtd">
<html xmlns="http://www.w3.org/1999/xhtml" xml:lang="en">
    <head>
        <title>Template</title>
        <meta name="description" content="Template"/>
        <meta name="author" content="Lee M. Cottrell" />
    </head>
    <body>
    <h3>Links</h3>
    <p><a href="country.html" target="content">Country</a></p>
    <p><a href="pop.html" target="content">Pop</a></p>
    <p><a href="rap.html" target="content">Rap</a></p>
    <p><a href="rock.html" target="content">Rock</a></p>
    </body>
</html>
```

Formatting Frames

Frames, like everything else in HTML, must be formatted. Unfortunately, CSS has no effect on the frames themselves. CSS can only affect the contents of the frames. CSS formats the documents within the frames, but the frames themselves need to be formatted within the frameset document.

Refer back to Table 12-1. With the exception of src and name, all of the other attributes format the frames. The most important of these are the frameborder and noresize attributes. Frameborder, when set to 0, will not display the border. Unfortunately, you do not have the ability to control which sides of the frame the border appears on. Additionally, to turn off borders between adjacent frames, both frames must have the frameborder set to 0. Failing to set both attributes will result in a transparent border. The following illustration shows the incorrect hiding of a frameborder.

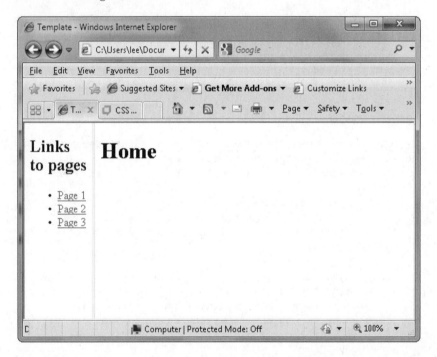

The next illustration shows the correct output. I set the colors of the pages to better illustrate the frames. Both frameborder attributes have been set to 0. Code Block 12-9 lists the frameset code for this illustration. In a three-column frame, there is no way to turn off borders between the first two frames and leave them on between the last two frames. The middle frame cannot both have borders on and off.

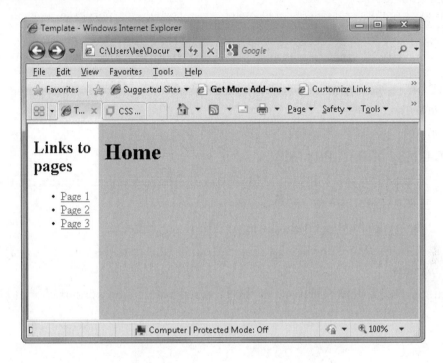

CODE BLOCK 12-9

```
<frameset cols="175, *">
<frame src="links.html" name="links" frameborder="0" ></frame>
<frame src="home.html" name="content" frameborder="0" ></frame>
</frameset>
```

The noresize property of frames dictates whether the user can resize your panes. The default is a resizable pane. Simply adding noresize to the frame turns this attribute on. From a design point of view, the proper choice is to disallow resizing. By keeping the frames a constant size, you can guarantee how your page looks. From a usability viewpoint, creating resizable frames allows a user to make the frame they care about adjustable. There is no right way. I typically do not allow resizable headers, while allowing resizable navigation and content panes. You will need to decide in accordance with the needs of your web site. Code Block 12-10 shows the noresize option added to the links pane of this frameset.

CODE BLOCK 12-10

```
<frameset cols="175, *">
<frame src="links.html" name="links" frameborder="0" noresize ></frame>
<frame src="home.html" name="content" frameborder="0" ></frame>
</frameset>
```

TIP   *The original HTML standard supported the scrolling option. This is deprecated in XHTML.*

Practice Formatting Frames

In this practice, you will set the formatting noresize and frameborder for the music site created earlier in the chapter.

1. Open the frameset.html file in your browser and editor.

2. Turn the frameborders off in each frame. Add frameborder="0" to each frame.

3. Save and view your page in the browser. Your frame borders should be invisible as in this image:

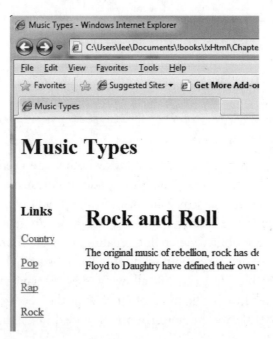

4. Do not allow the header pane to be resizable. Add the noresize attribute to the banner frame.

5. Save and refresh your page. The illustration shows that the content and navigation frames are resizable.

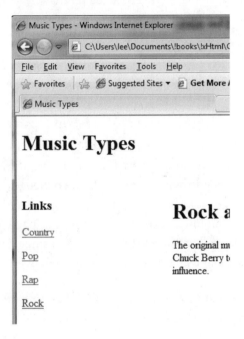

6. The final frameset code appears in Code Block 12-11.

CODE BLOCK 12-11

```
<!DOCTYPE html PUBLIC "-//W3C//DTD XHTML 1.0 Frameset//EN"
"http://www.w3.org/TR/xhtml1/DTD/xhtml1-frameset.dtd">
<html xmlns="http://www.w3.org/1999/xhtml" xml:lang="en">
    <head>
        <title>Music Types</title>
        <meta name="description"
        content="Music types frameset"/>
        <meta name="author" content="Lee M. Cottrell" />
    </head>
    <frameset rows="100,* ">
    <frame src="banner.html" name="banner" frameborder="0"
      noresize></frame>
        <frameset cols="10%, *">
            <frame src="navigation.html" name="navigation"
            frameborder="0"></frame>
```

```
                        <frame src="content.html" name="content"
                        frameborder="0"></frame>
                </frameset>
        <noframes>
                <body>
                <p>This page requires frames</p>
                </body>
        </noframes>
        </frameset>
</html>
```

iFrames

Frames do a nice job breaking your page into sections. However, your options are limited. Working with more than four frames is difficult. Also, placing frames wherever you need them to be can be a challenge. iFrames solve all of these problems.

The iFrame creates an independent object on your page. This object holds a web page. It can be placed anywhere on your page using traditional CSS methods. The iFrame is sizable using pixel widths and heights.

TIP *Firefox requires that you close iFrames with a closing tag. iFrames cannot self-close.*

To use an iFrame, you start with a standard HTML document. The frameset from this chapter disappears, replaced once again with the body tag. Place the iframe tag within the body, wherever you would like it to appear. Set the width and height properties as desired. Set the src property to the URL of the page you wish to appear. The optional id tag helps if you are going to target the iframe with a link. Be sure to close with a closing tag. Code Block 12-12 shows the code that generated the following illustration.

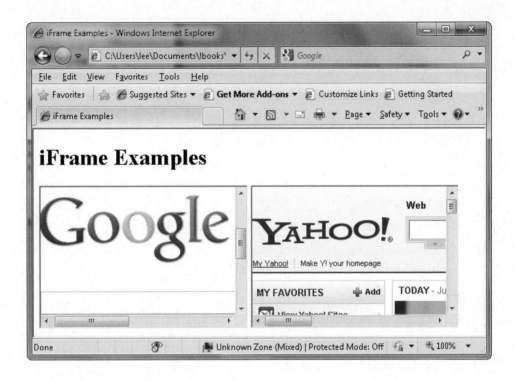

CODE BLOCK 12-12

```
<body>
<h1>iFrame Examples</h1>
<iframe src="http://www.google.com" width="300" height="200"
id="google"></iframe>
<iframe src="http://www.yahoo.com" width="300" height="200"
id="yahoo"></iframe>
</body>
```

Practice Creating iFrames

In this final section you will create a web page holding four iFrames. Each iFrame will hold one of the music pages created earlier. You will place the iframe inside of a div positioned using CSS.

1. Create a new document based on your template called **iframes.html**. Save it in the chapter12 folder.

2. Create a new CSS document called **chapter12.css**.

3. Link the iframes.html file to the chapter12.css file.

```
<link rel="stylesheet" href="chapter12.css" type="text/css"></link>
```

4. Inside of the CSS file create two generic classes called .left and .right.

```
.left{
}
.right{
}
```

5. Set the width and height of the .left class to 50% of the page. Set the float property to left. Set the clear option to clear both.

```
float:left;
width:50%;
height:50%;
clear:both;
```

6. Set the width and height of the .right class to 50%. Set the float property to right.

```
float:right;
width:50%;
height:50%;
```

7. Save your CSS document.

8. Switch to the iframes.html file in your editor.

9. Create a div tag using the .left class.

```
<div class="left">
</div>
```

10. Inside of this div, create an iframe utilizing 80% of the div size. Set the src to country.html.

```
<iframe src="country.html" width="80%" height="80%"></iframe>
```

11. Create a div tag using the .right class. Inside of this div, create an iframe utilizing 80% of the div size. Set the src to pop.html.

```
<div class="right">
<iframe src="pop.html" width="80%" height="80%"></iframe>
</div>
```

12. Create a div tag using the .left class. Inside of this div, create an iframe utilizing 80% of the div size. Set the src to rap.html.

```
<div class="left">
<iframe src="rap.html" width="80%" height="80%"></iframe>
</div>
```

13. Create a div tag using the .right class. Inside of this div, create an iframe utilizing 80% of the div size. Set the src to rock.html.

```
<div class="right">
<iframe src="rock.html" width="80%" height="80%"></iframe>
</div>
```

14. Save and view your page in a browser. It will look like this image:

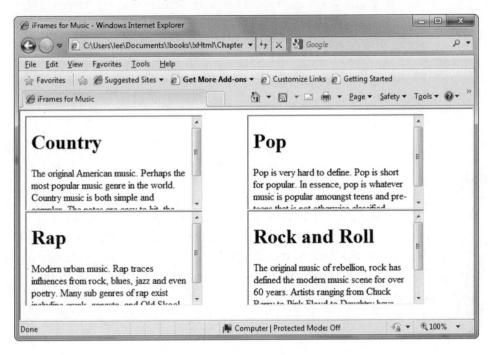

15. The final code listing for the iframes appears in Code Block 12-13.

CODE BLOCK 12-13

```
<!DOCTYPE html PUBLIC "-//W3C//DTD XHTML 1.0 Frameset//EN"
"http://www.w3.org/TR/xhtml1/DTD/xhtml1-frameset.dtd">
<html xmlns="http://www.w3.org/1999/xhtml" xml:lang="en">
    <head>
        <title>iFrames for Music</title>
        <meta name="description" content="iFrames for Music"/>
        <meta name="author" content="Lee M. Cottrell" />
    <link rel="stylesheet" href="chapter12.css" type="text/css">
</link>
    </head>
    <body>
    <div class="left">
        <iframe src="country.html" width="80%" height="80%">
</iframe>
    </div>
    <div class="right">
        <iframe src="pop.html" width="80%" height="80%">
</iframe>
    </div>
```

```
        <div class="left">
                <iframe src="rap.html" width="80%" height="80%">
        </iframe>
        </div>
        <div class="right">
                <iframe src="rock.html" width="80%" height="80%">
        </iframe>
        </div>
        </body>
</html>
```

Summary

In this chapter you created and formatted frames. Frames allow you to split your browser into several sections. As the developer, you have limited control over the size and positioning of the frames. Framesets can be simple or nested. Finally, iFrames provide a simple manner of creating individually scrolling regions on the page.

QUIZ

1. **Instead of a body tag, the _____ tag defines the frames for your web site.**
   A. windows
   B. panels
   C. frameset
   D. panes

2. **The _____ property of a frame controls the existence of a border.**
   A. border
   B. frameborder
   C. borderpane
   D. windowframe

3. **The attribute _____ names a frame.**
   A. name
   B. id
   C. content
   D. identification

4. **To change the content in a frame, the <a> tag must use the _____ attribute.**
   A. src
   B. target
   C. id
   D. title

5. **Which of the following does not need to be set on a document displayed within a frame?**
   A. body
   B. head
   C. meta
   D. title

6. **The _____ attribute of a frame or iframe describes the location of the content.**
   A. src
   B. href
   C. page
   D. content

7. **To support browsers without frame support, you need to _____ .**
   A. write JavaScript
   B. use css instead of frames
   C. create a noframes section
   D. require that your users upgrade their browsers

8. Creating independent scrolling objects on your screen requires _____ tags.
   A. iframe
   B. frameset
   C. region
   D. frame

9. The _____ attribute of a frame determines if the user can change its size.
   A. alterable
   B. morphable
   C. sizable
   D. noresize

10. Getting a frame to validate requires changing the doctype to _____ .
    A. xhtml1-frameset.dtd
    B. xhtml1-strict.dtd
    C. xhtml1-traditional.dtd
    D. xhtml1-frame.dtd

chapter 13

Creating a
Web Site

In this chapter, you will practice the steps to purchase, secure host, and publish a live web site. The chapter uses the popular hosting services Go Daddy and 1&1 for illustration. You can apply the skills in this chapter to any web hosting provider.

CHAPTER OBJECTIVES

In this chapter, you will

- Understand domain names
- Acquire web hosting
- Advertise a web site

Congratulations! You made it through the book. You deserve to brag about your accomplishment and show off your newly found skill. There is no better way to promote your HTML skills than to create a web site.

Throughout the book, I have used the term web site. In this context, a web site means a web page accessible by other people. Imagine Googling your web site name and seeing a link. This final chapter in the book will discuss how to obtain a domain name, select web hosting, get your page onto the Web, and advertise your page.

The skills discussed in this chapter are very lucrative. People pay hundreds of dollars to get a page on the Web. This is in addition to the fees to create the page. You will be able to provide this service to your friends, family, and employers.

Domain Names

The domain name is the name of your web site. It is how most people will access your site. You should choose it carefully.

Domain names have several components. The following illustration displays a typical domain name. There are three components of the name. The actual domain name is htmldemystified.com. The www stands for World Wide Web. Today, the name is there to follow convention. The rightmost part is the top-level domain, or suffix. The suffix .com indicates that this is a commercial entity, and htmldemystified is a second-level domain, or web site name.

www.htmldemystified.com

TIP *For a complete list of top-level domains, visit the Internet Assigned Names and Numbers web site at www.iana.org/domains/root/db/.*

The suffixes are the most confusing part. Domains ending in .com are the most popular choice for new domain names. However, there are hundreds of other choices. The suffix can indicate the country of the page, government affiliation, or educational status. Table 13-1 lists the more common suffixes available for your web page.

TABLE 13-1 Common Top-Level Domains

Top-Level Domain	Description
.biz	A suffix for a business entity.
.ca	The domain for a page hosted within Canada, and owned by a Canadian citizen.
.com	The most popular top-level domain. Use for commercial entities or for anyone desiring high visibility for their domains.
.info	A suffix intended for sites that pass information to their readers.
.me	A top-level domain for personal pages.
.net	An alternative to the .com suffix, typically reserved for Internet providers and network service companies.
.org	This suffix is usually reserved by charitable or nonprofit organizations.
.tv	A domain suffix for pages about television shows.
.us	The domain for a page hosted within the United States and owned by a United States citizen.

Subdomains

Web sites often have several subcomponents. An excellent way to organize the subcomponents of your site is through subdomains. The subdomain is a logical division of your web site. It is represented by a word preceding your domain name. In the next illustration, css and tables are subdomains of htmldemystified .com. Use a subdomain whenever you feel appropriate.

Choosing a Domain Name

Mark Twain once said that the difference between the right word and almost the right word is like the difference between lightning and a lightning bug. The same holds true for selecting a web site name. First, you want a name that is easy to remember and conveys the essence of your web site. Second, you want to choose an appropriate top-level domain. Refer back to Table 13-1 to see the choices for top-level domains. If in doubt, select .com as your suffix. Finally, you need to determine if the domain is available. The next section discusses how to determine if your domain name is available.

Obtaining a Domain Name

Getting a domain name requires visiting a domain registrar and requesting a name, and paying the yearly fee. Many registrars exist; I recommend 1and1.com or godaddy.com. Be leery of registrars that seem too good to be true.

Visit either 1and1.com or godaddy.com. Enter the desired domain name, select the top-level domain, and check its availability. Godaddy.com allows domain searching from the home page; 1and1.com requires that you click the Domains button to search for a domain. The next illustration shows the result of a 1and1.com domain name search. If it is not available, try another domain name until you find one you like that is available. If you must have the domain name, it is possible to purchase the domain from the current owner. Such transactions are legal, yet can be quite expensive.

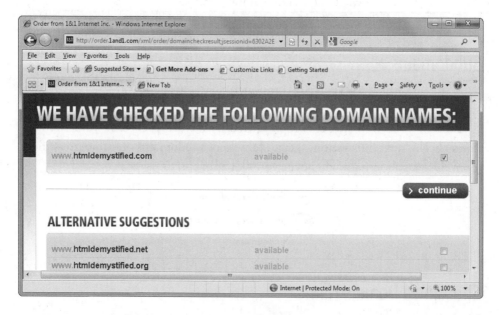

Often the domain you want is not available but is not in use. Often cyber-squatters own these domains. The cyber-squatter purchases domain names for potential resale later. Cyber-squatting is a lucrative business. Depending on the desirability of the domain name, the cyber-squatter can receive fees of $1000 or more for the transfer of the domain name. Cyber-squatting is quite legal unless you own the name you are trying to register. In this case, the squatter is breaking the law. The Internet Corporation for Assigned Names and Numbers, or ICANN, will help you resolve the case.

One of the first cases involving cyber-squatting involved the domain jimihendrix.com. Jimi Hendrix was a guitar player who died in 1970. His fame lived on. An American named Denny Hammerton purchased jimihendrix.com and then offered to sell it to the Jimi Hendrix estate for millions of dollars. In August 2000, the United Nations ruled that Mr. Hammerton had no claim on the name and had to transfer it to the Jimi Hendrix Foundation.

Quite often, you need to purchase more than one domain name. My first web client was for a manufacturing company in my area. Due to an oddity in their corporate structure, the company was known by several names. I registered each name and redirected them all to their primary corporate site.

Another reason to purchase multiple domain names is to protect your brand. Purchasing htmldemystifed.com will allow me to advertise this book online. However, if I do not also purchase htmldemystified.info, .com, .biz, .us, and .net, there is nothing stopping a book competitor from doing so. If you wish to create a unique presence on the Web, you should purchase all of the top-level domains that you can afford.

When you register a domain name, you have other choices to make. The first choice is whether the domain information will be publicly available or private. Private registration, which costs more, protects the identity of the web site ownership. The second choice is receiving a certified domain. The certified domain provides two benefits. First, it proves to the viewers that your site is legitimate. Second, it is the first step to obtaining a digital certificate. You need a digital certificate if your site will handle secure form processing.

Practice Obtaining a Domain Name

In this practice, you are going to find a domain name for a softball team. You will check two registrars for competing pricing.

1. The softball team name is Elliott Eagles. Decide upon a domain name for this site. I will use elliotteagles.com as a starting point.

2. Visit www.godaddy.com. Enter **elliotteagles**, and select .com for the top-level domain.

3. As of press time, elliotteagles.com was taken. Several other suffixes were available. Go Daddy offered several good alternatives. The following image shows the alternatives.

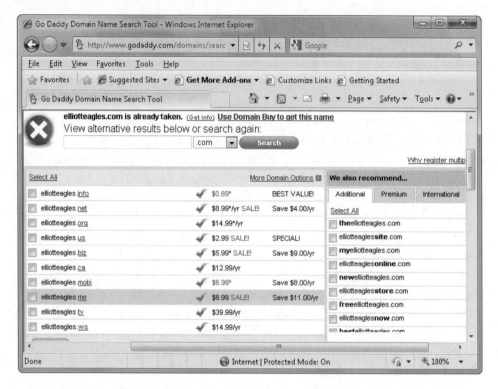

4. The manager of the team does not like any of the alternatives. Try elliotteaglessoftball.com. As of press time, this domain was available. If the domain is unavailable, continue trying domains until you find one that appeals to you.

5. Pricing is important. Check another registrar for another price.

6. Visit 1and1.com. Determine the price for obtaining the domain elliotteaglessoftball.com.

7. Whichever offers the lowest price might be the service you go with.

TIP   *Both godaddy.com and 1and1.com are excellent services. Their products are extremely competitive. Either service is outstanding.*

Acquiring Domain Hosting

To get your web page on the Web, you need hosting. Hosting stores your page and provides several services to support your page. Depending on your needs, hosting can be very inexpensive. Selecting the right web host is very important. You have a number of choices to make. The next illustration shows a subset of the features of two 1&1 hosting plans.

The first choice you need to make is what operating system your host will use. Your two choices are usually Windows or Linux. Both offer excellent hosting plans and are usually the same price. Either operating system will support the technologies discussed in this book. The difference is the support services they offer. A Windows host will usually support SQL Server databases and the

Still Struggling

I hosted my first personal web page with the cheapest hosting service I could find. I spent less than $0.75 per month. However, I got what I paid for. Technical support was nonexistent, the host never backed up my site, and the connection to the site was very slow. Today I spend about $3.00 per month for hosting. Despite paying more per month, I am much happier with my current hosting service. Remember that you typically get what you pay for.

ASP.Net scripting environment. A Linux host supports MySQL databases and the PHP and Perl scripting environments. If you will handle form processing, talk to whoever is writing your backend CGI scripts. They will tell you what to use. If you are not going to need scripting, either will work.

TIP   *Recall that scripting is necessary for creating interactive web sites.*

The second consideration is the amount of space. Beginner or home plans typically offer 10GB of space. That is 10 billion letters. While this may seem small when compared with your home computer, it is actually quite a lot of web room. Web pages are extremely small. Hundreds of thousands of web pages can easily fit in 10GB of space.

A third consideration is the e-mail provided by the service. Compare the number of e-mail addresses offered, the storage size for each account, and the spam service offered. A minimum for a beginner package is 100 e-mail addresses. While this seems like overkill for your family page, hosting a business might well require 100 or more e-mail addresses.

A fourth consideration is transfer or bandwidth limits. This is a limitation on the amount of data that can be transmitted from your web site. Larger values are better. However, for a personal site, 300GB per month is plenty. For a business site, consider nothing short of 1000GB per month, with unlimited the best choice. The following image shows the usage from one of my sites for 12 months.

traffic.html - Windows Internet Explorer

http://www.leecottrell.com/logs/traffic.html/

Month	Total		HTTP		FTP/SFTP		Mail	
	Megabytes	Requests	Megabytes	Requests	Megabytes	Requests	Megabytes	Quantity
2010-06	9.6	519	9.5	517	0.0	2	0.0	0
2010-05	18.2	2,539	18.0	2,538	0.1	1	0.0	0
2010-04	13.0	4,593	12.6	4,579	0.4	14	0.0	0
2010-03	28.4	3,830	26.3	3,816	2.2	14	0.0	0
2010-02	14.5	2,863	14.5	2,861	0.0	2	0.0	0
2010-01	106.3	4,309	87.3	4,251	19.0	58	0.0	0
2009-12	55.5	7,293	55.5	7,293	0.0	0	0.0	0
2009-11	37.3	6,327	37.3	6,318	0.1	9	0.0	0
2009-10	15.0	2,830	15.0	2,830	0.0	0	0.0	0
2009-09	12.2	2,395	12.1	2,379	0.1	16	0.0	0
2009-08	22.7	4,016	22.0	3,904	0.8	112	0.0	0

Done   Internet | Protected Mode: On   100%

Still Struggling

Understanding transfer amounts is tricky. I used to run an online component for my classes from my personal web site. I offered tests, assignments, and a web forum. At my peak time, 80 students accessed the site seven hours a day for five days a week. The highest transfer rate I experienced was150GB. Use this as a benchmark when comparing bandwidth limitations.

Another consideration is the price. A difference of $1.00 may seem trivial, but it can really add up. Ideally, you will hold your web page for several years. Spending $1.00 less per month over five years is a $60 savings. While this is not much, it is a dinner out for my family of four.

Finally, consider the cost of registering the domain at the site. Both 1and1 .com and godaddy.com offer incentives to register a domain and host your sites. Do the math and determine if it makes sense to register at a site different than your host.

TIP *If you plan to create several web sites for friends, family, and clients, find one hosting service and stick with it.*

Compare Web Hosting

The Elliott Eagles have decided on the domain name of elliotteaglessoftball .com. Now you need to find hosting. As with registering the domain, you will compare beginning hosting plans offered by godaddy.com and 1and1.com. Both services are excellent; you will make the decision as to which is best for your needs.

1. Open a web browser and visit www.1and1.com. Click the hosting link and select Linux hosting.

2. Find the basic, or beginner package. Determine the values for the following items.

   • Monthly price

   • Monthly transfer volume

- E-mail accounts
- Size of the MySQL database
- FTP users
- Incentives or sales
- Web site services offered

3. Visit www.godaddy.com. Determine the values for the following items for Linux hosting:

- Monthly price
- Monthly transfer volume
- E-mail accounts
- Size of the MySQL database
- FTP users
- Incentives or sales
- Web site services offered

4. Compare 1and1.com and godaddy.com. Whichever seems better is the hosting company to choose.

Free Web Hosting

You may not be able to get a free lunch, but you can get free web hosting. There are many sites dedicated to providing free hosting. Table 13-2 lists some of the more popular sites.

Free web hosting is not truly free. While you do not pay money, you do pay the host back with advertisements. The hosting service makes money advertising

TABLE 13-2 Popular Free Hosting Sites

Site	Description
Blogger.com	A free, ad–supported blog site.
Facebook.com	A social networking site originally intended for college students. It has gained extreme popularity with adults.
Geocities.com	A free, ad–supported service offered by Yahoo.
Myspace.com	A social networking site originally designed for bands, MySpace has enjoyed popularity with teens.
Webs.com	A free, ad–supported hosting service.

on your site. This is fine for a personal vanity page; it is completely unacceptable for a professional site. This illustration shows advertisements on myspace.com.

Another problem with free hosting is public perception of the site. Myspace .com and facebook.com, while excellent services, have security concerns. Both are excellent for a personal page, but do not use them for anything professional.

Not all is lost for free hosting sites. A few sites offer no strings attached hosting. One is the college or university that you may attend. Many offer their students personal web space. Another source is your ISP. Verizon and Comcast have offered personal web space to their customers. Check with your Internet provider for more details.

Publishing Your Page

Most hosting plans expect that you develop your site on your home computer and then transfer it to the hosting server. The most common tool to transfer your files is FTP.

TIP *FTP is likely to cause your security software to ask if FTP can access the Internet. FTP needs to open port 21, and perhaps an additional port. Allow FTP whatever it asks for.*

FTP stands for File Transfer Protocol. It is an old protocol designed to transfer files to other computers. FTP comes with all modern operating systems. However, the FTP client that comes with Windows is difficult to use. The next illustration shows Windows 7 FTP in action. Windows FTP is command-line based.

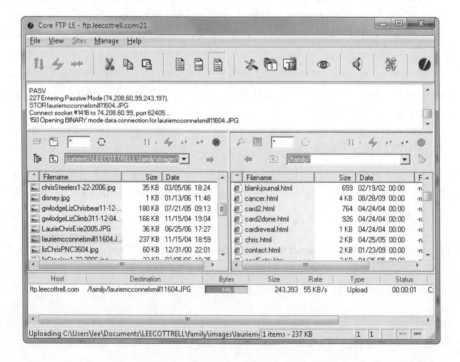

I do not recommend using the built-in FTP programs for your computer. There are several excellent, free FTP clients available. For the past several years, I have used CoreFTPLite for my web transfer needs. CoreFTPLite is free for home and educational usage. Get it at www.coreftp.com. This illustration shows CoreFTPLite in action.

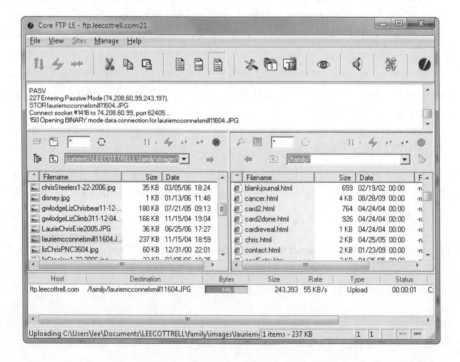

When you transfer your site to your host, you will need to transfer everything. Your host should provide directions on how to use FTP. You will need the FTP username and the password. Keep these closely guarded. If someone else gets your FTP account and password, they can change your web site.

Once you get the username and password, start CoreFTPLite. Most likely CoreFTPLite will default to the correct directory. Begin to transfer all of your .html files. In addition to the html files, you must transfer your images folder and all images. Pay extra attention to keeping the same folder structure. Finally, you must upload your JavaScript and CSS files as well.

Once you have uploaded your files, you should test the site. Visit your domain in the browser, test every link, and view every page. It is crucial that you determine the site is 100 percent functional before unleashing it upon the world.

Automatically Publishing Your Page

Web authoring tools like Dreamweaver and Expression Web provide built-in tools to transfer your web site to your host. You will need to get the FTP username and password from your hosting company. Start the publishing tool in your software. Enter the domain name, username, and password. Once the upload starts, your entire web site is uploaded automatically.

Advertising Your Site

You have spent time creating your site. Now you want people to find your site. You need to advertise your site. You will proceed differently, depending on the content in your site.

Before you panic, take heart. If you do nothing to advertise your site, the major search engines will eventually find you. The problem is eventually can be a long time. You need to take the steps to have your clients find you.

The first step is to tell people about your site. Tell your friends, hand out new business cards with your site, and e-mail your customers. Provide some incentive for people to use the site. Many of your clients are likely to be web-savvy and might prefer to use the site rather than actually dealing with you. If your site is well designed and has a practical function, then people will use the site.

A second step is to follow traditional advertising routes. Television and radio ads are effective. Roadside signs have become a popular method of advertising a web site.

These steps will eventually bring people to your site. However, if you are a business, you want people visiting your site *now*. You need a better method than word of mouth. Additionally, you want a search for your site to result in a good position for your link. A good position is one on the first page of links.

Both 1and1.com and godaddy.com offer services and incentives to help you promote your site. These services will get your site listed in the major search engines and guarantee a good position in the search results. Fees vary between hosting services, but the tools do work.

Another way to get a good search result is to pay for it. Both Google and Yahoo offer a payment plan that will guarantee you a search for your site that will result in your page featured at the top of the results. Google offers AdWords. Visit adwords.google.com for the complete details. Briefly, you provide a series of keywords that describe your site. Whenever someone Googles one of your keywords, your site is listed at the top in a shaded box. You pay Google a small fee whenever someone clicks your link. The next illustration shows the AdWords-sponsored site link for Google AdWords. Additionally, Google lists other sponsored links in the right side of the page.

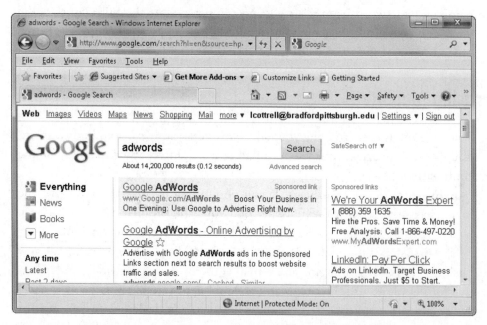

Yahoo! and Bing offer Sponsored Search. Sponsored Search works very much like AdWords. Visit advertising.yahoo.com for the complete details. You choose the keywords that describe your site. Your link appears at the top of the search results page. Again, you only pay when a user clicks the link. The following illustration shows the Yahoo! Sponsored Search links at the top of the search results page.

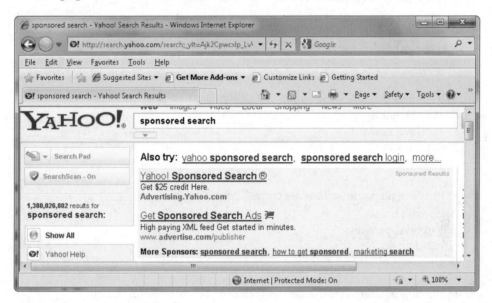

Summary

This is the final chapter of the book. You learned how to acquire a domain name and compared domain-hosting services. In particular, you examined the offerings of 1and1.com and godaddy.com. You understood the process of uploading a page to your host through FTP. Finally, you learned how to advertise your site in major search engines.

QUIZ

1. **This is the top-level domain for nonprofit companies.**
   A. .biz
   B. .be
   C. .com
   D. .org

2. **In the domain name softball.leecottrell.com, softball is a _____ .**
   A. domain name
   B. top-level domain
   C. subdomain
   D. URL

3. **In the domain name softball.leecottrell.com, com is a _____ .**
   A. domain name
   B. top-level domain
   C. subdomain
   D. URL

4. **In the domain name softball.leecottrell.com, leecottrell.com is a(n) _____ .**
   A. domain name
   B. top-level domain
   C. subdomain
   D. error

5. **A _____ purchases a domain name with express interest to resell it for a high value.**
   A. hacker
   B. cyber-squatter
   C. hosting service
   D. registrar

6. **The _____ protocol uploads pages to your host.**
   A. FTP
   B. PGP
   C. CSS
   D. HTTP

7. **This property of hosting services describes the amount of data your web site can send in a given month.**
   A. bandwidth
   B. web space
   C. e-mail addresses
   D. protocol

8. **If you need to use SQL Server and ASP.Net on your web site, then you need to select _____ hosting.**

   A. 1and1.com
   B. Microsoft Windows
   C. Linux
   D. godaddy.com

9. **Google offers _____ as a way for companies to advertise their web sites.**

   A. Sponsored Search
   B. Maps
   C. AdWords
   D. Linking

10. **Which of the following offers free web hosting?**

    A. godaddy.com
    B. myspace.com
    C. 1and1.com
    D. ICANN.com

Final Exam

1. The address for a web page is more correctly known as a _____.

   A. link

   B. hypertext

   C. URL

   D. nest

2. _____ developed the fundamental principles of the World Wide Web.

   A. Vint Cerf

   B. Tim Berners-Lee

   C. The United States Department of Defense

   D. Bob Kahn

3. Which of the following lines of XHTML code is correctly nested and closed?

   A. <p><b>First line</p></b>

   B. <b><p>Second line</p>

   C. <b><p>Third line</p></b>

   D. <b>Fourth line</p>

4. This helper language formats web pages.

   A. CSS

   B. JavaScript

   C. PHP

   D. Dreamweaver

5. The Internet first became functional in _____.

   A. 1960

   B. 1969

   C. 1973

   D. 1993

6. This is the version of HTML I recommend using.

   A. HTML 5

   B. HTML 4.01

   C. XHTML

   D. HTML 1

7. Which of the following is not part of the definition of well formed?

   A. All tags must be closed.

   B. Tags must be properly nested.

   C. Attributes may be null.

   D. Tags are in lowercase.

8. "Not to be supported in future releases" is the definition of _____.

   A. obsolete

   B. deprecated

   C. extensible

   D. nested

9. Deprecated tags and attributes have been replaced with _____.

   A. CSS properties

   B. newer HTML

   C. a strict DTD

   D. JavaScript

10. The _____ element of the head displays the name of the page in the caption bar of your browser.

   A. <meta>

   B. <style>

   C. <title>

   D. <link>

11. CSS rules are set using this format.

   A. property = value

   B. property:value;

   C. property = value;

   D. property:value

12. To display a horizontal rule on the page, use the _____ tag.

   A. <h1>

   B. <p>

   C.

   D. <hr />

13. Tags that self-close are known as _____ tags.

   A. deprecated

   B. empty

   C. handy

   D. property

14. Which of the following is the correct syntax for an attribute set on the <p> tag?

   A. <p>id="para1"</p>

   B. <p id=para1></p>

   C. <p id="para1"></p>

   D. <p id='para1'></p>

15. To create a paragraph, use the _____ tag.
    A.
    B. <p>
    C. <h1>
    D. <!-- -->

16. This is the name of the first page loaded in web sites.
    A. head.html
    B. first.html
    C. index.html
    D. begin.html

17. This HTML color code is green.
    A. #ff0000
    B. #00ff00
    C. #0000ff
    D. #000000

18. For images, the _____ property describes the images.
    A. alt
    B. title
    C. src
    D. tip

19. When setting a background image, you should also set a background color that _____.
    A. complements the background image
    B. overrides the background image
    C. matches the foreground color
    D. matches the predominate color in the background image

20. This image type is best suited for photographs.
    A. PNG
    B. GIF
    C. JPG
    D. BMP

21. To reserve space on the page for the image, you need to use the _____ and _____ attributes.

    A. length

    B. height

    C. width

    D. size

22. The _____ attribute of the img tag specifies the location of the image.

    A. alt

    B. title

    C. src

    D. tip

23. A small background image will repeat to fill the screen. This is the definition of _____.

    A. tiling

    B. scaling

    C. stretching

    D. filling

24. In CSS, the _____ function describes the location of the file.

    A. file

    B. location

    C. url

    D. place

25. This attribute of the <a> tag specifies the URL of the desired document.

    A. href

    B. title

    C. alt

    D. link

26. To access an external style sheet, use the _____ tag.

    A. <a>

    B. <style>

    C. <link>

    D. <head>

27. Intra-page links are identified with the _____ symbol.

    A. #

    B. $

    C. %

    D. !

28. This HTML target value creates a new window every time a link is clicked.

    A. new

    B. _popup

    C. _blank

    D. window

29. a:visited and a:link are examples of CSS _____.

    A. properties

    B. classes

    C. attributes

    D. pseudo-classes

30. A(n) _____ is a link to a page on a different site.

    A. internal link

    B. external link

    C. intra-page link

    D. targeted

31. A(n) _____ is a link to a page on the current web site.

    A. internal link

    B. external link

    C. intra-page link

    D. targeted

32. This attribute of the <a> tag creates a tooltip for the link.

   A. href

   B. title

   C. alt

   D. link

33. This tag is used by ordered and unordered lists to specify the list items.

   A. <li>

   B. <ol>

   C. <ul>

   D. <dt>

34. To create an ordered list, use the _____ tag.

   A. <ul>

   B. <ol>

   C. <dl>

   D. <li>

35. Which of the following items is the default bullet for an unordered list?

   A. circle

   B. disc

   C. triangle

   D. square

36. To change the numbering style for the ordered list, use the _____ property in a style section.

   A. number-style

   B. list-type

   C. list-style-type

   D. counter-style

37. This is the default style for the ordered list.

   A. upper-alpha

   B. decimal

   C. upper-roman

   D. numeric

38. To create a definition list, use the _____ tag.
    A. <ul>
    B. <ol>
    C. <dl>
    D. <li>

39. A list of items to take to school tomorrow is best rendered using a(n) _____.
    A. ordered list
    B. unordered list
    C. paragraph
    D. definition list

40. To create an unordered list, use the _____ tag.
    A. <ul>
    B. <ol>
    C. <dl>
    D. <li>

41. This HTML tag creates structured data.
    A. td
    B. th
    C. table
    D. h1

42. This tag creates a row in a table.
    A. tr
    B. td
    C. th
    D. caption

43. The _____ attribute of a table controls where on the outside of the cell borders appear.

A. frame

B. border

C. rules

D. width

44. The _____ attribute of a table controls the distance from the cell contents to the cell border.

A. cellspacing

B. cellpadding

C. border

D. width

45. The _____ tag is centered and bold by default in all browsers.

A. td

B. tr

C. th

D. caption

46. The _____ tag produces a title for the table above the table.

A. td

B. tr

C. th

D. caption

47. You want three cells in a row merged into one. Which of the following is the correct attribute and value?

A. rowspan="3"

B. rowspan="2"

C. colspan="3"

D. colspan="2"

48. The _____ tag creates a cell in the table.
   A. td
   B. tr
   C. th
   D. caption

49. This tag creates radio buttons, submit buttons, and text boxes.
   A. input
   B. control
   C. form
   D. data

50. The _____ attribute of a form describes how to send data to the CGI script.
   A. action
   B. name
   C. method
   D. encoding

51. The _____ attribute of input controls holds the data sent to the CGI script.
   A. name
   B. data
   C. value
   D. POST

52. The _____ attribute of a form describes the URL of the CGI script.
   A. action
   B. name
   C. method
   D. encoding

53. You wish to give your users a series of choices, of which they can select only one. Which of the following controls is the best?

    A. checkbox

    B. submit button

    C. text box

    D. radio button

54. This tag surrounds a group of form controls.

    A. legend

    B. label

    C. fieldset

    D. div

55. This tag joins a prompt to its corresponding control.

    A. legend

    B. label

    C. fieldset

    D. div

56. To make radio buttons work correctly, the _____ attribute must have the same data.

    A. value

    B. name

    C. data

    D. class

57. Which of the following is a correctly named generic class in CSS?

    A. header

    B. .header

    C. body.header

    D. class="header"

58. To center a block, set the margin-left and margin-right properties to _____.

   A. center

   B. dynamic

   C. auto

   D. fixed

59. This HTML tag applies formats to large sections of your page.

   A. div

   B. span

   C. body

   D. class

60. The CSS property of _____ provides space between the text and the border.

   A. space

   B. z-index

   C. margin

   D. padding

61. This HTML tag applies formats to small amounts of text on your page.

   A. div

   B. span

   C. body

   D. class

62. We divided a normal HTML page into _____ distinct regions.

   A. 2

   B. 3

   C. 4

   D. 5

63. The float property is sticky. To turn it off, use the CSS property _____.

   A. float

   B. clear

   C. padding

   D. reset

64. To hide an element without taking up any space, the _____ property is needed.

   A. display

   B. hidden

   C. visibility

   D. show

65. Most JavaScript lines end with a _____.

   A. period (.)

   B. dash (-)

   C. exclamation mark (!)

   D. semicolon (;)

66. JavaScript files have a ._____ extension.

   A. js

   B. jp

   C. css

   D. java

67. _____ is the "Write Less, Do More" library.

   A. Javascript.internet.com

   B. Jquery.com

   C. Devguru.com

   D. Google.com

68. A _____ is a named chunk of JavaScript code.

   A. variable

   B. function

   C. element

   D. object

69. To display text on the page using JavaScript, the _____ method of the document class is used.

    A. display

    B. page

    C. load

    D. write

70. For our greet and pageDate script to run, you created a variable of type _____.

    A. Time

    B. Calendar

    C. Date

    D. Clock

71. Making a decision in JavaScript requires the use of a(n) _____ statement.

    A. if

    B. decision

    C. then

    D. function

72. Programmers use _____ to store data for a program.

    A. objects

    B. classes

    C. variables

    D. functions

73. DOM stands for _____.

    A. Document Object Model

    B. Document Orientation Mode

    C. Document Object Maintenance

    D. Document Object Mode

74. To change a format in the web page, you access the style property of the
    _____ object.
    A. body
    B. document
    C. document.body
    D. page

75. The _____ event fires when the page comes into the browser.
    A. onload
    B. onpageload
    C. onbrowserload
    D. onloadpage

76. The _____ event fires when the mouse is over an object.
    A. onhover
    B. onmouseover
    C. onmouse
    D. onmousemove

77. The _____ property of JQuery allows you to change the contents of
    a tag.
    A. text
    B. src
    C. contents
    D. html

78. The _____ event fires when you click an object.
    A. onclick
    B. onmouse
    C. onmousepress
    D. onmousebutton

79. A _____ is data passed to a function.

    A. variable

    B. parameter

    C. constant

    D. value

80. To make the <a href> point to the current page, use the _____ symbol.

    A. $

    B. #

    C. @

    D. %

81. The most common type of animation.

    A. Flash

    B. MP4

    C. Wmv

    D. Ogg

82. The _____ tag is the easy way to create a background sound.

    A. object

    B. wav

    C. winamp

    D. embed

83. To play a video in Internet Explorer, you need the correct _____, set to a seemingly random series of letters and numbers.

    A. object

    B. clsid

    C. src

    D. name

84. Passing a value into the object tag is the job of the _____ tag.

    A. value

    B. param

    C. data

    D. send

85. Flash files are stored with a(n) _____ extension.

    A. fla

    B. swf

    C. wmv

    D. fsh

86. To play a sound on a click, you should use a _____ tag.

    A. sound

    B. embed

    C. a

    D. link

87. In HTML 5, the _____ tag will be used to play movies.

    A. embed

    B. video

    C. flash

    D. movie

88. The recommended tag for playing flash, sounds, or movies in Internet Explorer is the _____ tag.

    A. object

    B. embed

    C. video

    D. link

89. Instead of a body tag, the _____ tag defines the frames for your web site.

    A. windows

    B. panels

    C. frameset

    D. panes

90. The _____ property of a frame controls the existence of a border.
   A. border
   B. frameborder
   C. borderpane
   D. windowframe

91. The attribute _____ names a frame.
   A. name
   B. id
   C. content
   D. identification

92. To change the content in a frame, the <a> tag must use the _____ attribute.
   A. src
   B. target
   C. id
   D. title

93. This is the top-level domain for nonprofit companies.
   A. .biz
   B. .be
   C. .com
   D. .org

94. In the domain name softball.leecottrell.com, softball is a _____
   A. domain name
   B. top-level domain
   C. subdomain
   D. URL

95. In the domain name softball.leecottrell.com, com is a _____
   A. domain name
   B. top-level domain
   C. subdomain
   D. URL

96. In the domain name softball.leecottrell.com, leecottrell.com is a(n) _____
    A. domain name
    B. top-level domain
    C. subdomain
    D. error

97. A _____ purchases a domain name with express interest to resell it for a high value.
    A. hacker
    B. cyber-squatter
    C. hosting service
    D. registrar

98. The _____ protocol uploads pages to your host.
    A. FTP
    B. PGP
    C. CSS
    D. HTTP

99. This property of hosting services describes the amount of data your web site can send in a given month.
    A. bandwidth
    B. web space
    C. e-mail addresses
    D. protocol

100. If you need to use SQL Server and ASP.Net on your web site, then you need to select _____ hosting.
    A. 1and1.com
    B. Microsoft Windows
    C. Linux
    D. godaddy.com

Answers to Quizzes and Final Exam

Chapter 1

1. C	2. A	3. C	4. B	5. C
6. A	7. B	8. C	9. C	10. B

Chapter 2

1. A	2. C	3. B	4. D	5. B
6. C	7. B	8. C	9. B	10. B

Chapter 3

1. B	2. A	3. B	4. A	5. D
6. C	7. B, C	8. C	9. A	10. C

Chapter 4

1. A	2. C	3. A	4. C	5. D
6. B	7. A	8. B	9. A	10. A

Chapter 5

1. A	2. B	3. B	4. C	5. B
6. C	7. B	8. A	9. B	10. A

Chapter 6

1. C	2. A	3. C	4. B	5. C
6. D	7. C	8. A	9. B	10. A

Chapter 7

1. A	2. C	3. C	4. A	5. D
6. C	7. B	8. B	9. C	10. C

Chapter 8

1. B	2. C	3. A	4. D	5. B
6. B	7. B	8. A	9. D	10. B

Chapter 9

1. C	2. B	3. D	4. A	5. B
6. B	7. D	8. C	9. A	10. C

Chapter 10

1. A	2. C	3. A	4. B	5. D
6. A	7. B	8. B	9. B	10. C

Chapter 11

1. A	2. D	3. B	4. B	5. B
6. C	7. B	8. A	9. C	10. C

Chapter 12

1. C	2. B	3. A	4. B	5. D
6. A	7. C	8. A	9. D	10. A

Chapter 13

1. D	2. C	3. B	4. A	5. B
6. A	7. A	8. B	9. C	10. B

Final Exam

1. C	2. B	3. C	4. A	5. B
6. C	7. C	8. B	9. A	10. C
11. B	12. D	13. B	14. C	15. B
16. C	17. B	18. A	19. D	20. C
21. B, C	22. C	23. A	24. C	25. A
26. C	27. A	28. C	29. D	30. B
31. A	32. B	33. A	34. B	35. B

36. C	37. B	38. C	39. B	40. A
41. C	42. A	43. C	44. B	45. C
46. D	47. C	48. A	49. A	50. C
51. C	52. A	53. D	54. C	55. B
56. B	57. B	58. C	59. A	60. D
61. B	62. B	63. B	64. A	65. D
66. A	67. B	68. B	69. D	70. C
71. A	72. C	73. A	74. C	75. A
76. B	77. D	78. A	79. B	80. B
81. A	82. D	83. B	84. B	85. B
86. C	87. B	88. A	89. C	90. B
91. A	92. B	93. D	94. C	95. B
96. A	97. B	98. A	99. A	100. B

Index

DeMYSTiFieD®

Hard stuff made easy

The DeMYSTiFieD series helps students master complex and difficult subjects. Each book is filled with chapter quizzes, final exams, and user friendly content. Whether you want to master Spanish or get an A in Chemistry, DeMYSTiFieD will untangle confusing subjects, and make the hard stuff understandable.

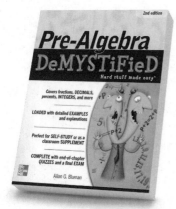

PRE-ALGEBRA DeMYSTiFied, 2e
Allan G. Bluman
ISBN-13: 978-0-07-174252-8 • $20.00

ALGEBRA DeMYSTiFied, 2e
Rhonda Huettenmueller
ISBN-13: 978-0-07-174361-7 • $20.00

CALCULUS DeMYSTiFied, 2e
Steven G. Krantz
ISBN-13: 978-0-07-174363-1 • $20.00

PHYSICS DeMYSTiFied, 2e
Stan Gibilisco
ISBN-13: 978-0-07-174450-8 • $20.00